KT-571-150

LE CORDON BLEU
QUICK & LIGHT

LE CORDON BLEU QUICK & LIGHT

JENI WRIGHT AND
LE CORDON BLEU CHEFS

First published in the United Kingdom in 2004
by Cassell Illustrated, a division of the Octopus
Publishing Group, 2–4 Heron Quays,
London E14 4JP

ISBN 1-84403-285-X

A CIP record for this book is available from the British Library.

Printed in China

Acknowledgments

Le Cordon Bleu and its publishers would like to express gratitude to the 80 Master Chefs from the Le Cordon Bleu schools around the globe, whose expertise and knowledge make books such as this possible, including:

Australia: Paul Beech, Hervé Boutin, Brian Lawes
Japan: Marc Bonard, Jean-Pierre Gestin, Dominique Gros, Bernard Guilhaudin, Hiroyuki Honda, Kenjii Hori, Manabu Kato, Tsuyoshi Kawamichi, Bruno Lederf, Eric Lepage, Cedric Maton, Minoru Nakamura, Olivier Oddos, Laurent Poilve, Atsushi Yamashita
Korea: Laurent Beltoise, Dominique Bourgoin, Marc Chalopin, Eric Ducellier, Eric Guibert, Jean-Jacques Tranchant
London: Yann Barraud, Christophe Bidault, David Bilsland, Alain Jacq, Franck Jeandon, Michael Katz, John Power, Julie Walsh
Mexico: Frédérik Berbille, Philippe Moulin, Christophe Letemple, Diego Perez-Turner
Ottawa: Armando Baisas, Hervé Chabert, Eric Chauffour, Frédéric Filliodeau, Philippe Guiet, Ludovic Chesnay, Laurent Pagès
Paris: Nicolas Bernardé (MOF), Jean-Claude Boucheret, Didier Chantefort, Xavier Cotte, Fabrice Danniel, Jean-François Deguignet, Frédéric Deshayes, Patrick Lebouc, Patrick Martin, Bruno Stril, Patrick Terrien, Marc Thivet
Peru: Jacques Benoit
USA: Kirk Bachmann, Mark Dowling, Jim Gallivan, Angela Goodman, William Hunt, John Paul Hutchins, Jack Kane, Michael Klein, Hervé Le Biavant, Heinz Lauer, Brian Mattingly, William McKenna, Michael Palmer, Brian Wilke, David Weir

And, last but not least, special thanks to all those on Le Cordon Bleu's administrative teams-- it is through their help and assistance that books such as this become reality.

Contents

Foreword

Welcome to Le Cordon Bleu *Quick & Light*, an enticing collection of mouth-watering and imaginative dishes that are healthy and light – where the emphasis is on natural fresh ingredients. These easy-to-prepare recipes, while based on French techniques, have a wide range of culinary influences, producing a creative marriage of flavours without the cream and butter often associated with classic cuisine. Here, you will find inspiring and delicious ideas for every day meals or for those more special occasions.

Founded in Paris in 1895, today Le Cordon Bleu has expanded around the globe with 25 schools in 15 countries. Newcomers to the Le Cordon Bleu team of schools include Peru, Korea, Lebanon and Mexico, as well as a third Japanese school, which recently opened in Kobe. Le Cordon Bleu's 80 Masterchefs share their knowledge with students of 70 different nationalities. These professionals also maintain close links with the culinary industry worldwide, including attendance and participation in over 60 culinary festivals and events each year.

Motivated students are drawn to Le Cordon Bleu's programs from all walks of life. Those with either professional aspirations, or simply a keen interest in the world of food and wine, benefit immensely from a Le Cordon Bleu education. Le Cordon Bleu's Masterchefs teach classic French techniques in the domain of world cuisine and pastry, guiding students in the development of their skills and potential.

Recently, developments in Le Cordon Bleu's curriculum have led to the establishment of Bachelors and Masters degrees in hospitality management in co-operation with international universities – the perfect complement to those skills acquired through the school's renowned Grand Diplôme courses.

And, in 2004, Le Cordon Bleu was selected by the Government of France to participate in a special new project, "*L'Institute des Hautes Etudes du Gout et de la Gastronomie*" ("The Institute for Advanced Studies of Taste and Gastronomy"), established by the French Ministry of Culture, for the preservation of the French culture and its enhanced development.

The name 'Le Cordon Bleu' evokes images of quality, tradition and unerring commitment to excellence at every level. This passionate dedication continues as Le Cordon Bleu enters its second century and continues to keep pace with a modern world of ever-changing lifestyles. Through its culinary arts programs, hospitality management degrees, publications, restaurants, bistros, bakeries, consultancies, gourmet and licensed products, Le Cordon Bleu continues to confirm its commitment to the promotion of the art of living and gastronomy – on a global scale.

Why not allow Le Cordon Bleu to bring the expertise of its chefs into your very own kitchen with its most recent publication, Le Cordon Bleu *Quick & Light*? The recipes are simple and delicious, prepared with minimal fuss and effort. The use of healthy cooking methods and low-fat ingredients make this book indispensable for those seeking the healthier option. It opens the door onto a whole new realm of creative possibilities...

Bon Appétit!

André J Cointreau
President and CEO
Le Cordon Bleu—l'Art Culinaire

1

SOUPS & STARTERS

First courses are generally only served for special occasions, so they need to be really good. First impressions count.

The first rule is to keep portions small and flavours delicate. Everyone is hungry at the beginning of a meal, so if you offer large portions, everyone is tempted to eat too much before the main course arrives. Remember that the first course is only a taste of things to come. If you serve small portions to whet the appetite, you are more likely to leave your guests looking forward to the rest of the meal.

Plan the whole meal together to get the balance right in terms of flavours and richness. If you are serving meat for the main course, choose a fish or vegetable first course; if fish is the main course, choose meat or vegetables to start. Read through the list of ingredients in each recipe and make sure not to serve similar flavours or cream in every course. By the same token, take care not to serve a strongly flavoured starter followed by a delicate main course.

Without doubt, the best first courses are those that can be prepared in advance. This will leave you free to concentrate on things like vegetables, most of which need to be cooked just before serving. If you have the first course ready before people arrive, then all you have to do is uncover the food just before you sit down.

Courgette and roasted garlic soup

This is a richly flavoured soup that can be served hot or cold. It goes especially well with warm focaccia, either plain or flavoured with onion or herbs. Serve it in summer or autumn when courgettes are most plentiful.

500 g (1 lb) courgettes
3 tablespoons olive oil
900 ml (1½ pints) hot vegetable stock
salt and freshly ground black pepper
flesh from 1 small head of Roasted Garlic (page 348)
200 ml (7 fl oz) double cream

Serves 4

Preparation time: 15 minutes
Cooking time: about 35 minutes

1 Trim and slice the courgettes. In a large saucepan, heat the olive oil over moderate heat. Add the courgettes and cook, stirring occasionally for 15 minutes or until they are soft.

2 Pour in the stock. Season to taste and bring to the boil. Cover and simmer for about 20 minutes until the courgettes are very soft and falling apart.

3 Pour the soup into a food processor or blender, add the roasted garlic flesh and purée until smooth. If serving hot, return to the pan, add about three-quarters of the cream and heat through. If serving cold, pour into a bowl and allow to cool, then stir in three-quarters of the cream, cover and refrigerate for at least 4 hours or overnight.

To Serve Pour into a soup tureen or individual bowls and swirl the remaining cream in the centre of the soup.

Chef's Tip

If you don't want to go to the trouble of roasting your own garlic, then removing the flesh from the skins, buy a jar of roasted garlic paste and keep it in the refrigerator. It is immensely versatile for adding an instant smoky garlic flavour to sauces, soups and casseroles. For this recipe you will need about 2–3 tablespoons.

Variation

If you prefer a smoother finish, work the soup through a sieve after puréeing.

Fresh tomato and pepper soup with basil

A brightly coloured soup for late summer when peppers and tomatoes are plentiful, ripe and full of flavour. Although it is served hot here, it is equally good chilled for a sunny al fresco meal.

Serves 4

Preparation time: 10 minutes
Cooking time: about 30 minutes

2 red peppers
500 g (1 lb) tomatoes, preferably Italian plum
1 small onion
1 garlic clove
2 tablespoons olive oil
800 ml (1⅓ pints) hot vegetable stock
good pinch of sugar
salt and freshly ground black pepper
fresh basil leaves, to serve

1 Roughy chop the peppers and tomatoes. Finely chop the onion and garlic, keeping all the vegetables separate.

2 In a large saucepan, heat the olive oil over low heat. Add the onion and stir for 2 minutes without colouring, then add the peppers and cook for 5 minutes. Add the tomatoes and garlic, cook for 10 minutes, then pour in the stock. Add the sugar and seasoning to taste. Bring to the boil, cover and simmer over moderate heat for 10 minutes.

3 Purée the soup in a food processor or blender until smooth, then strain through a fine sieve back into the pan. Bring to the boil, then lower the heat and adjust the seasoning to taste if necessary.

To Serve Pour into a soup tureen or individual bowls. Quickly shred the basil and sprinkle over the soup just before serving.

Variations

If you have a jar of pesto in the refrigerator, try adding a spoonful or two to the soup before puréeing. This is an especially good idea if you think the tomatoes might lack flavour. Red pesto will deepen the colour of the soup, green pesto will tone it down.

◆

For a rich, smoky flavour, use 2 chopped roasted red peppers instead of fresh peppers. You can buy them loose or in jars, or roast your own (page 348). Add them to the soup with the tomatoes in step 2.

Cucumber and dill soup

This ice-cold Scandinavian-inspired soup is delicious with delicate, wafer-thin Swedish crispbread. It is the perfect first course for a barbecue party. Serve in chilled bowls – white really shows up the glorious green colour.

1½ large cucumbers
1 small handful of fresh mint
1 small handful of fresh dill
500 ml (16 fl oz) cold chicken or vegetable stock
150 ml (¼ pint) natural yogurt
salt and freshly ground black pepper

To Serve
4 tablespoons natural yogurt
fresh dill and/or mint sprigs

1 Trim the ends off the cucumber and discard, then chop the cucumber into chunks and place in a food processor fitted with the metal blade. Add the mint and dill. Process until finely chopped, then add the stock through the feeder tube and process again until well mixed.

2 Strain the soup through a fine sieve into a bowl, then gradually whisk in the yogurt until evenly blended. Season to taste with salt and pepper.

3 Cover and refrigerate for at least 4 hours.

To Serve Whisk the soup well and taste for seasoning. Pour into individual soup bowls, swirl a spoonful of yogurt in the centre of each and garnish with mint and/or dill.

Serves 4

Preparation time: 20 minutes, plus cooling and chilling time
Cooking time: 40 minutes

Chef's Tips

Prepare the soup the day before, cover the bowl tightly with cling film and keep in the refrigerator overnight.

◆

Put the tureen or soup bowls in the refrigerator at the same time so they will be chilled as well.

Crab and ginger wonton soup

Pretty as a picture, this delicate soup is very low in fat and yet full of flavour. In China, wonton soups are served as a snack rather than a first course, but you may prefer to serve this soup for a lunch or supper.

1 small leek
2 carrots
4 fresh coriander sprigs
1 star anise
4 tablespoons rice wine
salt and freshly ground black pepper

Wontons
15 g (1/2 oz) pickled ginger
1 egg white
brown and white meat from 1 crab
40 g (1 1/2 oz) fresh white breadcrumbs
20 round wonton wrappers

Serves 4

Preparation time: 30 minutes
Cooking time: 25 minutes

1 Make the broth. Roughly chop and wash the green part of the leek and place in a large saucepan. Cut the white part into fine julienne strips, wash and set aside. Roughly chop 1 carrot and add to the pan. Cut the remaining carrot into julienne strips and set aside.

2 Strip the leaves from the coriander and set aside. Add the stalks to the pan with the star anise, rice wine, 1 litre (1 3/4 pints) cold water and salt and pepper to taste. Bring to the boil and simmer for 10 minutes, then cover and remove from the heat.

3 Make the wontons. Finely chop the ginger. Beat the egg white in a bowl until frothy, then transfer 2 teaspoons to a saucer. Mix the crab, ginger and breadcrumbs into the egg white in the bowl; season well. Place a little mixture in the centre of each wrapper. Brush a little reserved egg white around the edges of the wrappers, then gather them around the filling like purses. Twist just above the filling to seal tightly and expel any trapped air.

4 Strain the stock into a clean saucepan and discard the flavourings. Taste for seasoning, then bring to a simmer. Add the wontons and poach for 2 minutes. Add the carrot and poach for another minute, then add the leek and poach for a further 2 minutes.

To Serve Divide the wontons equally between 4 warm soup bowls and ladle in the broth. Sprinkle with the reserved coriander leaves and serve immediately.

Chef's Tips

Rice wine is made from fermented rice. It is used in Chinese cooking for its rich, mellow flavour and golden colour, and it is also served as a drink. The best kind is Shaoxing, which you will find in Chinese shops, but you can buy other good brands at most supermarkets. Dry or medium dry sherry can also be used instead; don't use the Japanese rice wine called sake, which is colourless.

Wonton wrappers are made from wheat flour, egg and water. They come in both round and square shapes, and are yellow in colour. For this recipe you need round wontons, about 7.5 cm (3 inches) in diameter. You can get them in oriental shops.

VICHYSSOISE

Classic vichyssoise is made with lots of butter and cream. This version only has a small amount of butter and no cream. It tastes so good you will hardly notice the difference. in fact you will probably prefer it to its rich predecessor.

300 g (10 oz) leeks
150 g (5 oz) onion
300 g (10 oz) potatoes
30 g (1 oz) butter
about 900 ml (1½ pints) chicken or vegetable stock
pinch of freshly grated nutmeg
salt and freshly ground black pepper

To Serve
4 tablespoons low-fat natural yogurt
1 tablespoon snipped fresh chives

Serves 4

Preparation time: 20 minutes, plus cooling and chilling time
Cooking time: 40 minutes

Chef's Tip

Keep some stock in the refrigerator while chilling the soup in case you need some for thinning the soup down before serving.

Variation

Serve the soup hot: after puréeing, return it to the rinsed pan and reheat until bubbling, stirring frequently. Add more stock if the consistency is too thick and stir until combined and heated through, then taste for seasoning.

1 Trim, slice and wash the leeks. Finely chop the onion. Peel and dice the potatoes. Melt the butter in a large saucepan, add the leeks and onion and stir to mix with the butter. Cover the pan and sweat the vegetables over low heat for 5–7 minutes until soft but not coloured. Stir them occasionally and take care not to let them brown.

2 Add the potatoes and stock. Bring to the boil, cover and simmer for about 30 minutes or until the potatoes are very soft. Season with the nutmeg and salt and pepper to taste.

3 Pour the soup into a food processor or blender and purée until smooth. Pour into a bowl and leave to cool, then cover and chill in the refrigerator for at least 4 hours, preferably overnight.

To Serve Stir the soup well and add a little more chilled stock if the consistency is too thick. Taste for seasoning. Ladle into chilled bowls and top with a spoonful of yogurt and a sprinkling of snipped chives. Serve well chilled.

Gazpacho

Naturally very low in fat and high in fibre, vitamins and minerals, this exquisite Spanish soup is a must for the summer months when tomatoes and peppers are ripe and full of flavour. For maximum visual impact, serve it in white bowls or a white tureen.

Serves 6–8

Preparation time: 20 minutes, plus chilling time

1 mild Spanish onion
1 cucumber
500 g (1 lb) ripe tomatoes
3 garlic cloves
1 large red pepper
90 g (3 oz) crustless white bread
200 ml (7 fl oz) tomato juice
3 tablespoons sherry vinegar
1 teaspoon caster sugar, or to taste
salt and freshly ground black pepper

To Serve
a little extra virgin olive oil
1 handful of shredded fresh basil leaves

1 Roughly chop the onion, cucumber, tomatoes and garlic. Quarter, core and deseed the red pepper. Break the bread into small pieces.

2 Place all of these ingredients in a food processor or blender and add the tomato juice, sherry vinegar, 600 ml (1 pint) cold water and salt and pepper to taste. Purée until the soup is mostly smooth, but retaining a little texture.

3 Pour the soup into a bowl and check the seasoning. Cover and chill in the refrigerator overnight. This will develop the flavours.

To Serve Stir the soup well and add a little cold water if the consistency is too thick. Taste for seasoning. Ladle into chilled bowls or a tureen and grind black pepper liberally over the surface. Swirl a little olive oil in the centre of the soup and garnish with shredded basil. Serve well chilled.

Chef's Tips

The peel of the cucumber gives the soup extra texture, but you can remove it before chopping the cucumber if you like. Sherry vinegar comes from Jerez in Spain, and you can buy bottles of it in most supermarkets. Its flavour is quite musky, which is good in a strong-flavoured soup like gazpacho. You can use sherry instead, or a red wine vinegar.

You may have to purée the soup in batches, depending on the size of your machine. This recipe makes about 1.8 litres (3 pints) of liquid.

Chilled watercress soup

With its tangy bite, watercress makes a really good chilled soup, and you will see there is no need to enrich it with cream, as so many recipes do. Serve for a first course or a light lunch, with fresh granary or wholemeal rolls.

1 large Spanish onion
500 g (1 lb) floury potatoes
125 g (4 oz) watercress
30 g (1 oz) butter
about 1.5 litres (2½ pints) vegetable stock or water
pinch of freshly grated nutmeg
salt and freshly ground black pepper

1 Finely chop the onion and dice the potatoes. Reserve 4 small sprigs of watercress for the garnish and roughly chop the rest.

2 Melt the butter in a large saucepan and sweat the onion over very low heat until soft but not coloured, about 10 minutes.

3 Add the potatoes, stock or water, nutmeg and salt and pepper to taste. Bring to the boil, cover and simmer for about 30 minutes or until the potatoes are very soft.

4 Pour the soup into a food processor or blender, add the watercress and purée until smooth. Strain through a fine sieve into a bowl and leave to cool, then cover and chill in the refrigerator for at least 4 hours, preferably overnight.

To Serve Stir the soup well and add a little more chilled stock if the consistency is too thick. Taste for seasoning. Ladle into chilled bowls and top each with a sprig of watercress. Serve well chilled.

Serves 4

Preparation time: 15–20 minutes, plus cooling and chilling time
Cooking time: 45 minutes

Chef's Tips

Floury potatoes are used instead of cream to thicken the soup and make it velvety smooth. The best floury varieties are Desirée, King Edward and Maris Piper.

◆

Keep some stock in the refrigerator while chilling the soup in case you need some for thinning the soup down before serving.

◆

Variation

Serve the soup hot: after puréeing, return it to the rinsed pan and reheat until bubbling, stirring frequently. Add more stock if the consistency is too thick and stir until combined and heated through, then taste for seasoning.

Carrot and coriander soup

Two types of coriander give this popular smooth soup great depth of flavour. Serve it as a stylish starter in elegant wide-rimmed bowls – it looks especially good against white or blue.

500 g (1 lb) carrots
1 onion
15 g (1/2 oz) coriander seeds
30 g (1 oz) butter
1 litre (1 3/4 pints) chicken or vegetable stock
a small handful of fresh coriander
salt and freshly ground black pepper

Serves 4

Preparation time: 20 minutes
Cooking time: 40–45 minutes

1 Roughly chop the carrots. Thinly slice the onion. Crush the coriander seeds with a mortar and pestle.

2 Melt the butter in a large saucepan and sweat the onion over low heat for about 5 minutes until soft. Add the chopped carrots and crushed coriander seeds, stir well and sweat for another 5 minutes.

3 Add the stock, coriander stalks and salt and pepper to taste. Stir and bring to the boil, then cover and simmer for 25–30 minutes or until the carrots are very soft.

4 Pour the soup into a food processor or blender and purée until smooth, then return to the rinsed pan and reheat. Meanwhile, chop the coriander leaves.

To Serve Taste the soup for seasoning, then ladle into warm bowls. Scatter the chopped coriander over the surface of the soup and serve immediately.

Chef's Tip

To heighten the spiciness of the coriander seeds, dry-fry them before crushing them in step 1. Heat them in a non-stick frying pan over low to moderate heat for 2–3 minutes, stirring constantly with a wooden spoon. Once you can smell their toasted aroma, it is time to remove them from the heat. Tip them into the mortar and crush them while they are still hot.

Summer minestrone

We tend to think of minestrone as a strongly flavoured red soup thick with tomatoes, beans and pasta, but there are many different types of minestrone in Italy. This one is delicate, fresh and green with new season's vegetables and herbs.

1 onion
1 celery stalk
1 garlic clove
100 g (3½ oz) fine green beans
1 courgette, weighing about 175 g (6 oz)
1 tablespoon olive oil
salt and freshly ground black pepper
1.2 litres (2 pints) vegetable or chicken stock
100 g (3½ oz) shelled fresh garden peas
150 g (5 oz) cooked white rice
2 tablespoons chopped soft fresh herbs (eg chervil, tarragon, parsley, basil)
shavings of Parmesan cheese, to serve

Serves 4–6

Preparation time: 15 minutes
Cooking time: 30–35 minutes

1 Finely dice the onion and celery. Crush the garlic. Cut the beans crossways into 2.5 cm (1 inch) pieces and cut the courgette into small even-size chunks.

2 Heat the oil in a large saucepan and sweat the onion, celery and garlic without colouring until soft, about 10 minutes. Add the beans and courgette, season well and cook, stirring, for 1 minute.

3 Add the stock and bring to the boil, then simmer for 15 minutes or until the vegetables are just cooked, adding the peas after 5 minutes.

4 Add the rice and about two-thirds of the herbs and stir well. Simmer for 1–2 minutes until the rice is hot.

To Serve Taste for seasoning and ladle into warm soup plates. Sprinkle with the remaining herbs, garnish with the Parmesan shavings and serve hot.

Chef's Tips

For authenticity, use a short-grain arborio or other risotto rice. To get 150 g (5 oz) cooked rice, you will need 60 g (2 oz) uncooked rice.

If you like you can dice the vegetables in a food processor, but take care not to overprocess them to a mush. If you have time, it is better to dice the vegetables with a sharp knife for this recipe. The finished soup will look more attractive if the vegetables are diced to a neat, uniform shape.

Variation

Use a small soup pasta (pastina) instead of rice. If you go to an Italian delicatessen you will find many different and unusual shapes to choose from. There is even a tiny shape called risoni, which looks like grains of rice. Use the same quantity of pasta as rice.

French onion soup

This is the perfect winter warmer. Everyone loves it, and it tastes best if made the day before, so it's the perfect thing for an informal midweek supper with friends or family.

- 2 large Spanish onions, total weight about 500 g (1 lb)
- 2 x 295 g cans condensed beef consommé
- 90 g (3 oz) butter
- salt and freshly ground black pepper
- 4 teaspoons plain flour
- 125 ml (4 fl oz) dry white wine
- 1 bouquet garni
- 6–9 slices of baguette
- 60–90 g (2–3 oz) Emmenthal, Gruyère or Jarlsberg cheese
- 2–3 tablespoons port or Madeira (optional)

Serves 2–3

Preparation time: 15–20 minutes
Cooking time: about 1 hour

1 Halve the onions lengthways and finely slice them. Make the consommé up to 1.2 litres (2 pints) with water and heat to boiling. Keep hot.

2 Melt the butter in a large saucepan over low heat. Add the onions, stir well and season with a generous pinch of salt. Cover and cook gently for 5 minutes. Remove the lid, increase the heat to moderate and cook the onions until a light golden brown in colour, 12–15 minutes. Stir frequently during this time and watch carefully towards the end of cooking, to prevent the onions catching on the bottom of the pan.

3 Stir in the flour and cook for 1–2 minutes, then add the wine and bring, to the boil. Cook for 1 minute, stirring constantly to loosen the browned pieces of onion on the bottom of the pan. Add the hot consommé and the bouquet garni, stir well and bring to the boil. Cover and simmer gently for 30 minutes.

4 Meanwhile, preheat the grill and lightly toast the slices of baguette on both sides. Leave the grill on. Thinly slice the cheese and arrange it on top of the baguette. Remove the bouquet garni from the soup, stir in the port or Madeira (if using), then season the soup to taste.

To Serve Ladle the soup into individual flameproof bowls. Top each serving with 3 slices of baguette and put under the grill until the cheese melts and bubbles. Serve.

Chef's Tips

Don't skimp on the browning time for the onions – this is essential to give the soup a good colour and flavour.

◆

If you don't have port or Madeira, you can use sherry or brandy, or leave it out altogether.

◆

If making the day before, cook the soup up to the end of step 3, then remove the bouquet garni. Cool, cover and refrigerate the soup. Before serving, reheat the soup until bubbling, preheat the grill and prepare the croûtes.

Lentil soup

This is a thick, textured soup, ideal for a hearty supper with crusty French bread and cheese. For a dinner party first course, it can be made to look elegant by being puréed, then sieved and served garnished with small celery leaves.

1 small onion
1 small carrot
1 small celery stick
1 garlic clove
90 g (3 oz) smoked bacon rashers
125 g (4 oz) French green lentils
1.5 litres (2½ pints) hot chicken or vegetable stock
1 bouquet garni
salt and freshly ground black pepper

Serves 2–3

Preparation time: 10 minutes
Cooking time: 1 hour

1 Finely chop the onion, carrot, celery and garlic. Cut the bacon into small pieces with scissors, discarding any rind.

2 Put the lentils in a large saucepan, cover with cold water and bring to the boil. Drain into a sieve, rinse under the cold tap, then return to the pan.

3 Add the stock to the lentils with the chopped vegetables, bacon and bouquet garni. Bring to the boil, then half cover and simmer over moderate heat until the lentils are very soft, about 1 hour. Stir occasionally during cooking and add a little water if the consistency of the soup is too thick

To Serve Remove the bouquet garni, then season the soup to taste. Serve hot.

Chef's Tips

French green lentils are sold in supermarkets, delicatessens and health food shops. The best are Le Puy lentils, which have a nutty flavour and retain their shape well during cooking. Although French chefs always use them, they are not essential for this soup – you could use red or orange lentils instead.

◆

You can cut down preparation time by chopping all the vegetables in a food processor fitted with the metal blade.

Corn and potato chowder

A favourite American soup that makes a warming and filling meal in winter. Serve with crusty baguette and follow with a green salad, or maybe some cheese and fresh fruit, such as apples and grapes.

1 small onion
2 garlic cloves
375 g (12 oz) potatoes
2 tablespoons olive oil
800 ml (1⅓ pints) hot chicken or vegetable stock
salt and freshly ground black pepper
1 x 198 g can sweetcorn with sweet peppers, drained
150 ml (¼ pint) double cream
chopped fresh parsley or coriander, to garnish

1 Finely chop the onion and garlic, keeping them separate. Peel the potatoes and cut them into small cubes. Heat the oil in a saucepan and cook the onion over low heat for 2–3 minutes until softened. Add the garlic and potatoes and cook, stirring, for a few minutes.

2 Add the hot stock, season and bring to the boil over high heat. Cover and simmer over low to moderate heat until the potatoes are very soft, about 30 minutes. Add the sweetcorn and peppers and the cream. Heat through, stirring, until bubbling.

To Serve Taste for seasoning and sprinkle with chopped parsley or coriander.

Serves 2–3

Preparation time: 10 minutes
Cooking time: about 40 minutes

Variation

There are many ways in which you can vary chowder. Some cooks like to use milk instead of stock, or half stock and half milk. Chopped bacon is often fried with the onion at the beginning, or cubed ham added at the end. Smoked fish chowder is a classic – cut 250 g (8 oz) smoked cod or haddock into large chunks and add them for the last 5 minutes. Flaked canned tuna is another popular fish to use: simply stir it in with the sweetcorn.

Prawn and ginger soup

A fusion of oriental and French cuisines takes place in this fresh-tasting soup. The ginger makes it spicy hot, while the herbs have a cooling effect. Serve with crisp prawn crackers.

2 medium celery sticks
1 garlic clove
30 g (1 oz) fresh root ginger
8–12 raw prawns in their shells
1 lemon grass stalk
2 star anise
15 g (1 oz) fresh dill sprigs
500 ml (16 fl oz) canned chicken consommé or chicken stock
salt and freshly ground black pepper
a few fresh chives or basil sprigs
1 egg white, to serve

Serves 4

Preparation time: 15 minutes
Cooking time: about 25 minutes

1 Roughly chop the celery and garlic and half the ginger and put them in a saucepan. Shell the prawns, and add the heads and shells to the pan. Bruise the lemon grass by smashing it with a pestle or the end of a rolling pin, then add to the pan with the star anise and dill stalks.

2 Pour in the consommé or stock and 250 ml (8 fl oz) water. Season with salt and pepper. Bring to the boil, then lower the heat, cover and simmer for 20 minutes.

3 Halve the prawns lengthways and remove any black intestinal veins. Cut the remaining ginger into very fine, needle-like threads. Chop the dill leaves and snip the chives or basil with scissors.

4 Strain the liquid and discard the solids. Return the liquid to the rinsed pan, add 250 ml (8 fl oz) water and bring to the boil. Lower the heat, add the prawns, ginger threads and herbs and simmer gently for 3 minutes. Taste for seasoning.

To Serve Lightly beat the egg white with a fork to loosen it without letting it become frothy, then pour it into the hot soup and stir it constantly to create fine threads. Pour the soup into warm bowls and serve immediately.

Chef's Tip

Raw prawns are grey – they only turn their more familiar pink colour when they are cooked. They are relatively easy to buy fresh or frozen at fishmongers or supermarkets with fresh fish counters, and you can use either for this soup. To remove the black intestinal veins, slit the prawns down their backs and ease out the veins with the point of the knife. Cooked prawns can also be used, but only heat them through for 1 minute or they may become tough and chewy.

Mixed greens with goat's cheese toasts

For variety of flavour, shape and texture, buy a bag of mixed greens from the supermarket. Good combinations are frisée, herbs, lamb's lettuce and rocket, sometimes labelled 'continental salad'.

30 g (1 oz) pine nuts
12 slices of baguette
3 crottins de Chavignol
125 g (4 oz) mixed greens

Dressing
2 tablespoons red wine vinegar or raspberry vinegar
salt and freshly ground black pepper
8 tablespoons olive oil

Serves 4

Preparation time: 20 minutes, plus cooling and chilling time
Cooking time: 40 minutes

1 Lightly toast the pine nuts under a hot grill. Toast the baguette until light golden on both sides. Slice each crottin into 4 discs and place 1 disc on each slice of toasted baguette. Leave the grill on.

2 Make the dressing: whisk the vinegar with salt and pepper to taste, then whisk in the oil. Toss with the mixed greens and divide between 4 plates.

3 Place the crottin toasts on a baking sheet and put under the hot grill for 3–5 minutes until the cheese is golden brown and bubbling.

To Serve Arrange the goat's cheese toasts on the salad and sprinkle the toasted pine nuts over the top. Serve immediately.

Chef's Tip

French crottins de Chavignol are sold at supermarkets and delicatessens. They are medium fat, hard goat's cheeses that are small and round, the perfect size and shape for cutting into discs for grilling. If you can't get them, buy a log of goat's cheese and slice it into rounds about 1.25 cm (½ inch) thick.

Smoked duck with broccoli and almonds

If you leave the glazed skin and fat on the smoked duck it will look attractive, but if you prefer to cut fat and calories, simply strip it off with your fingers before slicing the breast into thin strips.

Serves 4

Preparation time: 15–20 minutes

250 g (8 oz) broccoli florets
salt and freshly ground black pepper
30 g (1 oz) flaked almonds
1 smoked duck breast, weighing about 300 g (10 oz)

Dressing
3 tablespoons cider vinegar or red wine vinegar
5 tablespoons hazelnut oil
5 tablespoons sunflower oil

1 Divide the broccoli into tiny sprigs and trim the stalks. Blanch the sprigs in salted boiling water for 1 minute, drain and refresh immediately under cold running water. Drain again and leave to dry on kitchen paper.

2 Put the almonds in a non-stick frying pan and toss over moderate heat for about 3 minutes until evenly toasted. Turn into a bowl and set aside to cool.

3 Make the dressing. Put the vinegar in a large bowl, add salt and pepper to taste, then whisk in the oils. Add the broccoli and toss well to coat in the dressing. Set aside for at least 30 minutes.

4 Cut the smoked duck on the diagonal into thin slices.

To Serve Arrange the duck on individual plates, overlapping the slices slightly. Toss the almonds with the broccoli and spoon next to the duck. Drizzle any dressing from the bottom of the bowl over the broccoli, or over the duck if you prefer, and grind black pepper over the top.

Chef's Tips

Whole smoked duck breasts, usually imported from France, are sold at supermarkets, delicatessens, some butchers and gourmet food shops, or you can buy them ready sliced. Whole smoked chicken breasts are also available, and can be used in this recipe. They are smaller than duck breasts, so you will need 2 to serve 4 people.

◆

You can prepare this dish the night before. Toss the broccoli in the dressing and cover the bowl with cling film. Slice the duck, arrange on plates and cover with cling film. Just before serving, add the almonds and spoon the broccoli next to the duck.

Filo purses of fish

These crisp little pastries have a classic Scandinavian filling of salmon, lemon and dill. They look and taste delicate, and are very good with a crisp, dry white wine. They can be prepared in advance and baked at the last moment.

300 g (10 oz) salmon fillet, skinned
finely grated rind of 1 lemon
1 tablespoon chopped fresh dill
salt and freshly ground black pepper
1 x 275 g packet frozen filo pastry sheets, thawed
about 100 g (3½ oz) butter, melted and cooled
150 ml (¼ pint) crème fraîche
fresh dill sprigs, to garnish

Serves 6

Preparation time: 20 minutes
Cooking time: 10 minutes

1 Preheat the oven to 220°C (425°F) Gas 7. Cut the fish into 18 chunks and place them in a bowl. Add the lemon rind, dill, ½ teaspoon salt and plenty of pepper. Toss well to mix.

2 Cut the stack of filo sheets into a 15 cm (6 inch) square. Lay 1 sheet on a board and brush with melted butter. Lay another sheet on top and brush this with more butter. Place 3 pieces of fish in the centre of the square: top with ½–1 teaspoon crème fraîche.

3 Gather up the edges of the filo to form a purse, squeeze just above the filling, then twist once to create a drawstring effect. Place on a baking sheet and brush gently with a little more butter. Repeat to make 5 more purses. Bake for 10 minutes.

To Serve Place the purses on individual plates with a spoonful of the remaining crème fraîche alongside, topped with a sprig of feathery dill. Serve immediately.

Chef's Tips

Ready made filo pastry is available frozen in boxes from the freezer cabinets of most supermarkets. Be careful to handle it gently because it is paper thin, and keep it covered with a damp cloth until it is buttered or it may dry out and crack. In this recipe you will be left with quite a few trimmings; refreeze them to use on top of a pie at a later date.

◆

For an oriental flavour, use cod or monkfish instead of salmon, with 1 teaspoon mango chutney and 2 teaspoons chopped fresh coriander in place of the dill.

Layered vegetable terrine

Studded with rows of colourful vegetables, this chilled terrine is light, fresh and colourful. Serve it in summer when vegetables are at their best. Crusty French bread or ciabatta makes a good accompaniment.

a little olive oil
1 medium carrot, about 90 g (3 oz)
1 small courgette, about 100 g (3½ oz)
90 g (3 oz) trimmed French beans
125 g (4 oz) spinach leaves, any thick stalks removed
90 g (3 oz) baby sweetcorn
salt and freshly ground black pepper
1 x 12 g sachet powdered gelatine
400 ml (14 fl oz) tomato juice
1–2 teaspoons Worcestershire sauce, to taste
1 packet fresh basil leaves

Serves 6–10

Preparation time: 1 hour, plus at least 4 hours to chill the terrine

1 Brush a 23 x 12.5 cm (9 x 5 inch) loaf tin with oil, then line with cling film, letting it overhang the sides. Brush the film with a little oil. Peel the carrot and cut it into matchsticks. Cut the courgette into very thin rounds.

2 Cook each type of fresh vegetable separately in a saucepan of salted boiling water until just tender. Allow 2 minutes for each, except the sweetcorn, which needs about 6 minutes. As each type is cooked, rinse under cold running water, then spread out on a tea towel to dry. Cut the sweetcorn in half lengthways.

3 Sprinkle the gelatine over the tomato juice in a small pan. Leave until clear, then gently warm through, stirring to dissolve the gelatine. Add Worcestershire sauce and seasoning to taste and let cool to room temperature.

4 Line the tin with three-quarters of the spinach. Finely shred the basil. Layer the vegetables alternately in any order, spooning a little tomato mixture and basil over each layer. Finish with tomato and basil, then the remaining spinach. Cover with the overhanging cling film. Chill for 4 hours, or until set.

To Serve Unfold the cling film on the top and invert the terrine onto a plate. Remove the tin and cling film. Allow to come to room temperature, about 30 minutes.

Chef's Tips

When layering the vegetables in the tin, consider colour, bearing in mind what the terrine will look like when it is sliced.

◆

For a piquant touch, serve the terrine with curried mayonnaise: stir ¼ teaspoon ready made curry paste into 150 ml (¼ pint) mayonnaise and season with salt and a few drops of lemon juice.

◆

You can make the terrine up to 24 hours in advance and keep it, covered with cling film, in the refrigerator.

Seared scallops with roasted pepper coulis

A first course with an elegant presentation for a special occasion. Scallops are expensive, but they are quick and easy to cook, so this is a marvellous dish you can make at short notice.

8 large scallops
juice of 2 limes
90 ml (3 fl oz) olive oil
sea salt and freshly ground black pepper
fresh coriander leaves, to garnish

Coulis
175 g (6 oz) roasted peppers
1 garlic clove, roughly chopped
100 ml (3½ fl oz) olive oil
a little lime juice

Serves 4

Preparation time: 30 minutes
Cooking time: 2–3 minutes

1 Separate the corals from the scallops, then cut off and discard the rubbery muscles. Slice each scallop into 2–3 discs, depending on their thickness. Place the corals and scallops in a glass or stainless steel bowl. In a separate bowl, whisk together the lime juice, all but 1 tablespoon of the olive oil and plenty of pepper, then pour over the scallops. Cover and leave to marinate for 30 minutes.

2 Meanwhile, make the coulis: drain the peppers if necessary and place them in a food processor fitted with the metal blade. Add the garlic and olive oil and work to a purée. Strain and season to taste, then add lime juice to thin the coulis down a little.

3 Drain the scallops and corals and pat them dry. Heat the remaining oil in a non-stick frying pan until hot. Add the scallops and sear quickly and lightly over high heat until nicely coloured on each side, 2–3 minutes total cooking time. Remove with a slotted spoon.

To Serve Arrange the scallops and corals on individual plates and grind a little sea salt and black pepper over them. Spoon the coulis into the middle, garnish with coriander leaves and serve.

Chef's Tips

Delicatessens sell roasted peppers loose by the kilo/lb and in jars. Red or yellow peppers are the best colours for making coulis. If you like, you can roast peppers yourself – see page 348.

◆

Not all scallops come with their corals attached, but they do add a touch of colour and they taste really delicious, so try to get them if you can.

◆

Variation

Fresh salmon or tuna can be used instead of scallops.

Warm potato salad

Classic French recipes often include a raw egg in their dressings. Here a little ready made mayonnaise is used instead to create a salad dressing which has a similar texture and flavour.

625 g (1¼ lb) new potatoes
salt and freshly ground black pepper
2 celery sticks
1 small handful of fresh coriander
150 g (5 oz) lardons or thickly diced bacon or pancetta
2–3 teaspoons Dijon mustard, to taste
4 tablespoons olive oil
juice of ½ lemon
1 tablespoon bottled mayonnaise

Serves 4

Preparation time: 15 minutes
Cooking time: 20–25 minutes

1 Cook the potatoes in their skins in salted boiling water for 15–20 minutes until tender. Meanwhile, dice the celery and finely chop the coriander.

2 Drain the potatoes well and leave until cool enough to handle, then peel off the potato skins and thicky slice the potatoes or cut them into chunks. Put the potatoes in a warm bowl. Quicky dry-fry the lardons, bacon or pancetta in a nonstick frying, pan until browned and crispy. Remove with a slotted spoon and add to the potatoes.

3 Whisk together the mustard, oil and lemon juice in a jug, pour into the frying pan and stir over high heat to deglaze. Pour immediately over the potato mixture and shake the bowl so the dressing is evenly distributed.

4 Add the celery and mayonnaise and half the coriander. Fold gently to mix. Taste and add salt and pepper, and more mustard if you like.

To Serve Turn the salad into a serving bowl and sprinkle with the remaining coriander. Serve as soon as possible, while warm.

Chef's Tip

For salads, waxy potatoes are best. They hold their shape better than floury potatoes. The variety called Charlotte is a good one to use. In some supermarkets, waxy varieties are described as French-style or continental potatoes.

Individual cheese soufflés

These are simple to make – it's the large soufflés that are more tricky because it is difficult to judge whether they are cooked or not – so invest in a set of ramekins and impress your friends.

40 g (1½ oz) butter, plus extra for greasing
40 g (1½ oz) plain flour, plus extra for dusting
250 ml (8 fl oz) hot milk
100 g (3½ oz) Emmenthal, Grayère or Jarlsberg cheese, grated
3 egg yolks
¼–½ teaspoon English mustard powder, to taste
5 egg whites
pinch of salt

Serves 6

Preparation time: 20 minutes
Cooking time: 10–15 minutes

1 Brush six 150–200 ml (5–7 fl oz) ramekins with a little softened butter and dust with flour, shaking out any excess. Set aside in a cool place. Preheat the oven to 180°C (350°F) Gas 4.

2 Melt the butter in a medium saucepan and stir in the flour. Cook over low heat, stirring constantly, for 1 minute. Remove from the heat and whisk in the hot milk – the mixture will be very thick and stiff. Place over low heat and cook for 2–3 minutes, then stir in the grated cheese, egg yolks and mustard to taste. Keep the mixture warm.

3 In a large clean bowl, whisk the egg whites and salt until medium peaks form. Fold into the cheese sauce one-third at a time, taking care not to overmix.

4 Divide the mixture between the ramekins. Bake immediately for 10–15 minutes until well risen and golden.

To Serve Using oven gloves, quickly transfer the ramekins to individual plates. Serve immediately.

Chef's Tips

Check the volume of your ramekins before starting. Some will hold 250–300 ml (8 –10 fl oz), in which case the amount of soufflé mixture given here will be enough for four and you will need to increase the cooking time by 3–5 minutes.

◆

To help the soufflés rise evenly clean the rims of the ramekins before baking by pinching the dish with your thumb on the inside and turning the dish around.

◆

Variation

Instead of the mild cheese, you can use a mature Cheddar, or a crumbled blue cheese with 90 g (3 oz) sautéed mushrooms.

Beef carpaccio

This Italian classic originated in the famous Harry's Bar in Venice. In Italian restaurants it is usually served with a bottle of the best extra-virgin olive oil to sprinkle over the beef. You can do this too if you wish.

- 250–300 g (8–10 oz) piece of beef fillet
- salt and freshly ground black pepper
- 4–6 tablespoons Basil Coulis (page 349) or bottled pesto and a little olive oil
- 1 shallot or small onion
- 4 tablespoons drained capers
- 150 g (5 oz) block of Parmesan cheese

Serves 4

Preparation time: 15 minutes, plus 4 hours freezing

1 Trim any fat or sinew from the beef and discard. Wrap the beef very tightly in cling film and place it in the freezer for about 4 hours to harden.

2 About 1 hour before serving, cut the beef into wafer thin slices, using a sawing action with a very sharp knife. Arrange the beef on 4 plates, overlapping the slices slightly. Season with salt and pepper and drizzle with basil coulis or with pesto mixed to a runny consistency with olive oil. Finely chop the shallot or onion and sprinkle over the beef with the capers.

3 Take the block of Parmesan and a vegetable peeler and carefully shave thin slivers of cheese onto a plate. Pick up the shavings with your fingertips and place them delicately on the carpaccio. Cover the plates and leave at room temperature for 30–45 minutes, by which time the beef will have thawed.

To Serve Uncover the plates and serve immediately, with hot crusty bread.

Chef's Tip

Freezing the beef until hard is a technique used by oriental chefs. It is the best way to get wafer thin slices.

Variation

Make Quesadillas. Sandwich 2 tortillas with grated cheese, chopped jalapeño chillies and stoned black olives. Heat in a hot non-stick frying pan until the cheese starts to melt. Flip the sandwich over and heat the other side.

Crêpes with Wild Mushrooms

The combination of earthy wild mushrooms, garlic and cream makes a fabulously rich filling for crêpes. Serve before a simple main course of grilled or roast meat, poultry or fish, or as a supper dish on their own with a crisp salad to follow.

500 g (1 lb) mixed wild mushrooms
2 shallots
1 garlic clove
60 g (2 oz) butter
salt and freshly ground black pepper
100 ml (3½ fl oz) double cream
4 cooked crêpes
very finely chopped fresh fat-leaf parsley, to serve

Serves 4

Preparation time: 10 minutes
Cooking time: about 15 minutes

1 Thinly slice the mushrooms. Finely chop the shallots and garlic. Melt the butter in a large frying pan and sauté the mushrooms over high heat, stirring frequently until all of their liquid has evaporated and they are tender.

2 Turn the heat down to low and add the shallots and garlic. Cook for another minute, stirring constantly, without allowing the shallots and garlic to brown. Season with salt and pepper and stir in the cream. Increase the heat to moderate and cook until very thick, about 2 minutes. Remove from the heat and keep warm.

3 Gently warm the crêpes through in a very lightly buttered non-stick frying pan over low to moderate heat. Lay the crêpes on a clean surface and spoon one-quarter of the mushroom filling in the centre of each. Fold in the sides, then make into parcels or roll up into logs.

To Serve Place the crêpes seam-side down on individual plates and sprinkle with chopped parsley. Serve immediately.

Chef's Tip

Ready made buckwheat pancakes (crêpes) from Brittany are sold in packets in many supermarkets and delicatessens. Apart from the fact that they save time and trouble, they are very good, and lend this classic French dish a touch of authenticity. They are usually large, about 30 cm (12 inches) in diameter; if you make your own crêpes, a recipe for which is given on page 372, they are likely to be smaller, so you will need 2–3 crêpes per person.

Warm scallop salad

A quintessentially French salad for a special dinner party. The combination of crisp sautéed potatoes and melt-in-the-mouth scallops is absolutely delicious, and the presentation on a bed of red and green mixed leaves is really eye-catching.

Serves 4

Preparation time: 15–20 minutes
Cooking time: about 15 minutes

8 large scallops
500 g (1 lb) peeled small potatoes
leaves of ½ head of frisée lettuce
leaves of ½ head of radicchio
4 tablespoons olive oil
salt and freshly ground black pepper
6 tablespoons Balsamic Vinaigrette (page 360)

1 Remove the corals from the scallops and cut each coral into 2–3 pieces. Cut off and discard the rubbery muscles from the scallops, then slice each scallop into 2–3 discs. Cut the potatoes into discs. Tear the salad leaves into bite-sized pieces and arrange in mounds on individual plates.

2 Heat the olive oil in a frying pan until hot. Add the potatoes, sprinkle with salt and pepper and sauté over moderate heat for about 10 minutes until nicely coloured. Transfer to kitchen paper with a slotted spoon, sprinkle with salt and drain.

3 Season the scallops. Increase the heat under the pan to high, add the scallops and corals and sauté for 3–4 minutes until seared on all sides. Remove with a slotted spoon and arrange on top of the salad leaves with the potatoes.

4 Pour the vinaigrette into the pan and stir over high heat until sizzling.

To Serve Spoon the vinaigrette over the salads and serve immediately.

Chef's Tips

Vacuum-packed peeled potatoes, called pommes parisiennes, are ideal for sautéing. Look for them in the fresh vegetable sections of supermarkets. They are completely natural, with no additives or preservatives.

◆

Fresh scallops are best for salads. Frozen scallops tend to be watery when they are thawed.

Grilled mussels with lime and pesto

For a dinner party, these mussels can be arranged on a bed of coarse sea salt in individual gratin dishes. This way they will not only look good, but the salt will help to hold them steady.

1 kg (2 lb) fresh mussels
1 shallot or small onion
250 ml (8 fl oz) dry white or red wine
1 sprig of fresh thyme
1 bay leaf
salt and freshly ground black pepper
about 4 tablespoons bottled green or red pesto
fresh basil sprays and lime wedges, to garnish

Serves 4

Preparation time: 45 minutes
Cooking time: about 10 minutes

Chef's Tip

Before buying mussels, check that they don't have too many barnacles and beards attached. Some are sold quite clean, and you will find these save you an enormous amount of preparation time.

1 Rinse the mussels well in cold water and scrape off any barnacles with a small sharp knife. Pull off any hairy beards. Discard any mussels that are open or do not close when tapped sharply against the work surface.

2 Finely chop the shallot or onion and place it in a saucepan with the wine, thyme, bay leaf and salt and pepper. Cover tightly and bring slowly to simmering point. Add the mussels, cover the pan again and cook, bubbling briskly, until all the shells have opened, about 3–4 minutes.

3 Drain the mussels from the cooking liquid and cool them to room temperature. Detach the top shell of each mussel, then loosen the mussels from their bottom shells but leave them in place. Spoon a little pesto over each mussel, then arrange them in individual flameproof gratin dishes.

4 Minutes before serving, preheat the grill to high. Place the mussels under the grill for about 1 minute, watching all the time, until the pesto bubbles.

To Serve Tuck a few basil sprigs between the shells and serve immediately, with lime wedges for squeezing. French bread makes a good accompaniment.

Crab and tomato charlottes

These dainty little upside-down ramekins are very quick and easy to make, and the orange and basil dressing is a really delicious flavour contrast. They are ideal for a dinner party because they can be prepared up to a day ahead.

500 g (1 lb) large tomatoes
salt and freshly ground black pepper
375 g (3/4 lb) white crab meat
100 g (3 1/2 oz) half-fat crème fraîche
1 tablespoon tomato purée
2 teaspoons coarsegrain mustard
fresh basil leaves, to serve

Vinaigrette
4 sweet cherry tomatoes, preferably on the vine
1 handful of fresh basil leaves
4 tablespoons extra virgin olive oil
grated rind and juice of 1 orange
caster sugar, to taste (optional)

Serves 4

Preparation time: 15–20 minutes, plus chilling time

1 Line four 150 ml (1/4 pint) ramekins with cling film, letting it hang over the edges.

2 Peel the large tomatoes, then slice them lengthways into quarters and scrape out the cores and seeds. Cut a line across the centre of each quarter, on the inside. This will make them more flexible. Line the ramekins with the tomato petal shapes, arranging them rounded side out and as close together as possible. Sprinkle with salt and pepper.

3 Mix the crab with the crème fraîche, tomato purée, mustard and salt and pepper to taste. Spoon into the ramekins and cover with the overhanging cling film. Chill in the refrigerator for at least 4 hours, preferably overnight.

4 When ready to serve, make the vinaigrette. Finely dice the cherry tomatoes and finely shred the basil. Place in a bowl with the oil, orange rind and juice and whisk together, then taste and season. Add a small amount of sugar if the tomatoes and orange are sharp.

To Serve Unfold the cling film and place an inverted chilled plate on top of each ramekin. Turn the charlottes out on to the plates and remove the cling film. Spoon the dressing around the charlottes and scatter with basil leaves. Serve chilled.

Chef's Tips

You will need 5–6 large tomatoes to have enough quarters to line 4 ramekins. To peel them, cut a cross in the rounded ends and put the tomatoes in a bowl. Pour boiling water over the tomatoes, leave for 1–2 minutes until the skins start to peel back from the cuts, then drain and immerse in a bowl of cold water. The skins will peel off easily with your fingers.

◆

It is not always easy to get fresh white crab meat. Two 185 g cans of crab meat can be used instead.

◆

Variation

Garnish the top of each charlotte with a tiny cluster of black lumpfish roe as well as the basil.

Smoked trout with cucumber and cumin

Toasted cumin seeds give a spicy kick to the creamy dressing in this quick and easy Scandinavian-style starter. It can be prepared just before serving or several hours ahead. Served with nutty or seedy bread, it also makes an excellent lunch dish.

½ large cucumber
salt and freshly ground black pepper
1 tablespoon cumin seeds
250–300 g (8–10 oz) smoked trout fillets
150 g (5 oz) low-fat crème fraîche or natural yogurt

To Serve
about 90 g (3 oz) baby salad leaves
fresh dill or chervil sprigs

Serves 4

Preparation time: 45 minutes, including standing time

Chef's Tip

Packets of baby salad leaves are available at supermarkets. Try to get a packet which contains some red leaves like chard, lollo rosso or radicchio. A few fresh herb leaves will add extra flavour – dill goes especially well with the other flavours in this dish.

◆

Variation

Use smoked salmon, mackerel or eel instead of trout.

1 Peel the cucumber, cut it in half lengthways and scoop out the seeds with a sharp-edged teaspoon. Cut the flesh into thin strips, place in a colander and sprinkle with salt. Leave for 30 minutes.

2 Meanwhile, dry-fry the cumin seeds in a non-stick frying pan for a few minutes until toasted. Flake the trout into large pieces.

3 Rinse the cucumber under the cold tap, drain and pat dry with a clean tea towel or kitchen paper. Place in a bowl, sprinkle the toasted cumin seeds over the top and mix in the crème fraîche or yogurt. Season with pepper to taste.

To Serve Tear the salad leaves into bite-size pieces and arrange like nests around the edges of 4 plates. Spoon the cucumber mixture in the centre. Pile the trout attractively on top of the cucumber and garnish with sprigs of dill or chervil. Serve at room temperature.

HOT CRAB AND GINGER SOUFFLÉS

Crab and ginger are a favourite combination of flavours in the Far East. Here they're used with great success in a classic French soufflé recipe. Individual soufflés are easier to make than large ones because they are less likely to sink in the middle.

30 g (1 oz) butter
30 g (1 oz) dried white breadcrumbs
20 g (¾ oz) pickled ginger
30 g (1 oz) plain flour
300 ml (½ pint) hot milk
200 g (7 oz) crab meat (brown and white)
4 eggs, separated
salt and freshly ground black pepper

Serves 4

Preparation time: 20 minutes
Cooking time: 15–20 minutes

1 Preheat the oven to 190°C (375°F) Gas 5. Butter the insides of four 200 ml (7 fl oz) ramekin or soufflé dishes and coat with dried breadcrumbs. Finely chop the pickled ginger.

2 Melt the remaining butter in a saucepan, add the flour and stir over low to moderate heat for 1 minute. Stir in the pickled ginger and gradually whisk in the milk. Bring to the boil, stirring, then simmer for 2 minutes.

3 Remove the pan from the heat and stir in the crab meat and egg yolks. Season well.

4 In a clean bowl, whisk the egg whites until stiff. Fold into the crab mixture, then spoon into the prepared dishes and run the tip of a blunt knife around the inside of the rims. This will facilitate rising. Bake for 15–20 minutes or until risen and golden.

To Serve Quickly transfer the dishes to small plates and serve immediately.

Chef's Tips

Pungent pickled ginger, also called sushi ginger, is sold in jars at Japanese stores and in the oriental sections of large supermarkets. It is fresh root ginger that has been peeled, very thinly sliced and pickled in rice vinegar.

◆

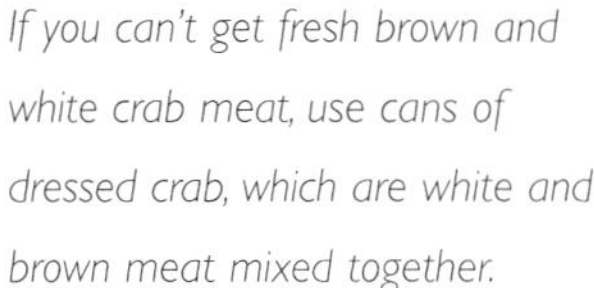

If you can't get fresh brown and white crab meat, use cans of dressed crab, which are white and brown meat mixed together.

Spiced prawn and squid skewers

This Asian-inspired dish is given extra flavour by being cooked on the barbecue, but it can equally well be cooked under the grill or on a ridged cast iron griddle pan on top of the stove.

16 large raw prawns in their shells
200 g (7 oz) prepared baby squid
2 tablespoons sesame seeds

Marinade
2.5 cm (1 inch) piece of fresh root ginger
2 garlic cloves
1 tablespoon light soy sauce
1 tablespoon sweet sherry
1 teaspoon chilli oil
1 tablespoon cornflour

To Serve
about 90 g (3 oz) mixed salad leaves
juice of 1 lime
lime wedges

Serves 4

Preparation time: 20 minutes, plus marinating time
Cooking time: 6–8 minutes

1 First make the marinade. Grate the ginger into a large bowl. Crush the garlic and add to the ginger with the remaining marinade ingredients. Whisk well to mix.

2 Remove the shells from the prawns and cut the squid into 2.5 cm (1 inch) pieces. Add the prawns and squid to the marinade and stir to mix, then cover and marinate in the refrigerator for up to 4 hours.

3 Soak 8 short wooden skewers in a bowl of warm water for at least 30 minutes. Prepare the barbecue for cooking.

4 Add the sesame seeds to the fish and marinade and stir to coat evenly, then thread the prawns and squid alternately on the drained skewers. Spoon over any marinade and barbecue for 3–4 minutes on each side.

To Serve Arrange a small bed of salad leaves on each plate and top with the skewers of fish. Squeeze a little lime juice over the skewers and serve immediately, with lime wedges as a garnish.

Chef's Tips

You can buy ready prepared whole baby squid pouches from supermarkets and fishmongers. Don't buy squid rings because they are difficult to thread on skewers.

◆

Wrap fresh root ginger well and keep it in the freezer. When it is frozen hard, ginger is very easy to peel and grate.

Chilli oil is available from Chinese and Indian shops and the oriental sections of supermarkets. Made with dried red chillies, it is bright orange and fiery hot. If you prefer an oil with a milder taste, use sesame oil.

Chinese pickled vegetables with chilli dip

This is an excellent starter for an oriental meal and it needs to be made well ahead of time, so it is good for entertaining. Tell your guests to put a little of the chilli dip on the side of their plates and to taste it with caution to begin with.

100 g ($3^1/_2$ oz) carrot
100 g ($3^1/_2$ oz) mooli
100 g ($3^1/_2$ oz) drained canned water chestnuts
4 tablespoons rice vinegar
90 g (3 oz) Chinese leaves, to serve

Dip
3 mild red chillies
60 g (2 oz) pickled ginger
1 teaspoon tomato purée

Serves 4

Preparation time: 15 minutes, plus marinating time

1 Cut the carrot and mooli into 2.5 cm (1 inch) cubes. Halve or quarter the water chestnuts. Mix all the vegetables together with the rice vinegar. Cover and set aside for 2–3 hours, mixing occasionally.

2 Meanwhile, halve and deseed the chillies, then pound them to a paste with the pickled ginger. Use a pestle and mortar for pounding, or the small bowl and blade of a food processor. Mix in the tomato purée and turn into a small serving bowl.

To Serve Shred the Chinese leaves and pile them up on a platter. Drain the pickled vegetables and place on top of the leaves. Serve at room temperature, with the bowl of chilli dip alongside.

Chef's Tips

Mooli is Japanese white radish, sometimes called daikon. You can get it in most supermarkets and greengrocers, and Asian stores of course. Its beauty lies in its pure white flesh, which has a very crisp texture when raw.

◆

Water chestnuts are not chestnuts at all, but crisp white bulbs with a brown skin. Canned water chestnuts are peeled and ready to eat, either raw or heated through in stir-fries.

◆

When buying red chillies, the larger and fatter they are the milder they are most likely to be. The very tiny, skinny ones are usually the hottest.

Aubergine and cumin dip

This is similar to the Middle Eastern aubergine dip, baba ghanoush. It has a creamy consistency and a smoky flavour laced with garlic, and is delicious in summer served with fresh vegetable crudités or pitta bread.

3 large aubergines, total weight about 750 g (1 ½ lb)
4 teaspoons olive oil
2 shallots
2 garlic cloves
½ teaspoon cumin seeds
1 x 200 g carton Greek yogurt
salt and freshly ground black pepper

To Serve
about 1 tablespoon extra virgin olive oil
pinch of paprika

Serves 4–6

Preparation time: 20 minutes, plus chilling time
Cooking time: 45 minutes

1 Preheat the oven to 180°C (350°F) Gas 4. Cut the aubergines in half lengthways and score a criss-cross pattern in the flesh. Place the aubergines cut side up on a baking sheet and brush with half the oil. Bake for 45 minutes or until the flesh is soft, especially around the edges.

2 Remove the aubergines from the oven and leave for a while until they are cool enough to handle.

3 Meanwhile, finely chop the shallots and crush the garlic. Heat the remaining oil in a non-stick frying pan, add the shallots and garlic and stir over low heat for a few minutes until softened. Turn into a food processor. Add the cumin seeds to the pan and fry for a few minutes until toasted, then tip them into the food processor.

4 Scoop the aubergine flesh out of the skins into the food processor. Add the yogurt and work to a purée, then add salt and pepper to taste. Turn the dip into a shallow serving dish and swirl the surface to make it level. Cover and chill in the refrigerator for at least 4 hours.

To Serve Drizzle a little oil over the surface of the the dip and sprinkle with paprika. Serve chilled.

Chef's Tip

Greek yogurt comes in 3 different varieties. When it is made with cow's milk, it is available with 10 g fat or 0 g fat per 100 g. Made with sheep's milk, it usually contains about 6 g fat per 100 g. You can use any of these in this recipe, according to personal taste. The cow's milk yogurt containing 10% fat will give the creamiest result; the other two yogurts will give the dip a slightly sharper taste.

◆

Variation

Halve, deseed and finely chop 1 mild green chilli, then fry with the shallots in step 3.

Roast red pepper pâté

Intensely flavoured with smoky roast vegetables and garlic, this pâté-cum-dip is at its best served with a selection of brightly coloured, crisp crudités and warm pitta bread. Make it for a summer barbecue party when peppers and tomatoes are plentiful and cheap.

500 g (1 lb) red peppers
500 g (1 lb) ripe plum tomatoes
1–2 tablespoons olive oil
3 garlic cloves in their skins
1 handful of fresh basil leaves
1 teaspoon sea salt
2–3 teaspoons lemon juice
freshly ground black pepper
a few fresh basil leaves, to serve

Serves 4

Preparation time: 30 minutes, plus cooling, chilling and bringing to room temperature
Cooking time: 1 1/2 hours

1 Preheat the oven to 170°C (325°F) Gas 3. Cut the peppers and tomatoes in half lengthways and remove the cores and seeds. Place the peppers and tomatoes in a large roasting tin and sprinkle with 1 tablespoon oil. Roast for 1 1/2 hours, stirring and turning occasionally and adding the garlic cloves for the last 30 minutes.

2 Allow the vegetables to cool, then peel off and discard the skins from the peppers and garlic. Put the vegetables in a food processor and add the basil and salt. Work to a rough paste, then add another tablespoon oil and lemon juice and pepper to taste. If the mixture is not moist enough, add some of the roasting juices from the vegetables.

3 Transfer the mixture to a serving bowl, cover tightly with cling film and chill in the refrigerator for at least 4 hours, preferably overnight.

To Serve Let stand at room temperature for about 30 minutes, then unwrap and scatter with basil leaves.

Chef's Tips

Plum tomatoes are the ones used for canning, but they are widely available fresh as well. When ripe, they are good for roasting because they have a good colour, rich flavour and juicy flesh. The best kind are the ones that have been ripened on the vine in the sun, and these are easy to get in the summer and early autumn.

A little goes a long way with this pâté because it has a strong flavour. The quantities given here are ample for 4 people, but you can easily double or triple the recipe if you want to make more.

Chicken and Vegetable Spring Rolls

Spring rolls are usually deep fried, but these are the uncooked type made from rice paper, so they are lighter and healthier. The contrast between the soft wrappers and the shredded filling is extremely good.

- 1 carrot
- 3 celery sticks
- 4 spring onions
- 1 small smoked chicken breast
- 2 garlic cloves
- 2.5 cm (1 inch) piece of fresh root ginger
- 2 tablespoons chopped fresh coriander
- 10 round rice paper wrappers

Dipping Sauce

- 1 red chilli
- 1 spring onion
- 1 teaspoon grated fresh root ginger
- 4 tablespoons light soy sauce
- 1 tablespoon sesame oil
- 1 tablespoon clear honey
- 1 tablespoon rice or white wine vinegar
- juice of 1 lime

Serves 4

Preparation time: 30–40 minutes

1 Very finely shred the carrot, celery and spring onions into julienne sticks. Blanch the carrot and celery in boiling water for 1–2 minutes, until just softened. Drain and plunge into cold water, then drain well.

2 Shred the chicken, discarding the skin and any bones, and place in a bowl. Finely chop the garlic and add to the chicken, then grate the ginger into the bowl. Add the blanched vegetables, spring onions and coriander. Mix well.

3 Dip a sheet of rice paper in a bowl of warm water for 10–20 seconds, then place about 3 tablespoons of the filling in the centre. Fold in the sides of the paper, then roll it up in the opposite direction to make a cylindrical parcel. Seal the open edge with water and place the parcel seam side down on a damp tea towel. Cover with another damp tea towel and repeat until all the ingredients are used.

4 Make the dipping sauce. Very finely shred the chilli (removing the seeds if you prefer) and the spring onion. Set aside a few pieces for garnish, then mix the rest with the remaining sauce ingredients.

To Serve Arrange the spring rolls with the bowl of dipping sauce and garnish with the reserved shredded chilli and spring onion.

Chef's Tip

Rice paper wrappers are translucent white and round, usually about 22 cm ($8^{1/2}$ inches) in diameter. You can buy them, fresh or frozen, at oriental stores. They do not need cooking, but they are brittle when you buy them so they must be dipped in water to make them soft enough to roll. To prevent them drying out during preparation, always keep them well covered with a damp tea towel, as you would with filo pastry.

Variation

If you find smoked chicken difficult to get, you can use smoked duck instead – or ordinary roast or poached chicken.

Blackened sweetcorn with chive vinaigrette

A recipe for autumn when corn is at its sweetest and best. Serve as a first course with crusty French bread to mop up the tangy dressing. Pierce the ends of the sweetcorn with small corn-on-the-cob skewers and provide plenty of napkins.

4 corn-on-the-cob
sea or rock salt and freshly ground black pepper

Chive Vinaigrette
125 ml (4 fl oz) extra virgin olive oil
grated rind and juice of 1 lemon
2 tablespoons snipped fresh chives

Serves 4

Preparation time: 10 minutes
Cooking time: 15 minutes

1 Preheat the grill to hot. Remove the papery husks, silks and fibres from the outside of the corn cobs and place the corn under the grill for about 15 minutes, turning several times until the corn is mottled black and charred.

2 Meanwhile, whisk together the ingredients for the vinaigrette.

To Serve Remove the corn from the grill and place on plates. Spoon the chive vinaigrette over the hot corn and sprinkle generously with salt and pepper. Serve hot.

Chef's Tips

Never add salt to the water for boiling corn-on-the-cob because it toughens the kernels. For a sweeter flavour, add a pinch or two of sugar if you like.

◆

Use best quality extra virgin olive oil for dressings like this one in which the flavour is of paramount importance. Keep a bottle especially for salads and for sprinkling over cooked foods just before serving. Check the label: it should say 'cold-pressed' or 'from the first cold pressing'. This type of olive oil tastes fruity; some kinds are peppery hot.

Spicy cheese, tomato and basil soufflés

Sun-dried tomatoes and basil give these summery little soufflés a Mediterranean flavour, while chilli and Parmesan give them a spicy kick. They are good served with warm olive or tomato ciabatta.

- a little softened butter, for coating
- 75 g (2½ oz) finely grated Parmesan cheese
- 1 teaspoon mild chilli powder
- 4 pieces of sun-dried tomato
- 4 eggs, separated
- 2 tablespoons dry white wine
- 1 tablespoon tomato juice
- salt and freshly ground black pepper
- 1 tablespoon shredded fresh basil
- 4 small fresh basil sprigs, to serve

Serves 4

Preparation time: 20–30 minutes

Cooking time: 8–10 minutes

Chef's Tip

This recipe uses the kind of sun-dried tomatoes you buy in packets. They are soaked in water before use to make them easier to chop and less chewy. If you prefer, you can use sun-dried tomatoes which are packed in olive oil. These do not need soaking before use, but they should be drained on kitchen paper to remove excess oil.

1 Preheat the oven to 220°C (425°F) Gas 7. Butter the insides of four 200 ml (7 fl oz) ramekin or soufflé dishes. Mix the Parmesan and chilli powder together, put 1 tablespoon of this mixture into each dish and turn to coat the inside thoroughly.

2 Put the sun-dried tomato pieces in a bowl, cover with boiling water and set aside. Put the egg yolks and wine in a heatproof bowl over a pan of hot water. Whisk until thick and foamy, remove from the heat and stir in the tomato juice and seasoning to taste.

3 Drain the sun-dried tomatoes well, squeeze out as much excess water as possible, then finely chop them.

4 In a clean bowl, whisk the egg whites until stiff. Fold them into the yolk mixture with the sun-dried tomatoes, basil and the remaining spiced Parmesan. Spoon into the prepared dishes and run the tip of a blunt knife around the inside of the rims. This will facilitate rising. Bake in the oven for 8–10 minutes or until risen and golden.

To Serve Quickly transfer the dishes to small plates, garnish with basil sprigs and serve immediately.

SOUPS & STARTERS

quick and easy ideas

NIBBLES AND NUTS

• Dry-fry assorted nuts – cashews, peanuts, almonds, macadamias – in a small non-stick frying pan with 1 tablespoon Persian Spice Rub (page 347). Tip onto kitchen paper and leave to cool.

CIABATTA WITH DIPS

• Serve each person with a small bowl of best-quality olive oil and chunks of fresh ciabatta for dipping.

• For a peppery bite, grind black pepper over the top.

• Add a few finely chopped black or green olives to the oil, or a spoonful of tapenade (olive and anchovy paste).

• Or add a few chopped canned anchovies or sun-dried tomatoes to the oil.

BRUSCHETTA AND CROSTINI

• Lightly toast thin slices of baguette, then spread with pesto or sun-dried tomato paste.

• Cover with thin slices of mozzarella or goat's cheese, then top with mixed dried herbs, canned anchovy fillets, sardines or tuna, or pan-fried thinly sliced scallops.

• Grill or bake in a hot oven for a few minutes until the cheese melts. Serve hot, garnished with sprigs of fresh herbs.

quick and easy ideas

Antipasto

• Arrange a few thin slices of salami, bresàola or other cured or cooked meats on individual plates.

• Next to the meat, arrange quartered hard-boiled eggs or quails' eggs, black and green olives, bottled artichoke hearts and mushrooms, cherry tomatoes, roasted peppers, sliced mozzarella.

• You can serve just one or two of these Italian antipasto ingredients, or as many as you like.

• The aim with antipasto is to present a dish that is as colourful as it is tasty. Alternative ingredients could be chunks of tuna, strips of anchovy (draped across the hard-boiled eggs), tiny radishes, celery hearts or flageolets.

• It is customary to offer extra-virgin olive oil and wine vinegar at the table, so that your guests can dress the vegetables if they wish.

Melon

• Cut baby melons (charentais, cantaloupe or ogen) in half and scoop out the seeds. Cut a very thin slice from the base of each, then stand the melon halves upright on individual plates. Pour port or Madeira into the centre.

• Cut chilled ripe cantaloupe or ogen melon into thin slices, removing the seeds and skin. Arrange the slices in a fan shape and sprinkle with a little lemon juice. Serve with wafer-thin slices of Parma ham, sprinkled with freshly ground black pepper.

SOUPS & STARTERS

quick and easy ideas

Smoked salmon

• Serve thin slices of smoked salmon topped with a spoonful of soured cream and a little caviar or black lumpfish roe. Accompany with lemon or lime wedges and thinly sliced and buttered pumpernickel, rye or wholemeal bread.

• Make roulades by rolling smoked salmon slices around a filling of cream cheese, plain or mixed with finely chopped dill or snipped chives, or with chopped prawns. Garnish with dill fronds or whole chives.

• Line ramekins with shiny sliced smoked salmon, letting the slices overhang the edges. Fill with taramasalata and cover with the overhanging salmon. Turn out upside down onto individual plates and garnish with slices of black olives.

Soup

• Dress up canned tomato soup or consommé by adding a spoonful or two of sherry, vermouth, port or Madeira.

• Whisk a little dry white wine and cream or crème fraîche into a canned smooth soup such as chicken, mushroom or tomato, and serve swirled with cream, feathering it with the handle of a teaspoon.

• Whisk a spoonful or two of bottled pesto or Roasted Garlic flesh (page 348) into vegetable soups.

• Just before serving, sprinkle soup with chopped or shredded fresh herbs, or a single sprig or leaf.

• A liberal sprinkling of black pepper can also be used as a garnish, or a little freshly grated nutmeg, finely grated or shredded cheese, or Parmesan curls.

quick and easy ideas

Parma ham with figs

• Place wafer-thin slices of Parma ham (prosciutto di Parma) on individual plates. For an attractive presenttion, roll them up into cone shapes.

• Cut a cross in the tops of fresh figs, open the figs out to make flower shapes, then place next to the ham.

Prawns

• Serve cooked tiger or king prawns in their shells with Aïoli (garlic mayonnaise, page 365) for dipping. Provide finger bowls and napkins.

• Toss peeled cooked prawns with crème fraîche or mayonnaise (or both), lime juice, grated fresh root ginger and chopped fresh coriander. Season with a dash of fish sauce and serve in Little Gem lettuce cups. Add a little chopped fresh chilli) if you like a hot flavour.

Avocado

• Cut ripe avocados in half and remove the stones. Fill the centres with flaked crabmeat mixed with mayonnaise, soured cream or fromage frais, or a mixture of these, sprinkled with lemon or lime juice and seasoned with salt, pepper and a drop or two of Tabasco.

• Alternate thin slices of ripe avocado, plum tomatoes and mozzarella on a platter, overlapping them slightly. Drizzle with Basil Coulis (page 349) or Balsamic Vinaigrette (page 360).

• Arrange thin slices of avocado alternately with pink grapefruit slices and drizzle with Vinaigrette (page 360).

2

Fish & shellfish

It is hard to beat fish and shellfish for low-fat protein. They are both lighter and easier to digest than poultry and meat – and quicker to cook. Oily fish has the added bonus of containing unsaturated oils, and these can help prevent heart disease if eaten regularly. Fish and shellfish deserve to be eaten more often.

Most of the recipes in this chapter concentrate on the healthier methods of cooking fish – poaching, baking, grilling, barbecuing and chargrilling. Fat is kept to a minimum with these cooking methods and yet the end results are beautifully tender, tasty and moist. The secret is not to overcook, because the delicate flesh of fish and shellfish quickly becomes dry. Always cook for the least amount of time and err on the side of caution. Remember that the flesh continues to cook in its own heat for a while after the fish is removed from the oven or hob.

The variety and choice of fish and shellfish are forever increasing and many are interchangeable in recipes. Fishmongers are immensely knowledgeable, and usually more than happy to give advice about what is best to buy on the day. If you don't see what you want, ask your fishmonger to recommend an alternative. This is far better practice than sticking rigidly to a recipe.

Open ravioli of red mullet

Squares of fresh lasagne are stacked on top of each other with diamonds of red mullet in between and fresh green vegetables all around. The dish is served like a warm salad, with a drizzle of cool basil vinaigrette.

750 g (1 ½ lb) young broad beans in their pods
1 small courgette
12 red mullet fillets, skinned
2 teaspoons olive oil
6 sheets of fresh lasagne
fresh basil leaves, to serve

Basil Vinaigrette
30 g (1 oz) fresh basil leaves
4 tablespoons extra virgin olive oil
1 tablespoon lemon juice
salt and freshly ground black pepper
½ teaspoon sugar

Serves 4

Preparation time: 30 minutes
Cooking time: about 15 minutes

Chef's Tip

For a very special chef's garnish, thinly slice 1 small black truffle and arrange the slices decoratively on top of the pasta just before serving.

1 Preheat the oven to 150°C (300°F) Gas 2. Make the vinaigrette. Purée the basil and oil in a food processor or blender, adding the lemon juice towards the end. Season with salt and pepper and set aside.

2 Shell the broad beans and thinly slice the courgette. Cut each mullet fillet diagonally into 2–3 diamond shapes and season. Heat the oil in a non-stick frying pan and pan-fry the fish, skin side up, for 2–3 minutes. Transfer the fish, skin side up, to an oiled baking sheet, cover with foil and place in the oven for 5 minutes to finish cooking.

3 Blanch the beans and courgette in boiling water for 2 minutes. Drain both vegetables; remove the skin from the broad beans. Place the vegetables in a heatproof dish, cover and keep warm in the oven.

4 Cut the pasta sheets in half to make shapes that are roughly square. Cook in a large saucepan of salted boiling water for 3–4 minutes or until al dente. Drain well and place in a single layer on a clean cloth.

To Serve Layer the pasta and fish on 4 warm plates, starting and finishing with pasta and letting the fish peep out. Scatter the beans and courgette around. Mix the sugar into the vinaigrette, spoon it over and around, then grind black pepper over the top. Garnish with basil leaves and serve immediately.

WARM SALAD OF SMOKED SALMON AND SORREL

This is a dish of contrasting colours, textures and flavours which complement each other superbly well. The saltiness of smoked salmon, sweetness of pink grapefruit and sharpness of sorrel taste very good together. Serve for a light lunch, with crusty bread.

2 pink grapefruit
400–500 g (14 oz–1 lb) smoked salmon
6 black peppercorns
1 bay leaf
100 g (3½ oz) sorrel leaves
4 tablespoons extra virgin olive oil
salt and freshly ground black pepper

Serves 4

Preparation time: 15–20 minutes
Cooking time: 5–7 minutes

1 Preheat the oven to 180°C (350°F) Gas 4. Cut 3 long strips of peel from one of the grapefruit, avoiding the white pith. Put the strips in a shallow baking dish. Peel both fruit totally, cutting off and discarding all the remaining peel and pith. Segment the grapefruit over a bowl, catching the juice. Place the the segments in another large bowl.

2 Place the smoked salmon, peppercorns and bay leaf in the baking dish. Pour cold water over the fish to just cover it, then bake in the oven for 5–7 minutes or until the fish has just turned pale. While the fish is cooking, wash, dry and shred the sorrel.

3 Remove the salmon with a slotted spoon and discard the cooking liquid, grapefruit peel and flavourings. Drain the salmon well and add it to the bowl of grapefruit segments with the sorrel. Fold the ingredients very gently together until evenly combined.

4 Whisk the oil in a jug with 3 tablespoons of the reserved grapefruit juice and season generously with pepper. Drizzle the dressing over the salad and toss gently.

To Serve Turn the salad into a serving bowl and serve immediately.

Chef's Tip

Don't buy expensive, perfect slices of smoked salmon. Smoked salmon trimmings, sometimes called cocktail salmon, are good enough for cooking, and they are much cheaper than the slices.

◆

Variations

If you prefer a milder flavour for the dressing, use half olive oil and half sunflower oil.

◆

If sorrel is difficult to get, use watercress instead. It will give the salad a more peppery bite than sorrel. Cut off and discard the ends of the watercress stalks, then tear the rest of the watercress into small sprigs.

◆

If you have a bottle of dry white wine open, use it to cook the smoked salmon rather than water, or use half wine and half water.

Mackerel with peanuts and chillies

The robust flavours of spring onions, garlic and chillies hold their own against mackerel, a fish with a strong flavour. The mackerel looks and tastes good served Asian style, broken into large pieces on a mound of fragrant jasmine rice.

8 mackerel fillets
4 spring onions
60 g (2 oz) natural unsalted peanuts, skinned
2 green chillies
1 garlic clove
2 tablespoons peanut oil
salt
lime or lemon wedges, to serve

Serves 4

Preparation time: 10–15 minutes, plus marinating time
Cooking time: 6–8 minutes

Variation

For a different serving idea, arrange the mackerel fillets on a bed of noodles. Soak 200 g (7 oz) Chinese dried cellophane noodles in 1 litre (1¾ pints) boiling vegetable stock or water for 3 minutes and drain thoroughly before serving.

1 Cut several slits in a lattice pattern in the mackerel skin. Place skin-side down on a non-metallic tray. Remove the green tops from the spring onions and cut into fine strips. Place these in iced water in the refrigerator and reserve for the garnish. Thinly slice the white parts of the onions and scatter over the fish.

2 Crush the peanuts with the flat side of a large knife blade. Halve, deseed and finely chop the chillies. Crush the garlic.

3 Sprinkle the peanuts, chillies and garlic over the fish, drizzle half of the oil over and sprinkle with a little salt. Cover and set aside at cool room temperature for 1 hour, turning once.

4 Preheat the grill or prepare the barbecue for cooking. Brush the fish with the remaining oil and grill or barbecue for 3–4 minutes on each side or until cooked through.

To Serve Transfer the fish to warm plates and garnish with the drained spring onion tassels. Serve hot, with lime or lemon wedges for squeezing.

Salmon in Vodka with Red Cabbage

This is an inspired dish from northern Europe. It combines traditional sweet and sour red cabbage braised with onion, apple, sugar and wine with the delicate flavour of salmon. Serve it for a dinner party main course, with new potatoes or Mash (page 367).

- 4 thick salmon fillets, each weighing 150–175 g (5–6 oz), skinned
- 125 ml (4 fl oz) vodka
- 4 tablespoons cold fish stock
- 2 tablespoons chopped fresh dill
- ½ small red cabbage, weight about 500 g (1 lb)
- salt and freshly ground black pepper
- 1 red onion
- 2 garlic cloves
- 1 small cooking apple
- 30 g (1 oz) butter
- 1 tablespoon soft brown sugar
- 90 ml (3 fl oz) red wine
- 4 fresh dill sprigs, to serve

Serves 4

Preparation time: 30–60 minutes, including marinating time
Cooking time: 30–35 minutes

Chef's Tip

Look for wild salmon at the fishmonger or supermarket. It has more flavour than farmed salmon, which tends to be bland, but it is more expensive. For a special occasion, you will find it well worth the extra cost.

1 Make sure all the bones in the fish have been removed, then place the fish in a shallow non-metallic baking dish. Mix the vodka, stock and dill together, pour over the fish and cover with cling film. Marinate in the refrigerator for 30–60 minutes.

2 Finely shred the red cabbage, place in a colander and sprinkle with salt. Finely chop the onion and crush the garlic. Peel, core and finely chop the apple.

3 Preheat the oven to 180°C (350°F) Gas 4. Melt the butter in a large saucepan and sweat the onion and garlic over low heat until soft. Rinse the cabbage and shake off the excess water, then add the cabbage to the pan with the apple, sugar, pepper to taste, wine and 75 ml (2½ fl oz) cold water. Cook for 3 minutes, stirring, then cover and cook, stirring occasionally, for about 25 minutes until the liquid has been absorbed. The cabbage should be tender but still a little crisp.

4 Meanwhile, uncover the dish of salmon, place it in the oven and bake for 15 minutes or until just cooked.

To Serve Place the red cabbage on warm plates, arrange the salmon on top and spoon over the cooking liquid. Garnish each serving with a sprig of dill and serve immediately.

Plaice with Wild Mushrooms

Simple and quick, this dish is given a wild earthy flavour from the mushrooms, which also make it more satisfying. Here, chanterelles, girolles and trompettes des morts are used for colour and flavour contrast, but you can use any type of mushroom you like.

2 shallots
100 g (3½ oz) assorted wild or exotic mushrooms
300 ml (½ pint) fish stock
100 ml (3½ fl oz) dry white wine
1 bouquet garni
a little butter
salt and freshly ground black pepper
12 small plaice fillets, skinned
1 tablespoon low-fat crème fraîche
lemon juice
2–3 tablespoons chopped fresh parsley
fresh flat-leaf parsley sprigs, to serve

Serves 4

Preparation time: 10–15 minutes
Cooking time: 20 minutes

1 Preheat the oven to 190°C (375°F) Gas 5. Finely chop the shallots and slice the mushrooms. Put the stock, wine and bouquet garni into a saucepan. Add 300 ml (½ pint) cold water, bring to the boil and boil until reduced to 400 ml (14 fl oz).

2 Meanwhile, butter a shallow flameproof dish. Season the fish, fold each fillet into three, skinned side inwards, and place in the dish. Sprinkle the shallots and mushrooms over the fish.

3 Strain the stock into the dish. Bring to the boil, cover and place in the oven. Bake for 5–8 minutes or until the fish is white. Transfer the fish to a warm platter, leaving the mushrooms and shallots behind. Cover the fish and keep hot.

4 Boil the sauce for a few minutes, stirring constantly until reduced. Add the crème fraîche, a squeeze of lemon juice and 2 tablespoons parsley. Stir to mix, then taste for seasoning and add more lemon juice and parsley if you like.

To Serve Coat the fish with the sauce, garnish with parsley sprigs and serve immediately.

Chef's Tips

There is a recipe for a light fish stock on page 356, but if you don't have the time to make your own, use chilled fresh or canned fish stock, available at most supermarkets and delicatessens. Both of these have a very good flavour, and are better than using stock cubes.

You will need 3 whole plaice to get 12 fillets. Ask your fishmonger to fillet them for you and remove the skin. If they are very small you may prefer to leave the skin on because it is very fiddly to remove and may tear the delicate flesh of the plaice.

Variation

For a special occasion, use lemon sole instead of plaice.

Cod and baby vegetables en papillote

There is hardly any fat at all in this dish, making it ideal when you are entertaining guests who are on low-fat diets. It is easy to manage too, because it can be prepared in advance and popped in the oven while you are eating the first course.

Serves 4

Preparation time: 20 minutes
Cooking time: 40 minutes

- 200 g (7 oz) mixed baby vegetables
- 100 g (3½ oz) sugarsnap peas
- 100 g (3½ oz) baby new potatoes
- 4 cod steaks, each weighing about 200 g (7 oz)
- salt and freshly ground black pepper
- 15 g (½ oz) chilled butter

Dressing

- grated rind and juice of ½ small orange
- juice of 1 small lemon
- 1 tablespoon chopped fresh coriander
- 1 teaspoon crushed Sichuan peppercorns
- ¼ teaspoon sea salt

1 Preheat the oven to 190°C (375°F) Gas 5. Put a large saucepan of water on to boil. Trim the vegetables if necessary and halve them if they are not tiny. Cut 4 large circles of greaseproof paper and foil, about 30 cm (12 inches) in diameter. Place a circle of greaseproof paper over a circle of foil, then place a piece of fish on top, just off centre. Season. Repeat with the remaining circles and fish.

2 Add salt to the water, then boil each type of vegetable separately for 2–3 minutes until just tender. The potatoes may take a little longer. Remove to a colander with a slotted spoon.

3 Mix all the dressing ingredients and taste for seasoning. Put the vegetables on top of the fish and spoon the dressing over them (you may not need all of it). Dice the butter and scatter over the vegetables, then fold the paper and foil over to make half-moon shapes. Fold and pleat the edges so they are sealed and there are 4 neat parcels.

4 Put the parcels on a baking sheet and bake for 20–25 minutes, depending on the thickness of the fish. Open up the parcels for 5 minutes at the end.

To Serve Place a parcel on each of 4 plates, or remove the fish and vegetables from the parcels and place them on warm plates, whichever you prefer.

Chef's Tips

For colour and flavour contrast, the best baby vegetables for this dish are turnips, carrots and courgettes. When buying the new potatoes, choose the smallest you can find.

◆

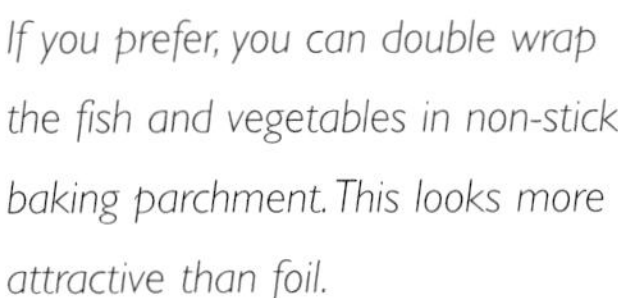

If you prefer, you can double wrap the fish and vegetables in non-stick baking parchment. This looks more attractive than foil.

◆

Variation

You can use other fish besides cod. Haddock, hake and salmon are all suitable, or a more unusual fish like red mullet or sea bream.

Monkfish in nori

Nori seaweed protects the delicate flesh of fish during roasting in the oven. It is used here as a tasty low-fat alternative to bacon rashers, which are often wrapped around monkfish for roasting.

2 monkfish tails, each weighing about 750 g (1 ½ lb), filleted (see Chef's Tips)
2 red hot chillies
finely grated rind and juice of 1 lime
125 ml (4 fl oz) mirin
2 tablespoons rice vinegar
1 tablespoon light soy sauce
2 tablespoons sesame oil
1 x 25 g packet dried nori

Serves 4

Preparation time: 20 minutes, plus marinating time
Cooking time: 15–20 minutes

1 Remove any skin and membrane from the 4 pieces of monkfish, if this has not already been done. Place the fish in a shallow non-metallic dish. Halve, deseed and finely chop the chillies, then mix them with the lime rind and juice, mirin, vinegar, soy sauce and half the sesame oil. Pour over the fish, cover with cling film and marinate in the refrigerator for about 1 hour.

2 Preheat the oven to 180°C (350°F) Gas 4. Dampen 3 sheets of nori and lay them flat on a board. Overlap them slightly so there are no gaps in between. Lift one of the monkfish fillets out of the marinade and place it on the nori, then wrap the nori around the fish, leaving a little room for the fish to swell. Place the parcel in a baking dish. Repeat with the remaining nori and fish, reserving the marinade.

3 Brush the parcels with the remaining oil and bake in the oven for 15–20 minutes. To test for doneness, pierce the fish through the nori with a skewer. The fish should feel tender but still slightly firm. Remove the fish from the oven and pour the cooking juices into a saucepan. Add the reserved marinade, bring to the boil and simmer for a few minutes.

To Serve Slice the parcels of fish crossways with a very sharp knife. Arrange the slices on warm plates, spoon the sauce over and serve.

Chef's Tips

Monkfish tails come with a central bone running through them. Ask your fishmonger to remove the bone from each tail – he will cut the tails lengthways in two so you will have 4 pieces of fish altogether. The tough membrane can be removed at the same time.

Mirin is sweet rice wine. You can buy it in Japanese shops and the oriental sections of supermarkets.

Nori is a Japanese seaweed rich in vitamins and minerals. It is sold as dried roasted sheets in packets in the oriental sections of supermarkets and at health food shops. Sheets of nori are shiny and dark green, like stiff crinkled paper. For this recipe they need to be dampened so they are pliable enough to wrap around the fish.

TUNA WITH BOK CHOI AND MUSHROOMS

Tuna is meaty and satisfying, yet very low in fat. It needs only an hour to marinate in this recipe, then all you have to do is quickly chargrill it and stir-fry the vegetables, making this an ideal dish for entertaining at short notice.

Serves 4

Preparation time: 15 minutes, plus marinating time
Cooking time: 6–8 minutes

4 pieces of tuna fillet, each weighing 150–175 g (5–6 oz)
3 red hot fresh chillies
2 garlic cloves
250 ml (8 fl oz) red wine
300 g (10 oz) bok choi
125 g (4 oz) button mushrooms
salt and freshly ground black pepper
1 tablespoon olive oil

1 Place the pieces of tuna in a single layer in a non-metallic dish. Thinly slice the chillies and garlic, sprinkle them over the tuna and pour in the wine. Cover and marinate in the refrigerator for 1 hour. Meanwhile, coarsely chop the bok choi (both the stalks and the leaves) and halve the mushrooms lengthways.

2 When ready to cook, heat a ridged cast iron griddle pan until very hot. Lift the tuna out of the marinade, drain on kitchen towels and season with a little salt. Pour the marinade into a small pan, add salt and pepper to taste, then simmer for a few minutes until reduced by about half. Remove from the heat, cover and keep hot.

3 Dip a wad of kitchen paper in oil and wipe it over the hot griddle pan. Place the tuna on the pan and chargrill it until done to your liking, about 3 minutes on each side for rare fish in the centre, 4 minutes on each side for medium to well-done.

4 Meanwhile, heat the remaining oil in a wok or large deep frying pan until very hot. Add the bok choi and mushrooms and stir-fry over high heat for about 3 minutes. Season.

To Serve Cut the pieces of tuna in half. Mound the vegetables on warm plates and top with the tuna and marinade. Serve hot.

Chef's Tip

Bok choi, sometimes spelled bok choy or called pak choi, is a member of the cabbage family. You can get it in oriental supermarkets, although many greengrocers and supermarkets also stock it. It is easy to recognize by its thick, creamy white stalks and dark green leaves. It has a mild, peppery taste.

◆

Variation

If you prefer not to chargrill the fish and stir-fry the vegetables at the last moment, this dish can be made in another way that does not involve last-minute cooking. Chargrill the tuna for 3 minutes on each side until pink in the centre, place in the marinade and leave to cool, then chill for several hours in the refrigerator. Serve cold on a bed of raw mushrooms and bok choi, with the marinade poured over.

Herbed filo sole parcels with tomato sauce

This is a delicate-looking main course. Serve with new potatoes tossed in chopped fresh herbs, extra virgin olive oil and a drop or two of balsamic vinegar. A fresh vegetable like mangetouts or sugarsnap peas would also be nice.

200 g (7 oz) button mushrooms
4 tablespoons olive oil
juice of 1/2 lemon
salt and freshly ground black pepper
8 rectangular sheets of filo pastry
2 heaped tablespoons fresh chervil leaves
4 sole fillets

Tomato Sauce
300 ml (1/2 pint) tomato juice
1 teaspoon finely chopped fresh tarragon
15 g (1/2 oz) fresh white breadcrumbs

Serves 4

Preparation time: 30 minutes
Cooking time: 15 minutes

1 Preheat the oven to 200°C (400°F) Gas 6. Finely chop the mushrooms. Heat 1 tablespoon of the oil in a sauté pan, add the mushrooms and lemon juice and cook over low to moderate heat for 3–4 minutes until completely dry. Season.

2 Lay 1 sheet of filo flat on the work surface and brush with oil. Lay one-quarter of the chervil leaves on top, spreading them out in an even pattern. Cover with another sheet of filo and brush with oil.

3 Pat a fish fillet dry and place it lengthways on the pastry. Season the fish and top with the mushroom mixture, then fold in the 2 short sides of the pastry. Fold in the 2 long sides, then place the parcel, join side down, on a baking sheet and brush with more oil. Repeat with the remaining pastry, chervil and fish.

4 Bake for 15 minutes or until the pastry is golden around the edges and the fish is tender in the centre when pierced through the pastry with a skewer. Meanwhile, gently heat the tomato juice, tarragon and breadcrumbs in a small pan, whisking until smooth and thickened. Remove from the heat and add salt and pepper to taste.

To Serve Place the fish parcels on warm plates and spoon the sauce alongside. Serve hot.

Chef's Tips

The most convenient way to buy filo pastry is frozen. It is available in rectangular boxes at supermarkets and Middle Eastern stores. The exact size of the filo sheets is not important for this recipe. Once the sheets have thawed, cover them with cling film or a damp cloth to prevent them drying out.

◆

Use lemon sole. It is less expensive than Dover sole, and easier to get.

◆

Buy a carton or bottle of natural tomato juice, the type you would normally buy for drinking. It is concentrated and strained so the consistency is rich and smooth, ideal for making sauces. Check the label to see if salt has been added and take care with the seasoning.

SALMON FISH CAKES WITH LEMON AND DILL

Homemade fish cakes are far superior to any that you can buy. For one thing, you can be sure of what's in them. These are extra tasty because they are packed with fresh salmon and herbs and served with a tangy, yogurt-based sauce.

300 g (10 oz) salmon fillet
125 ml (4 fl oz) hot fish stock
125–150 ml (4–5 fl oz) hot semi-skimmed milk
3 baked potatoes
2 tablespoons chopped fresh dill
2 tablespoons chopped fresh parsley
salt and freshly ground black pepper
1 egg yolk
2 eggs
about 125 g (4 oz) dried breadcrumbs
lemon wedges, to serve

Dressing
200 ml (7 fl oz) low-fat natural yogurt
finely grated rind of 1 lemon
¼ bunch of fresh dill

Makes 8

Preparation time: 40 minutes
Cooking time: 1½–1¾ hours, including baking time for potatoes

Chef's Tips

The best potatoes for baking are the large, floury main crop types such as Desirée, King Edward and Maris Piper. These have a light and fluffy texture when cooked. To bake potatoes, prick them in several places with a skewer or fork, then bake in a 200°C (400°F) Gas 6 oven for 1¼ hours or until tender.

◆

The fish cakes can be prepared up to the end of step 3, then kept in the refrigerator for up to 24 hours before cooking. If you refrigerate them uncovered, the breadcrumb coating will harden and be extra crisp when baked.

1 Preheat the oven to 190°C (375°F) Gas 5. Put the salmon in a baking dish with the stock and 125 ml (4 fl oz) milk. Cover with foil and poach in the oven for 5–6 minutes or until the fish flakes easily with a fork. Remove the fish with a slotted spoon and drain on kitchen paper.

2 Flake the fish, discarding the skin and any bones. Cut the baked potatoes in half, then scoop out the flesh and mash with a fork. Add the fish and herbs to the potato and mix thoroughly. Season well with salt and pepper and moisten with the egg yolk. Add a little milk if the mixture seems dry.

3 Divide the mixture into 8 equal pieces and pat into small cakes. Beat the eggs in a shallow dish with a pinch each of salt and pepper. Coat the fish cakes with beaten egg mixture, then the breadcrumbs.

4 Place the fish cakes on a baking tray and bake for 15 minutes or until golden, turning them over halfway. Meanwhile, mix the yogurt, lemon rind and dill together to make the dressing.

To Serve Place the fish cakes on a warm platter with the bowl of dressing in the centre. Garnish with lemon wedges and serve.

Salmon and scallop wraps

This is a very special dish for a dinner party. If you are lucky enough to buy scallops with the orange coral (roe) attached, these can be pulled off and chopped, then heated through in the sauce at the last minute. They look pretty and taste delicious.

8 large scallops
4 thin slices of skinless salmon fillet, each weighing about 150 g (5 oz)
3 shallots
about 2 tablespoons dry vermouth
65 g (2½ oz) watercress leaves
2 tablespoons low-fat crème fraîche
salt and freshly ground black pepper

Preparation time: 15 minutes
Cooking time: 20 minutes

1 Preheat the oven to 200°C (400°F) Gas 6. Pat the scallops dry with kitchen paper if necessary. Put the salmon slices between 2 sheets of cling film and flatten them with the bottom of a saucepan. Remove the cling film and cut each slice of salmon in half crossways. Wrap each scallop in a slice of salmon, skinned side inwards.

2 Place the fish parcels with their joins underneath in a baking dish. Finely chop the shallots and scatter them over the fish. Pour in water to come halfway up the fish. Cover with foil and bake for 10 minutes. Meanwhile, chop the watercress, reserving a few sprigs for the garnish.

3 Remove the fish with a slotted spoon to a serving platter, cover and keep warm. Strain the cooking liquid into a measuring jug and make up to 500 ml (18 fl oz) with water. Pour into a saucepan, add 2 tablespoons vermouth and boil until reduced by about half

4 Lower the heat and add the watercress and crème fraîche. Heat through, stirring, then add seasoning to taste. If you like, add a splash more vermouth.

To Serve Pour the sauce over the fish parcels and garnish with the reserved watercress. Serve immediately.

Chef's Tip

Fresh scallops are better than frozen for this recipe because frozen scallops tend to be watery after thawing. They must be absolutely fresh, so buy and cook them within 24 hours, keeping them in the refrigerator until you are ready to cook. To prepare scallops, pull off the tough crescent-shaped muscle on the side. This must be discarded because it is chewy and will spoil the finished dish.

◆

Variation

An aniseed liqueur such as Pernod can be used instead of vermouth.

Brochettes of Fish with Ginger and Lime

Three different types of fish provide contrasts of colour, texture and flavour in these succulent grilled kebabs. The cooking juices are used to make an oriental-style sauce, which tastes delicious when served with fragrant Thai rice.

250–375 g (8–12 oz) monkfish fillet
250–375 g (8–12 oz) salmon fillet
250–375 g (8–12 oz) cod fillet
2 limes
2.5 cm (1 inch) piece of fresh root ginger
3–4 tablespoons light soy sauce
freshly ground black pepper
lime wedges, to serve

Serves 4

Preparation time: 10 minutes, plus marinating time
Cooking time: 10 minutes

1 Skin all of the fish and cut it into even-size cubes. Finely grate the lime rind and squeeze the juice. Peel and finely grate the ginger. Put the lime rind and juice in a non-metallic dish with the ginger and 2 tablespoons soy sauce. Stir together. Place the fish in the dish and stir gently, making sure that all the cubes are coated in marinade. Cover with cling film and marinate in the refrigerator for 1 hour.

2 Meanwhile, put 8 wooden skewers to soak in a bowl of warm water. Preheat the grill.

3 Drain the skewers and thread the fish on them, alternating the different types. Place on the rack under the grill and cook the fish for 4 minutes on each side.

4 Transfer the skewers to warm plates and keep hot. Pour the cooking juices into a small pan, add a few tablespoons of cold water and 1–2 tablespoons soy sauce to taste. Bring to the boil, stirring.

To Serve Spoon the sauce over the brochettes, then grind black pepper over them. Serve with wedges of lime for squeezing.

Chef's Tips

It is quite tricky to skin fish without tearing the flesh, so get your fishmonger to skin the fish fillets if possible. If you have to do it yourself, lay each fillet skin side down and grip the tail end with your fingers dipped in salt. Cut between the fish and the skin at this end, then work the knife away from you using a sawing action at a low angle until you reach the other end of the fillet.

If you keep root ginger in the freezer you will find it easier to grate when it is frozen hard than when it is fresh.

Moules marinière

This classic dish is naturally light and low in fat, yet not often thought of as such. Serve with a crusty baguette for mopping up the delicious juices. The quantities given here are enough for a first course for four people or a main course for two.

Serves 4

Preparation time: 30 minutes

Cooking time: 10–15 minutes

1 kg (2 lb) live mussels
1 onion
1 garlic clove
1 tablespoon olive oil
200 ml (7 fl oz) dry white wine
1 bay leaf
1 tablespoon fresh thyme leaves
2 tablespoons chopped fresh parsley
salt and freshly ground black pepper

1 Rinse the mussels well in cold water and scrape off any barnacles with a small sharp knife. Pull off any hairy beards. Discard any mussels that are open or do not close when tapped sharply against the work surface. Give the closed mussels a final wash. Finely chop the onion and crush the garlic.

2 In a deep saucepan with a close-fitting lid, sweat the onion in the oil until softened. Add the garlic and stir for 1 minute, then add the wine, bay leaf, thyme and drained mussels. Stir well, cover tightly and cook rapidly until the mussels have opened, about 5–10 minutes.

3 Remove from the heat and add the parsley and seasoning.

To Serve Ladle the mussels and liquid into large bowls, discarding any mussels that have not opened. Serve immediately.

Chef's Tip

Fresh mussels can be bought from September to April, when there is an 'r' in the month. They are alive when you buy them, with their shells tight shut. Those that are open and do not close when tapped sharply should be discarded because they have died and are not safe to eat, so always buy slightly more than you need to allow for wastage. Frozen mussels are available all year round.

◆

Variation

Use dry Normandy cider instead of the white wine.

Clam and black bean salad

In the United States, both clams and black beans are favourite ingredients and here they come together in this dramatic-looking salad which is full of flavour. Serve it with crusty French bread.

1 kg (2 lb) small live clams
150 ml (¼ pint) dry white wine
2 garlic cloves
3 shallots
250 g (8 oz) dried black beans, soaked in cold water overnight
4 large ripe tomatoes
1–2 tablespoons chopped fresh dill, to taste
salt and freshly ground black pepper

Serves 4–6

Preparation time: 40 minutes, plus soaking time
Cooking time: about 1½ hours

1 Wash the clams in several changes of cold water and scrub them well. Discard any that are open or do not close when tapped sharply against the work surface. Pour cold water into a large saucepan to come about 4 cm (1½ inches) up the sides. Add the wine. Finely chop the garlic and shallots. Add the garlic and one-third of the shallots to the pan. Bring to the boil, tip in the clams and cover the pan tightly. Cook over moderate heat for 10 minutes, shaking the pan often.

2 Tip the clams into a colander set over a bowl to catch the cooking liquid. Check that all the clams have opened, discarding any that have not. Remove most of the clams from their shells, reserving a few in shell for the garnish.

3 Strain the cooking liquid through a muslin-lined sieve. Make up to 1.6 litres (2¾ pints) with cold water, return to the rinsed pan and bring to the boil. Drain the beans and add to the pan with half the remaining shallots. Boil hard for 10 minutes, then simmer until the beans are tender, 50–60 minutes. If necessary, top up with more water during cooking.

4 Halve, deseed and dice the tomatoes. Drain the beans and mix them with the shelled clams, tomatoes and remaining shallots. Add dill and seasoning to taste.

To Serve Turn the salad into a serving bowl and garnish with the reserved clams in their shells. Serve at room temperature.

Chef's Tips

Use small clams, which may be labelled palourdes, Venus or amandes. These have sweet, tender flesh and are the most suitable varieties for salads. Soak them in a bowl of cold water for 2 hours before use. Clams are very sandy and this helps draw out the sand and make them less gritty.

Black beans, sometimes called turtle beans, have always been popular in north, central and south America, and now you can get them here, both in supermarkets and health food shops. They come from the same family as red kidney beans, but are slightly sweeter.

Bouillabaisse

A classic bouillabaisse is usually served with rouille (a chilli-flavoured mayonnaise) and croûtes made from fried or toasted bread. This simple version dispenses with these finishing touches and is therefore much lighter, but it is equally good.

300 g (10 oz) monkfish
300 g (10 oz) conger eel
300 g (10 oz) red gurnard
300 g (10 oz) cod
1 John Dory
300 g (10 oz) sea bass
1 small leek
1 celery stick
1 small bulb of fennel
1 onion
2 garlic cloves
3 tablespoons olive oil
1.8 litres (3 pints) fish stock
2 pinches of saffron threads
1 bouquet garni
salt and freshly ground black pepper
a few heaped tablespoons peeled and diced tomato, to serve

Serves 6

Preparation time: 20 minutes
Cooking time: 25–30 minutes

1 Remove all skin and bone from the fish and cut the flesh into about 5 cm (2 inch) chunks. Thinly slice the leek and wash thoroughly. Thinly slice the celery and fennel, reserving the feathery tops for the garnish. Finely chop the onion and crush the garlic.

2 Heat the oil in a large saucepan and sweat the vegetables and garlic until soft, about 10 minutes. Add the stock, saffron, bouquet garni and salt and pepper to taste, stir well and bring to the boil.

3 Lower the heat to a gentle simmer, then add the chunks of fish. Simmer until the fish is just cooked, about 10–15 minutes. Take care not to overcook the fish or it will fall apart.

To Serve Taste the soup for seasoning and ladle into warm soup plates. Top with the diced tomato and the reserved celery and fennel tops. Serve immediately.

Chef's Tip

Bouillabaisse comes from the French port of Marseille in the Mediterranean, where it is made with many different kinds of locally caught fish. The fish suggested here can be bought when they are in season from good fishmongers, but if you find red gurnard or John Dory hard to get, you can use any other white fish such as cod, haddock, hake, sole, red snapper, sea bream or whiting. Conger eel is an oily fish; mackerel or herring can be substituted for it.

Baked fillets of cod with a herb crust

This is a very quick and easy dish, and it has the added bonus that it can be prepared several hours ahead of time, ready to pop in the oven when you need it. Serve with Braised Celery in Tomato Sauce (page 216) and new potatoes for a low-fat lunch or dinner.

15 g (½ oz) softened butter
1 shallot
2 garlic cloves
a few rosemary, thyme and marjoram sprigs
a small handful of fresh parsley leaves
2 tablespoons olive oil
60–90 g (2–3 oz) fine fresh white breadcrumbs
salt and freshly ground black pepper
4 pieces of cod fillet, each weighing about 175 g (6 oz)

Serves 4

Preparation time: 20 minutes
Cooking time: 25 minutes

1 Preheat the oven to 180°C (350°F) Gas 4. Brush a baking dish with the butter. Chop the shallot and garlic. Strip the leaves off the herb sprigs and chop them finely. Chop the parsley finely, keeping it separate from the other herbs.

2 Heat the oil in a small frying pan and sweat the shallot and garlic with the rosemary, thyme and marjoram. Remove from the heat.

3 Put the breadcrumbs in a bowl with the parsley. Add the shallot mixture and mix well, then season generously with salt and pepper.

4 Season the fish, then press the breadcrumb and herb mixture all over it. Place it in the baking dish and sprinkle the remaining crumbs on top. Bake for 20 minutes or until the fish flakes easily with a fork and the crust is golden.

To Serve Place the fish on warm plates and serve immediately.

Chef's Tips

Make the breadcrumbs from stale bread in a food processor, working them until they are very fine, then spread them out on a tray and leave them to dry for a few hours – or overnight if possible.

You can use fish with the skin on or skinless fillets, whichever type you find easiest to get. Cod is a soft, flaky-textured fish, which has a tendency to break easily. Cooking it with the skin on helps keep the fillets together.

Variation

Haddock fillets may be used instead of cod.

Scrambled egg and smoked salmon tarts

These crisp little filo tarts make the most delicious brunch or lunch. The filo cases can be prepared a few hours ahead of time, so all you have to do is scramble the eggs just before serving.

2 tablespoons olive oil
30 g (1 oz) butter
2 shallots
12 rectangular sheets of filo pastry (see Chef's Tip)
salt and freshly ground black pepper
100–150 g ($3^1/_2$–5 oz) thinly sliced smoked salmon
8 eggs
6 tablespoons semi-skimmed milk

Serves 4

Preparation time: 20–30 minutes
Cooking time: about 12 minutes

1 Preheat the oven to 190°C (375°F) Gas 5 and put a large baking sheet in the oven to heat at the same time. Brush the insides of four 10–12.5 cm (4–5 inch) tart tins lightly with oil. Melt half the butter in a small pan, then pour it into a bowl and mix in the remaining oil. Chop the shallots very finely.

2 Cut 24 discs out of the filo, about 2.5 cm (1 inch) larger than the tins. Brush 1 disc lightly with oil and butter and place it in a tin, tucking the filo into the inside edge. Brush another disc with oil and place on top of the first. Repeat with a third disc. Sprinkle with a quarter of the shallots and salt and pepper to taste, then place 3 more discs on top, brushing the layers with oil and butter. Prick the base of the filo all over with a fork, then fill with crumpled foil. Repeat with the remaining 3 tart tins.

3 Put the tins on the hot baking sheet and bake blind for 5 minutes. Remove the foil, return the tins to the oven and bake for a further 2 minutes or until the pastry is golden brown. Set aside to cool a little in the tins. Cut the smoked salmon into thin ribbons. Beat the eggs with the milk and season well.

4 Melt the remaining butter in a non-stick pan and scramble the eggs over low heat for 3–4 minutes, stirring all the time with a wooden spoon. Stir off the heat for 1 minute.

To Serve Transfer the filo cases to plates, then spoon in the scrambled egg and pile the smoked salmon on top. Serve immediately.

Chef's Tip

Filo pastry is available frozen in boxes at most supermarkets and Middle Eastern stores. Most boxes contain rectangular sheets in a roll, which must be thawed before they can be unrolled. Sizes vary according to manufacturer, so you may need more or less sheets than the number given here, which is based on the sheets being 30 x 18 cm (12 x 7 inches). Filo pastry is very fragile and dries out very quickly when it is exposed to air. Always keep the pieces you are not actually working with covered with cling film or a damp cloth.

Pan-fried scallops with mango and chilli salsa

Delicate scallops hardly need any cooking, in fact the less you cook them the better – they can go rubbery and tough if overcooked. Serve this special dish for two with boiled white or saffron rice and a bottle of champagne or dry white wine.

Serves 2

Preparation time: 20 minutes
Cooking time: 3–4 minutes

6 large scallops
2 tablespoons olive oil
15 g (1/2 oz) unsalted butter
2 fresh coriander sprigs, to serve

Salsa
2 large ripe plum tomatoes
1 small ripe mango
15–30 g (1/2–1 oz) fresh coriander leaves
1 large shallot
juice of 1 lime
1/4 teaspoon Tabasco
salt and freshly ground black pepper

1 First make the salsa. Peel and dice the tomatoes. Peel, stone and dice the mango. Chop the coriander. Finely chop the shallot. Put all these ingredients in a bowl and add the lime juice, Tabasco and salt and pepper to taste. Stir well to mix, then cover and chill in the refrigerator until ready to serve.

2 Pat the scallops dry with kitchen paper. Heat the oil in a non-stick frying pan, add the butter and stir until foaming. Add the scallops to the pan and cook for 3–4 minutes, turning them once until lightly golden on both sides and tender to the touch.

To Serve Spoon the salsa on to 2 plates. Sit the scallops on top and garnish each serving with a sprig of coriander. Serve immediately.

Chef's Tip

Scallops are usually sold off the shell at supermarkets and fishmongers. Make sure they are fresh and have not been frozen and thawed, because frozen scallops tend to be watery and flabby. Before cooking, always pull off the tough muscle at the side of each scallop, but don't remove the orange coral if it is attached. The coral is a great delicacy – and it looks attractive too.

Scrambled eggs with smoked salmon

For a quick and nutritious after-work supper, nothing beats scrambled eggs on toast. Here they are given a luxurious touch with smoked salmon and cream. Serve them, moist and creamy, to contrast with the crispness of the toast.

125 g (4 oz) smoked salmon
1 small handful of fresh chives
6 large eggs
salt and freshly ground black pepper
2 tablespoons double cream
30 g (1 oz) butter

Serves 2

Preparation time: 5 minutes
Cooking time: 5–8 minutes

1 Cut the smoked salmon into thin strips. Snip the chives finely with scissors, reserving a few whole stems for the garnish. Break the eggs into a bowl, season, then add the cream. Whisk lightly, just enough to break up the yolks a little.

2 Heat the butter until foaming in a medium non-stick sauté pan or a wide shallow saucepan. Add the eggs and cook over low heat, stirring constantly and slowly with a wooden spatula until the eggs are only just beginning to set. They should still be creamy and moist.

3 Remove from the heat and gently stir in the smoked salmon. Taste for seasoning.

To Serve Spoon onto buttered toasted rye bread, muffins or bagels, garnish with the reserved chives and serve immediately.

Chef's Tips

Look for packets of smoked salmon trimmings in your supermarket. They are less expensive than whole slices.

◆

To accompany the scrambled eggs, sauté 200 g (7 oz) chanterelle mushrooms and 1 tablespoon finely chopped shallot in 60 g (2 oz) butter. Mix in 1 tablespoon finely chopped fresh parsley.

◆

Variation

For a luxurious brunch dish, replace the smoked salmon with 60 g (2 oz) caviar. Don't stir it into the eggs, simply spoon it on top of the eggs just before serving and garnish with a sprig of chervil. For a less expensive dish that looks equally impressive use lumpfish roe instead of caviar.

Omelette Arnold Bennett

This classic recipe was created for the writer by the chefs at the Savoy in London. It is still on the menu there. In the Savoy recipe the eggs are separated, the whites lightly beaten and folded into the yolks. This version is quicker and simpler.

175–200 g (6–7 oz) smoked haddock fillet
about 400 ml (14 fl oz) milk and water, mixed half and half
100 ml (3½ fl oz) double cream
2 large eggs
pinch of cayenne pepper
freshly ground black pepper
2 teaspoons sunflower oil
30–60 g (1–2 oz) Parmesan cheese
snipped fresh chives, to garnish

Serves 2

Preparation time: 10–15 minutes
Cooking time: about 10 minutes

1 Put the smoked haddock in a small pan and add enough milk and water to cover the fish. Heat to simmering point, then half cover and poach over low heat for 5 minutes.

2 Remove the fish with a slotted spoon and drain, then break it into its natural flakes, removing any skin and bones. Drain the fish again, place in a bowl and fold in half the cream. Beat the remaining cream with the eggs, cayenne and black pepper. Preheat the grill.

3 Heat the oil in an omelette pan or frying pan which can safely be used under the grill. When very hot, pour in the egg mixture. Stir with a wooden spatula until setting around the edges, then spoon the haddock and cream over the middle. Cook for a further 2–3 minutes or until the omelette has set underneath.

4 Grate the Parmesan over the omelette, then flash under the grill for 1–2 minutes until golden brown.

To Serve Slide the omelette out of the pan onto a plate and sprinkle with chives. Serve hot, cut into wedges.

Chef's Tip

One of the secrets of a good omelette is the pan in which you cook it. French chefs keep a well-seasoned cast iron pan especially for omelettes, never using it for anything else. It is not washed after use, but simply wiped with kitchen paper. A good quality, heavy non-stick pan is also good for omelettes, and 15–18 cm (6–7 inches) is the perfect size for a 2-egg omelette to serve 2 people. This is by far the easiest size to make, so if you are serving 4, it is better to make 2 separate omelettes than 1 large one.

Egg pancakes with salmon and herbs

A fusion of oriental-style pancakes and Scandinavian filling makes a very tasty supper dish for 2 people. Serve with a leafy green or mixed salad tossed in Vinaigrette (page 360).

4 large eggs
about 2 teaspoons sunflower oil

Filling
1 shallot or 2 spring onions
2 tablespoons sunflower oil
1 tablespoon sesame oil
300 g (10 oz) salmon fillet
¼ teaspoon each ground cumin and coriander
1–2 tablespoons chopped fresh dill
salt and freshly ground black pepper
fresh dill sprigs, to garnish

Serves 2

Preparation time: 20 minutes
Cooking time: about 20 minutes

1 First make the filling. Finely chop the shallot or spring onions. Heat the oils in a frying pan until hot, add the salmon and fry over moderate heat for 3 minutes on each side. Remove the pan from the heat and lift the salmon out with a fish slice. Flake the salmon, discarding any skin and bones.

2 Return the pan to the heat, add the shallot or spring onions and the spices and stir for 1 minute. Add the salmon, dill and seasoning and toss to combine. Remove from the heat and keep hot while making the pancakes.

3 Beat the eggs with 100 ml (3½ fl oz) water, a little salt and plenty of pepper. Lightly oil a 15–18 cm (6–7 inch) omelette or frying pan and heat until very hot. Pour in one-quarter of the egg mixture and cook like an omelette until set on top and golden underneath, 2–3 minutes. Slide out of the pan onto a plate and keep hot. Repeat with the remaining egg mixture to make 4 pancakes altogether, stacking them on top of each other.

To Serve Spoon one-quarter of the filling in the centre of each pancake, fold one side over the filling to cover it, then bring the other side over to overlap slightly. Arrange a sprig of dill in the centre of each pancake and serve immediately.

Chef's Tips

These pancakes are extra good if you put a spoonful of crème fraîche on top of the filling before folding, or if you serve them with a separate bowl of crème fraîche mixed with chopped fresh dill and salt and pepper.

◆

They also make a very good first course for 4 people. Use 2 large eggs and 4 tablespoons water to make 4 very thin pancakes and top the filling with crème fraîche before folding.

Fish with tomatoes and olives

Heady with Provençal aromas and flavours of tomatoes, garlic and thyme, this makes an excellent main course for midweek entertaining. Serve it with couscous, rice, Mashed Potatoes (page 239) or pasta and follow with a tossed green salad.

1 x 700–800 g can whole peeled tomatoes
1 small onion
4 garlic cloves
60 g (2 oz) stoned green or black olives
125 ml (4 fl oz) olive oil
1 bay leaf
2 fresh thyme sprigs
salt and freshly ground black pepper
4 thick cod fillets, each weighing about 175 g (6 oz)
fresh thyme sprigs, to garnish (optional)

Serves 4

Preparation time: 10 minutes
Cooking time: 35 minutes

1 Tip the tomatoes into a sieve placed over a bowl and let the juice run through. Turn the tomatoes into a food processor and, using the pulse button, chop them lightly. Finely chop the onion and garlic. Quarter the olives lengthways.

2 Heat two-thirds of the oil in a large, deep sauté pan over low heat. Add the onion and cook for 2–3 minutes without colouring, then add the tomato liquid, garlic, bay leaf and thyme. Increase the heat to moderate and cook. stirring occasionally, until reduced by half. Add the tomatoes and simmer over low heat, stirring occasionally, for 30 minutes or until the sauce is thick.

3 About 10 minutes before the sauce is ready, cook the fish. Season the fish fillets and heat the remaining oil in another large, deep sauté pan. Pan-fry the fish over moderate heat for 6 minutes, turning once.

4 Remove the bay leaf and thyme from the sauce, then pour the sauce over the fish and sprinkle in the olives and seasoning to taste. Shake the pan to coat the fish in the sauce.

To Serve Place the fish fillets on warm plates with the sauce spooned over and around. Garnish with thyme (if using) and serve immediately.

Chef's Tip

Thick cod fillets are very white and meaty, but delicate in texture, so take care not to let them break up during cooking. If you leave the skin on, this will help keep the fillets intact, but you may prefer to remove it – most people prefer fish served without skin.

◆

Variations

Tuna or swordfish steaks or monkfish fillet can be used instead of cod.

◆

To save time, you can use chopped tomatoes or bottled passata (sieved tomatoes), some brands of which have onion, garlic and herbs added. In this case, simply simmer for 10–15 minutes before adding the fish.

Salmon fillets with sesame crust

This is an excellent main course if you are entertaining a friend after work, and it is easy to increase the quantities if there are more than two of you. Broccoli or mangetouts would make a good accompaniment, or a mixed vegetable stir-fry.

4 tablespoons sesame seeds
2 thick salmon fillets, each weighing 150–175 g (5–6 oz), skinned
salt and freshly ground black pepper
2–3 tablespoons oyster sauce
1 tablespoon sunflower oil
1 tablespoon sesame oil

To Serve
2 lime wedges
oyster sauce

Serves 2

Preparation time: 5 minutes
Cooking time: about 10 minutes

1 Dry-fry the sesame seeds in a non-stick frying pan over moderate heat for 2–3 minutes until lighty toasted. Preheat the grill.

2 Cut each salmon fillet in half, then season with salt and pepper. Brush generously with oyster sauce and coat with the toasted sesame seeds.

3 Heat the oils in a non-stick frying pan until hot. Place the salmon in the pan and cook over moderate to high heat until the edges have become firm, about 3 minutes. Cook the salmon on one side only – do not turn it over.

4 Using a fish slice and keeping the fish the same way up, transfer the salmon to the grill pan. Finish cooking under the grill for about 3 minutes.

To Serve Arrange the salmon fillets on warm plates with lime wedges for squeezing. Serve extra oyster sauce in a small bowl alongside.

Chef's Tip

Salmon fillets are sold in packets in the fresh fish sections of supermarkets. Look for fillets that are about 2.5 cm (1 inch) thick. They should be boneless, but always check for any fine pin bones before cooking, and pull them out with tweezers or your fingertips. Rinse the fish before using and pat dry with kitchen paper.

THAI FISH CAKES

If you have a food processor, nothing could be quicker and easier than these spicy hot fish cakes, and they can be prepared up to the frying stage the day before. Serve the with a mixed salad or stir-fried vegetables.

500 g (1 lb) cod fillets, skinned
1 medium red pepper
1 large egg
2 tablespoons fish sauce
1 tablespoon red or green Thai curry paste
finely grated rind of 1 lime
1 large handful of fresh coriander leaves
good pinch of salt
4–6 tablespoons sunflower oil

To Serve
lime wedges
fish sauce (optional)

Serves 4

Preparation time: 10 minutes
Cooking time: 5–10 minutes

1 Cut the fish into chunks, checking carefully that there are no bones. Roughly chop the red pepper, removing the core, seeds and spongy ribs. Put the fish and red pepper in the bowl of a food processor and add the egg, fish sauce, curry paste, lime rind, coriander leaves and salt. Work to a coarse purée.

2 Heat about 2.5 cm (1 inch) oil in a frying pan until very hot. Remove the blade from the food processor bowl, then scoop out the fish mixture in heaped spoonfuls, about the size of the palm of your hand. Drop the mixture into the hot oil and flatten slightly with the back of the spoon.

3 Cook the fish cakes over moderate to high heat for 2–3 minutes on each side until golden brown. The mixture makes about 16 fish cakes, so you will need to cook them in 2–3 batches to avoid overcrowding the pan. Remove them with a slotted spoon, drain on kitchen paper and keep hot.

To Serve Arrange on a warm platter with lime wedges and serve hot. Fish sauce can be served in a small bowl, to be sprinkled over the fish cakes or used as a dip.

Chef's Tips

If you prepare the mixture the day before, turn it into a bowl, cover and refrigerate. Use within 24 hours.

◆

Don't overwork the mixture in the food processor because this will toughen the fish, and only fry the fish cakes for the time given in the recipe. Overcooked fish cakes tend to be rubbery.

◆

Variation

For a first course, make the fish cakes half the size. For pre-dinner nibbles or canapés, make them bite-sized and serve them on cocktail sticks. They can even be served cold, and taste good with a dip made of mayonnaise flavoured with Thai curry paste.

Salmon with rosemary cream

A fabulous main course for a midweek supper party. The rosemary cream sauce tastes divine, and it can be made the day before, so all you have to do on the night is quicky pan-fry the fish. Serve with baby new potatoes and mangetouts.

Serves 4

Preparation time: 2–3 minutes
Cooking time: about 25 minutes

- 500 ml (16 fl oz) fish stock
- 1 fresh rosemary sprig
- 200 ml (7 fl oz) double cream
- 90 g (3 oz) butter
- salt and white pepper
- 1 tablespoon sunflower oil
- 4 thick salmon fillets, each weighing 150–175 g (5–6 oz)
- 4 fresh rosemary sprigs, to garnish

1 Put the fish stock and rosemary in a saucepan and bring to the boil, then simmer gently until the stock has reduced to about half its original volume. Add the cream and continue simmering until reduced by about half again. Strain and discard the rosemary. Whisk 60 g (2 oz) of the butter into the reduced stock and cream mixture and season to taste. Set aside.

2 Check the salmon and remove any pin bones. Rinse the fish and pat dry. Melt the remaining butter with the oil in a frying pan over moderate heat. Season the salmon, place the fillets flesh side down in the pan and cook for 2–3 minutes, depending on the thickness of the fish. Carefully turn the salmon over and cook the skin side for 2–3 minutes. Remove and blot on kitchen paper.

To Serve Gently reheat the sauce, then spoon in a pool on 4 warm plates. Place a salmon fillet on top, drizzle with a little more sauce and garnish with a sprig of rosemary. Serve immediately.

Chef's Tips

Look for cans of fish stock in your supermarket – it has a much better flavour than fish stock cubes. A 425 g can will yield the right volume for this recipe.

◆

If you can't get fresh rosemary sprigs, use about 1 tablespoon dried rosemary and tie it in a small piece of muslin.

Prawns with Orange and Ginger

A speedy stir-fry that takes next to no time to prepare and cook. You can make it as hot and spicy as you like – the sweet tang of the fresh oranges provides a refreshing contrast to the heat of the chillies. Serve with noodles or rice for a complete meal.

- 5 cm (2 inch) piece of fresh root ginger
- 2 garlic cloves
- 1 tablespoon sesame oil
- ¼–½ teaspoon crushed dried chillies, or to taste
- salt and freshly ground black pepper
- 500 g (1 lb) peeled raw tiger king prawns, thawed if frozen
- 1 large red pepper
- 6 spring onions
- 2 large oranges
- 1 tablespoon sunflower oil

Serves 3–4

Preparation time: 5 minutes, plus 10–15 minutes marinating
Cooking time: 8 minutes

1 Peel the ginger and grate it into a bowl. Finely chop the garlic and add to the ginger with the sesame oil, crushed chillies and black pepper to taste. Add the prawns and toss until coated. Cover and leave to marinate at room temperature for 10–15 minutes.

2 Meanwhile, thinly slice the red pepper. Thinly slice the spring onions on the diagonal, keeping the white and green parts separate. Peel and segment the oranges, catching the juice in a bowl (there should be 3–4 tablespoons), then cut the segments in half crossways and add them to the bowl.

3 Heat a wok or large, deep sauté pan over moderately high heat until hot. Add the prawns and stir-fry for a few minutes until the prawns turn pink all over. Remove with a slotted spoon and set aside on a plate.

4 Heat the sunflower oil in the pan. Add the red pepper and the white parts of the spring onions and stir-fry for 5 minutes or until softened. Mix in the orange segments and juice, then return the prawns and any juices to the pan and stir until mixed and heated through.

To Serve Taste for seasoning and serve immediately, sprinkled with the green parts of the spring onions.

Chef's Tip

Fully peeled raw tiger king prawns are sold both frozen and chilled in supermarkets. If they are frozen, they should be thawed for a maximum of 2–3 hours before cooking. If you don't have this amount of time, put them in a sieve and hold them under the cold tap, separating them with your fingers until they soften. Dry them well on kitchen paper.

Fish kebabs with lime and rosemary

A fresh and light main course, good in summer with a delicate accompaniment such as boiled white rice or new potatoes and a leafy green salad tossed in Curry Lime Vinaigrette (page 361).

Serves 4

Preparation time: 5 minutes, plus 10 minutes marinating
Cooking time: 5 minutes

4 thick salmon fillets, each weighing 150–175 g (5–6 oz), skinned
salt and freshly ground black pepper

Marinade
2 garlic cloves
1 small fresh rosemary sprig
100 ml (3½ fl oz) olive oil
2 tablespoons lime juice

To Serve
lime slices
2 fresh rosemary sprigs

1 Check the salmon and remove any fine pin bones. Rinse the fish and pat dry. Cut the fish into 2 cm (¾ inch) cubes, place them in a shallow dish and sprinkle with salt and pepper.

2 Make the marinade. Finely chop the garlic and the rosemary leaves. Place in a jug with the olive oil and lime juice and whisk until blended.

3 Pour the marinade over the fish, turn the cubes until they are well coated, then cover and leave to marinate for 10 minutes. Meanwhile, preheat the grill.

4 Thread the cubes of fish on kebab skewers and grill for 5 minutes, turning once. Heat the marinade in a small saucepan.

To Serve Arrange the skewers on warm plates and spoon over the hot marinade. Serve immediately, with the lime slices and rosemary sprigs.

Chef's Tip

You can marinate the fish for slightly longer than 10 minutes if you like, but don't marinate it for longer than 1 hour because the lime juice has the effect of 'cooking' the fish, as in the Mexican raw fish dish called ceviche. There is nothing wrong in this, but the salmon will overcook and become too soft during grilling if it has been marinated for too long.

Grilled fish with mustard beurre blanc

A main course that is quintessentially French. The sauce is velvety smooth and rich. Serve with plain vegetables, such as new potatoes and French beans or mangetouts, or follow with a crisp green salad tossed in Vinaigrette (page 360).

8 fish fillets (eg mackerel or trout), each weighing about 90 g (3 oz)
4 tablespoons sunflower oil

Sauce
2 shallots
100 ml (3½ fl oz) dry white wine
1 tablespoon white wine vinegar
100 ml (3½ fl oz) double cream
100 g (3½ oz) cold butter, diced
1 tablespoon wholegrain mustard
salt and freshly ground black pepper

Serves 4

Preparation time: 5 minutes
Cooking time: about 15 minutes

1 Preheat the grill.

2 Make the sauce. Finely chop the shallots and place them in a saucepan with the wine and vinegar. Bring to the boil, then cook over moderate heat for about 5 minutes until dry. Add the cream, simmer for 2–3 minutes, then whisk in the cold butter a few pieces at a time. Be sure that each batch of butter has completely melted and been whisked in before adding more. Strain the sauce into a warm bowl, stir in the mustard and season to taste. Cover and keep warm.

3 Place the fish fillets on a lighty oiled baking sheet, brush with oil and sprinkle with salt and pepper. Grill for 5–6 minutes.

To Serve Arrange 2 fish fillets on each of 4 warm plates and spoon over the sauce. Serve immediately.

Chef's Tips

Beurre blanc (white butter) is a classic French chef's sauce that is quick and easy to make. It goes well with chicken, vegetables and eggs as well as fish.

Trout fillets are sold in packets at supermarkets. Fresh fillets of mackerel are not always so readily available, but your fishmonger will fillet whole fish for you. For this recipe you will need 4 mackerel.

Thai prawns

Garlicky and chilli hot, this quick and easy stir-fry makes an impressive supper dish for friends. Have the ingredients prepared before they arrive, then you can toss everything in the wok at the last minute. Serve with jasmine-scented Thai rice.

12 raw jumbo prawns in their shells, thawed if frozen
125 g (4 oz) broccoli florets
1 large red pepper
3–4 garlic cloves
2 tablespoons sunflower oil
1 fresh chilli
3 tablespoons fish sauce
1 tablespoon sugar
freshly ground black pepper
1 small handful of Asian basil, stalks removed

Serves 4

Preparation time: 15 minutes
Cooking time: 10–15 minutes

1 Remove the heads and shells from the prawns, and any black intestinal veins. Wash and dry the prawns and cut them in half if they are very large. Divide the broccoli into tiny sprigs and trim the stalks. Cut the red pepper into thin strips. Crush the garlic finely.

2 Heat the oil in a wok or deep sauté pan over moderate to high heat. Add the garlic and stir-fry until lightly browned, then add the whole chilli and the prawns and stir-fry until the prawns turn pink all over, 3–4 minutes. Remove with a slotted spoon and set aside on a plate.

3 Add the broccoli, red pepper, fish sauce and sugar. Season to taste with pepper and stir-fry for 5–8 minutes until the vegetables are cooked – the broccoli should be bright green and the red pepper just beginning to wilt.

4 Return the prawn mixture to the wok with any juices that have collected on the plate. Add the basil leaves and stir-fry for 1–2 minutes, just long enough to heat the prawns through and let the flavour of the basil infuse.

To Serve Turn into a warm serving bowl and remove the whole chilli. Serve hot.

Chef's Tips

Fish sauce (nam pla) is an essential flavouring in almost every savoury dish in South-East Asia, especially in Thai cooking. It is a very thin, strong and salty sauce, often combined with sugar in stir-fries. You can get it easily at oriental greengrocers and most large supermarkets, and it keeps almost indefinitely, so is well worth buying.

◆

Fresh Asian basil, also called holy basil, can be bought in bunches in oriental greengrocers. It is more peppery than European sweet basil, but the two are interchangeable in most recipes.

SEAFOOD FRICASSEE

Rich, creamy and luxurious, this is a main course for a very special dinner party. The chefs in Paris serve it in a copper chafing, dish and it looks sensational. Serve with plain boiled rice, and follow with a salad.

1 kg (2 lb) large mussels
500 g (1 lb) skinless salmon fillet
12 large scallops
2 shallots
1 large handful of fresh flat-leaf parsley
1 fresh thyme sprig
1 bay leaf
400 ml (14 fl oz) dry white wine
12 large raw Mediterranean prawns in their shells
400 ml (14 fl oz) double cream
salt and freshly ground black pepper

Serves 4–6

Preparation time: 45 minutes
Cooking time: about 20 minutes

Variations

For garlic lovers, add 2–4 chopped garlic cloves with the herbs at the beginning.

◆

For a hint of spice, sweat the shallots in 20 g (¾ oz) butter with 1–2 teaspoons curry powder or garam masala before adding the wine.

1 Scrub the mussels well and remove any beards and barnacles with a small sharp knife. Discard any mussels that are open or do not close when tapped sharply against the work surface. Cut the salmon into 2.5 cm (1 inch) cubes. Separate the corals from the scallops, then cut off and discard the rubbery muscles. Cut the scallops in half. Finely chop the shallots. Separate the parsley leaves from the stalks and chop the leaves.

2 Put the shallots, parsley stalks, thyme, bay leaf and wine in a large saucepan and boil over high heat until reduced by about half. Add the mussels and prawns, cover and cook over moderate heat until the mussels open and the prawns are pink, about 5 minutes. Remove the mussels and prawns with a slotted spoon. Shell the prawns.

3 Strain the liquid through a fine sieve into a clean pan and bring to the boil. Reduce the heat to low, add the scallops, corals and salmon, cover and cook for 3 minutes only. Remove the fish and shellfish with a slotted spoon.

4 Reduce the liquid until syrupy, add the cream and simmer until the sauce coats the back of a spoon. Season well. Add the salmon, scallops and prawns, shake to coat in the sauce, then arrange the mussels on top. Cover and heat gently for 2–3 minutes.

To Serve Sprinkle with the chopped parsley and serve immediately.

Spiced prawns with sweet and sour sauce

This Chinese recipe is simple as well as quick. For a special meal for two, serve it with boiled or steamed rice or stir-fried vegetables. With other dishes as part of a Chinese meal, it is enough to serve 4–6 people.

20 raw tiger king prawns, peeled and deveined
1 tablespoon five-spice powder
1 large egg
2 tablespoons cornflour
about 600 ml (1 pint) groundnut oil, for deep-frying

Sauce
1½ teaspoons cornflour
3 tablespoons light malt vinegar
3 tablespoons sugar
3 tablespoons tomato ketchup
1 tablespoon soy sauce
pinch of salt

Serves 2–6

Preparation time: 10 minutes
Cooking time: about 15 minutes

Variations

Langoustines or strips of white fish, chicken or pork can be used instead of the prawns.

◆

Ready made garam masala can be used instead of the five-spice powder.

1 Sprinkle the prawns with the spice powder and set aside. Beat the egg in a bowl, add the cornflour and beat well to make a batter. Mix together all the ingredients for the sauce in a small saucepan. Stir until smooth.

2 Heat the oil in a wok until very hot but not smoking. Dip about one-quarter of the prawns in the batter, then deep-fry them in the hot oil for 2–3 minutes until golden. Remove with a slotted spoon. Drain and keep hot on kitchen paper. Repeat with the remaining prawns and batter.

3 Bring the sauce to the boil, stirring. Add a little water to thin it to a runny consistency and stir vigorously.

To Serve Arrange the prawns on warm plates, spoon the sauce alongside and serve immediately.

Scallops with tomato and saffron

A simple dish that can be made very quickly at short notice – good for an informal supper party. Fresh scallops are best, but you can use frozen ones as long as they are thoroughly thawed and dried before cooking.

Serves 4

Preparation time: 10 minutes
Cooking time: about 25 minutes

1 x 700–800 g can whole peeled tomatoes
2–3 shallots
20 large scallops
90 ml (3 fl oz) olive oil
salt and freshly ground black pepper
1 large pinch of saffron threads or 1 sachet saffron powder
125 ml (4 fl oz) dry white wine

1 Tip the tomatoes into a sieve placed over a bowl and let the juice run through. Turn the tomatoes onto a board and coarsely chop them, then put them back in the sieve and let them drain for 10 minutes. Finely chop the shallots. Separate the corals from the scallops, then cut off and discard the rubbery muscles. Cut the scallops in half.

2 Heat 2 tablespoons of the oil in a frying, pan over moderate to high heat. Season the scallops and sear them for 1 minute on each side in the hot oil. Transfer them to a plate with a slotted spoon.

3 Add the shallots to the pan and cook for 1 minute. Pour in the liquid from the tomatoes, add the saffron and cook over moderate heat for 5–8 minutes or until the liquid has reduced by about half. Set aside.

4 In a separate pan, cook the tomatoes and wine in the remaining oil over moderate heat until thick, 5–10 minutes. Season well to taste, then add the saffron sauce and scallops. Cook for 2 minutes only, just until very hot.

To Serve Taste for seasoning, then spoon over hot boiled rice or pasta.

Variations

For additional flavour, fry some chopped bacon or sliced button mushrooms with the shallots.

◆

Use cubes of monkfish fillet or large raw Mediterranean or tiger king prawns instead of scallops.

Fish soup

This is a very special main-meal soup with a delicate but absolutely delicious flavour. Serve it for a Scandinavian-style Sunday lunch or supper party. It can be spooned over boiled rice in deep soup plates, or served solo with crusty French bread.

1 small onion
2 small carrots
2 medium leeks (white and pale green leaves only)
15 g (½ oz) butter
1 tablespoon olive oil
250 ml (8 fl oz) dry white wine
1 large pinch of saffron threads or 1 sachet saffron powder
salt and freshly ground black pepper
500 g (1 lb) skinless thick cod or haddock fillet
500 g (1 lb) skinless thick salmon fillet
6–8 large scallops
250 g (8 oz) raw peeled tiger king prawns, thawed if frozen

To Serve
2 tablespoons chopped fresh dill
4 tablespoons cream or crème fraîche

Serves 4

Preparation time: 15–20 minutes
Cooking time: 35 minutes

Chef's Tip

This is the perfect dish for entertaining because the cooking liquid actually improves in flavour if made the day before. Cook it up to the end of step 2, let it cool, then cover and refrigerate overnight. Before serving all you need to do is bring the liquid to simmering point and continue from the beginning of step 3.

1 Thinly slice the onion, carrots and leeks. Melt the butter with the oil in a large saucepan or flameproof casserole. Add the sliced vegetables, cover and cook over low heat for 15 minutes. Stir occasionally during this time.

2 Stir in the wine and bubble briskly until evaporated, then add 900 ml (1½ pints) water and the saffron. Bring to the boil. Season, cover and simmer for 15 minutes.

3 Cut the white fish and salmon into 5 cm (2 inch) cubes. Separate the corals from the scallops, then cut off and discard the rubbery muscles. Cut the scallops in half. Add the white fish and salmon to the soup and barely simmer for 3 minutes. Add the prawns, scallops and corals and simmer for 3 minutes only.

To Serve Sprinkle in half the dill and add the cream. Shake the pan gently to mix without breaking up the fish. Serve hot, sprinkled with the remaining dill.

Monkfish with olive and tomato sauce

A sophisticated dish made simple by using ready prepared ingredients from the supermarket. Serve it for a maximum of 4 people – any more than this and you will find the last-minute cooking and serving difficult to manage.

625 g (1¼ lb) monkfish fillets
2 tablespoons plain flour
salt and freshly ground black pepper
2 ripe tomatoes
1 tablespoon extra-virgin olive oil
2 tablespoons chopped fresh flat-leaf parsley or coriander
pinch of sugar
375 g (12 oz) prepared cabbage
90 g (3 oz) butter
4 tablespoons bottled olive and tomato sauce
90 ml (3 fl oz) dry white wine or water

Serves 4

Preparation time: 20 minutes
Cooking time: about 15 minutes

1 Trim the monkfish if necessary, cut into 16 medallions and coat in the flour seasoned with salt and pepper. Peel the tomatoes and cut them in half. Squeeze out the seeds, then dice the flesh finely. Place in a bowl and mix with the olive oil, half the herbs, the sugar and salt and pepper to taste. Cover and refrigerate. Cut the cabbage into ribbons if this has not already been done.

2 Melt 60 g (2 oz) of the butter in a large sauté pan until foaming. Add the monkfish and sauté over moderate to high heat for 3 minutes on each side until golden and just cooked through. Remove with a slotted spoon and keep hot.

3 Melt the remaining butter in the pan, add the cabbage and salt and pepper to taste and stir-fry over high heat for 3–4 minutes or until wilted. Remove with a slotted spoon and arrange in the centre of 4 warm plates. Keep hot.

4 Add the sauce to the pan with the wine or water. Stir to mix and bring to the boil. Lower the heat, stir in the remaining herbs, then return the monkfish to the pan and quickly coat with the sauce.

To Serve Arrange 4 medallions on each mound of cabbage, spooning the sauce over them. Spoon a little of the tomato mixture in the centre and serve immediately.

Chef's Tips

Olive and tomato sauce is sold in small jars like pesto. It is available in supermarkets and delicatessens, and makes an excellent sauce for pasta, chicken, steaks and chops as well as fish. Once the jar is opened, it keeps for 2 weeks in the refrigerator, so it is well worth buying.

◆

Bags of ready prepared greens are sold in the fresh chilled cabinets. They are washed and ready to cook, often with the leaves cut up or shredded into ribbons (as called for in this recipe), so they save an immense amount of time.

Baked fish with ginger and rice wine

With its subtle oriental flavour, this very quick Chinese dish will certainly inspire compliments. Serve with bowls of boiled or steamed rice and colourful and crisp stir-fried vegetables.

5 cm (2 inch) piece of fresh root ginger
4 spring onions
1 tablespoon sesame oil
salt and freshly ground black pepper
4 star anise
4 thick fish fillets, each weighing about 150 g (5 oz)
125 ml (4 fl oz) rice wine

Serves 4

Preparation time: 10 minutes
Cooking time: about 15 minutes

1 Preheat the oven to 220°C (425°F) Gas 7. Peel and grate the ginger. Thinly slice the spring onions on the diagonal. Brush the bottom of a roasting tin with the sesame oil and sprinkle with salt and pepper.

2 Place the star anise in the tin, spacing them well, and place 1 fish fillet on top of each. Sprinkle with the ginger and spring onions. Pour the rice wine over and around the fish.

3 Place the tin on the hob. Bring the wine to the boil, then cover the tin tightly with foil and put in the oven. Bake for about 10 minutes until the fish flakes easily when tested with the tip of a sharp knife. The exact cooking time will depend on the fish and the size of the fillets.

To Serve Lift the fish out of the tin with a fish slice and place on warm plates. Spoon the juices and flavourings around and serve immediately.

Chef's Tips

Any boneless fish fillets can be used. Cod, haddock, brill, sea bass, mullet or monkfish are all suitable, depending on your budget and the season. Leave the skin on the fish, so that it retains its shape.

◆

Frozen root ginger is much easier to grate than fresh, so keep a packet of it in the freezer. It will thaw instantly when it is grated.

Sole with smoked salmon

This is an impressive and elegant dish for a special dinner party. Serve it with a plain accompaniment such as boiled new potatoes tossed with butter and chopped fresh herbs, and a simple green vegetable like courgettes or mangetouts.

Serves 4–6

Preparation time: 30 minutes
Cooking time: about 20 minutes

2 large shallots
a knob of softened butter
salt and freshly ground black pepper
12 sole fillets, skinned
4–6 tablespoons finely chopped fresh herbs
150–175 g (5–6 oz) sliced smoked salmon
400 ml (14 fl oz) dry white wine
400 ml (14 fl oz) double cream
fresh herbs, to garnish

1 Preheat the oven to 180°C (350°F) Gas 4. Finely chop the shallots. Brush the inside of a large flameproof casserole with butter, then sprinkle with the chopped shallots and a little salt and pepper.

2 Trim off any ragged edges from the sole. Using the flat of a large chef's knife, lightly pound each fillet on the skinned side. Sprinkle this same side with pepper and herbs.

3 Cut the smoked salmon into narrow strips and fit them on top of the sole fillets, over the herbs. Roll up each fillet from the broadest end and secure with a wooden toothpick. Stand the rolls upright in the prepared casserole, pour the wine over and bring to the boil over moderate heat. Quickly cover with buttered baking parchment or foil, then the casserole lid. Cook in the oven for 12 minutes.

4 Remove the fish with a slotted spoon, cover with the parchment or foil and keep hot. Place the casserole on the hob and bring the cooking liquid to the boil. Add the cream and boil, stirring, until reduced to your liking. Taste for seasoning.

To Serve Remove the toothpicks from the fish and arrange the fish rolls on warm plates. Spoon the sauce over and garnish with fresh herbs. Serve immediately.

Chef's Tip

Supermarkets and fishmongers sell individual sole fillets, but if you have to ask for whole fish to be filleted you will need 3 whole fish to get 12 fillets. Buy lemon sole (it is less expensive than Dover sole) and ask the fishmonger to remove the skin.

GRILLED RED MULLET NIÇOISE

A lovely light dish to serve on a summer's evening – preferably outside so you can smell the fish cooking on the barbecue. The sauce has an exquisite Provençal flavour from the tomatoes, garlic, anchovies and black olives.

4 ripe tomatoes, total weight about 375 g (12 oz)
1 garlic clove
5 black olives
4 tablespoons olive oil
2–4 drained canned anchovy fillets
30 g (1 oz) butter, softened
freshly ground black pepper
1 tablespoon capers (optional)
4 fresh red mullet, each weighing about 250 g (8 oz)
2 fresh herbs sprigs (basil, rosemary or thyme), to garnish

Serves 2

Preparation time: 10–15 minutes
Cooking time: about 25 minutes

1 Peel the tomatoes and cut them in half. Squeeze out the seeds, then dice the flesh. Finely chop the garlic. Stone the olives and cut each one in half or into quarters. Heat 2 tablespoons of the olive oil in a saucepan over moderate heat. Add the tomatoes and garlic and simmer for 10–15 minutes or until most of the liquid has evaporated. Meanwhile, light the barbecue or preheat the grill.

2 Using a fork, mash the anchovies with the butter. Off the heat, stir the anchovy butter into the tomatoes. Season with pepper and stir in the olives and capers (if using). Keep hot.

3 Make 3 diagonal slashes on either side of each red mullet. Brush with the remaining olive oil and season with salt and pepper. Barbecue or grill for 2–3 minutes on each side.

To Serve Spoon the tomato mixture onto warm plates and arrange the fish on top or to the side. Garnish with a sprig of fresh herbs and serve immediately, with a fresh baguette and a well-chilled dry white or rosé wine.

Chef's Tips

Finely chopped fresh basil, rosemary or thyme can be added to the tomatoes.

◆

The sauce can be made ahead of time and quickly reheated just before serving.

◆

Whole fresh red mullet are not always available. Frozen red mullet fillets can be used instead – allow 6 fillets for 2 people, thaw them and barbecue or grill for only 1–2 minutes on each side.

FISH

quick and easy ideas

Fish fillets and steaks

• Top fish with shredded fresh root ginger and lemon grass, julienned vegetables, crème fraîche, grated lemon rind and chopped fresh parsley or coriander. Wrap in foil and bake in the oven.

• Pan-fry salmon fillets in oil and butter. Make a simple noisette butter. Deglaze pan with lemon juice, swirl in a knob of butter and stir over high heat until foaming and turning colour. Season and pour over salmon. Serve with lemon wedges.

• Grill fish and serve topped with Maître d'Hôtel Butter (page 353).

• Or serve with anchovy butter. Mash canned anchovies, beat into softened unsalted butter and season with a few drops of lemon juice and black pepper. Tapenade (anchovy and olive paste) can be used instead of anchovies.

• Or mix softened butter with grated rind and juice of lemon or orange and salt and pepper. If using orange, add 1 teaspoon sun-dried tomato paste or tomato purée.

• If you prefer, pan-fry fish and remove, then add flavoured butter to pan, let it sizzle, then pour over fish.

3

POULTRY, GAME & MEAT

Meaty main courses often seem the most difficult if you're trying to cook healthily, but really it is only a question of choosing your cut of meat wisely and using the best cooking method for it. Animals are bred lean these days. Even pork, which once had a reputation for being a fatty meat, now has the minimum amount of fat. Venison, which you can now buy in supermarkets, is even lower in fat and cholesterol than chicken without its skin.

The rules are simple. For maximum interest and perfect nutritional balance, combine small amounts of meat with fresh fruit and vegetables. It tastes better and is better for you. Marinating works wonders with lean protein. It tenderizes fibres and injects flavour at the same time. Follow it up with a healthy cooking method like grilling, barbecuing or chargrilling and you've got the perfect complement to marinating. These two are close cousins when it comes to healthy cooking.

In this chapter you will find a variety of different birds and cuts of meat, none of which is difficult to get at the supermarket or butcher, but suggestions are given for alternatives which can also give more variety. There are recipes for everyday meals, when you are in a rush after work, and recipes for dinner parties and other special occasions when you can cook at your leisure.

Chicken with Sage and Lemon en Papillote

Fresh, light and summery, this dish is very simple and quick to make. Serve it for a simple after-work supper, with new potatoes and a fresh green vegetable or a mixed salad tossed in vinaigrette dressing.

4 skinless boneless chicken breasts
salt and freshly ground black pepper
2 tablespoons finely shredded fresh sage
grated rind and juice of 2 lemons
4 fresh sage sprigs, to serve

Serves 4

Preparation time: 20 minutes
Cooking time: 15 minutes

1 Preheat the oven to 200°C (400°F) Gas 6. Cut 4 pieces of foil, each about 30 cm (12 inches) square.

2 Place a chicken breast in the centre of a square of foil and season generously with salt and pepper. Sprinkle one-quarter of the sage and lemon rind over the top, then drizzle with a little lemon juice. Wrap the foil around the chicken to make a parcel and fold over the edges to seal. Repeat with the remaining ingredients.

3 Place the chicken parcels on a baking sheet and bake in the oven for 15 minutes or until the chicken has cooked through. Unwrap a parcel and pierce one of the chicken breasts with a skewer – the juices should run clear not pink or red.

To Serve Unwrap the chicken and place on warm plates. Spoon the cooking juices over the chicken, drizzle with the remaining lemon juice and garnish with fresh sage sprigs. Serve immediately.

Chef's Tips

Skinless boneless chicken breasts are very easy to get at supermarkets, ideal for quick evening meals after work. If you can get chicken breasts described as 'part-boned' or 'suprêmes', buy these instead. They are not as easy to get as boneless breasts, but they have juicier flesh, so are well worth seeking out.

◆

Foil measuring 300 mm (30 cm/12 inches) wide is the best size for making papillotes.

◆

The parcels can be prepared the day before and kept in the refrigerator overnight. If you have the time, let them come to room temperature for about 30 minutes before putting them in the oven.

Turkey fillets poached in Madeira

The combination of ingredients in this recipe may seem unusual at first sight, but they give a truly delicious end result. Serve on bed of plain boiled rice or noodles and follow with a crisp green salad tossed in a mustard-flavoured vinaigrette.

625 g (1 1/4 lb) turkey breast fillet
125 g (4 oz) ready-to-eat dried apricots
300 ml (1/2 pint) chicken stock
125 ml (4 fl oz) Madeira
grated rind of 1 orange
salt and freshly ground black pepper
2 teaspoons cornflour
about 1 tablespoon chopped fresh coriander, to serve

Serves 4

Preparation time: 10 minutes
Cooking time: about 20 minutes

1 Cut the turkey into strips. Halve the apricots lengthways.

2 Heat the stock and Madeira in a sauté pan, add the apricots and orange rind and bring to the boil. Add the turkey and stir well, then season generously with salt and pepper. Cover and simmer gently for 10–15 minutes until the turkey is tender, stirring occasionally.

3 Remove the turkey and apricots with a slotted spoon and keep them hot in a warm serving dish. In a small bowl, mix the cornflour with 1 tablespoon cold water, then stir into the sauce. Bring to the boil and simmer for 2–3 minutes, stirring all the time until the sauce has thickened. Taste for seasoning.

To Serve Pour the sauce over the turkey and sprinkle with the chopped coriander. Serve immediately.

Chef's Tips

Turkey fillet is naturally low in fat and cholesterol and there's no added fat in this recipe, which makes it exceptionally light. For convenience, buy turkey breast fillet that is already cut into strips. Most supermarkets sell it in packets, often labelled 'turkey for stir-fries'.

◆

Madeira is a fortified red wine from the Portuguese island of the same name. There are both sweet and dry varieties – the dry is most suited to savoury dishes like this one. It is easy to get hold of at wine merchants and supermarkets, but you could also use a dry sherry, port or vermouth, or a dry Italian Marsala wine.

◆

Variation

Skinless boneless chicken breasts can be used instead of turkey.

Quails with roast pepper sauce

Quail meat is tender, delicate and low in fat, and it benefits from being served with a pungent-flavoured sauce as here. Rosemary also has a special affinity with quail, and is often cooked or served with it in the Mediterranean.

2 tablespoons clear honey
4 quails
a few fresh rosemary sprigs, to serve

Sauce
2 red peppers
a little olive oil
200 g (7 oz) low-fat natural yogurt
salt and freshly ground black pepper

Serves 2

Preparation time: 20–30 minutes
Cooking time: 40–55 minutes

1 Make the sauce. Preheat the oven to 200°C (400°F) Gas 6. Halve the peppers lengthways and remove the cores and seeds. Put the peppers skin side up on a baking sheet, brush with a little oil and roast in the oven for 30–40 minutes or until the skin has blackened and blistered. Remove the peppers from the oven, put them in a plastic bag and leave to cool for 10–15 minutes. Leave the oven on.

2 Unwrap the peppers and peel off the skins. Place the flesh in a food processor or blender, add 4 tablespoons cold water and work to a purée. Turn the purée into a bowl, mix in the yogurt and add salt and pepper to taste. Cover and set aside.

3 Gently warm the honey in a small saucepan. Place the quails on a rack in a roasting tin, season and brush with the warmed honey. Roast in the oven for 10–12 minutes or until tender when pierced in the thickest part of a thigh with a skewer. Remove from the oven and leave to rest for 5 minutes.

To Serve Arrange the quails on a warm platter and garnish with a few sprigs of rosemary. Hand round the sauce separately.

Chef's Tip

Quails are immensely popular along the Mediterranean coastlines of southern France and Italy, where you often see them spit-roasted on long metal skewers over open fires. Here, inexpensive farmed quail is available all year round at butchers and supermarkets. Always serve 2 birds per person because they are very tiny and do not have an abundance of flesh.

Smoked chicken and papaya salad

This makes an excellent cold lunch in summer. Serve it very simply, with fresh crusty bread. It can also be served as a first course, in which case it will serve 6 people.

Serves 4

Preparation time: 15 minutes, plus standing time

30 cm (12 inch) piece of cucumber
salt and freshly ground black pepper
2 ripe papayas
2 smoked chicken breasts, each weighing 175–200 g (6–7 oz)
1 cos lettuce heart

Dressing
5 cm (2 inch) piece of fresh root ginger
3 tablespoons sunflower oil
2 tablespoons hazelnut oil
1 teaspoon white wine vinegar
1–2 teaspoons Dijon mustard, to taste
pinch of sugar

1 Peel the cucumber, halve it lengthways and scoop out the seeds. Cut the flesh lengthways in half again, then cut across these pieces to make small chunks of cucumber. Place in a colander, sprinkle generously with salt and leave to stand for 30–60 minutes.

2 Rinse the cucumber thoroughly and pat dry. Peel, halve and deseed the papayas, then cut the flesh lengthways into neat slices. Remove the skin from the chicken breasts and cut the chicken lengthways into slices of a similar size. Shred the lettuce heart.

3 Make the dressing. Finely grate the ginger into a bowl, add the other ingredients and whisk until well combined. Season to taste.

To Serve Toss the lettuce and cucumber together, then divide between 4 plates, heaping it up in the centre. Arrange slices of chicken and papaya alternately on top and spoon the dressing over them. Leave to stand for 20–30 minutes for the flavours to mingle. Serve at room temperature.

Chef's Tip

A quick and easy way to remove cucumber seeds is to run a melon baller in a channel down the inside of the halved cucumber. If you haven't got a melon baller, use a sharp-edged teaspoon.

Variation

Smoked duck can be used instead of smoked chicken, and mangoes instead of papayas.

Guinea fowl with a dry sherry sauce

Both the guinea fowl and the richly reduced sauce have superb flavours in this simple recipe. Serve it in winter with mash and a fresh green vegetable. Brussels sprouts and chestnuts would be ideal.

175 g (6 oz) shallots
15 g (½ oz) butter
1 tablespoon olive oil
4 guinea fowl breasts, each weighing 125–175 g (4–6 oz)
400 ml (14 fl oz) dry sherry
500 ml (18 fl oz) hot brown or chicken stock
salt and freshly ground black pepper
1–2 teaspoons chopped fresh flat-leaf parsley, to serve

Serves 4

Preparation time: 15 minutes
Cooking time: 20–25 minutes

1 Preheat the oven to 180°C (350°F) Gas 4. Thinly slice the shallots. Heat the butter and oil in a deep sauté pan and seal the guinea fowl breasts, skin side down, for 4–5 minutes until golden brown.

2 Remove the breasts from the pan and place them, skin side up, on the rack of a roasting tin. Finish cooking them in the oven for 10–15 minutes or until tender when pierced with a skewer.

3 Meanwhile, add the shallots to the pan and cook over moderate heat for 5–7 minutes, stirring them frequently until they are golden brown. Remove with a slotted spoon and keep hot. Deglaze the pan with about three-quarters of the sherry, reducing it to a syrup. Add the stock to the pan and bring it to the boil, then boil rapidly until reduced by about half.

4 While the sauce is reducing, remove the guinea fowl from the oven and cover it with foil. Leave it to rest in a warm place.

5 Add the remaining sherry to the sauce and season to taste, then strain the liquid through a fine sieve into a clean pan. Cover and keep hot until ready to serve.

To Serve Slice the guinea fowl on the diagonal and arrange on warm plates. Place a few of the cooked shallots over the guinea fowl and sprinkle with chopped parsley, then spoon the sauce over and around. Serve immediately.

Chef's Tip

Guinea fowl is an excellent alternative to chicken because it has more flavour. Although strictly speaking it isn't a game bird, it tastes more like game than chicken, and is often sold in the game or specialist meat and poultry sections of large supermarkets. It is available all year round.

Variation

Chicken suprêmes (breasts with the wing bone attached) may be substituted for the guinea fowl. If you find them difficult to slice, serve them whole.

Roast chicken with red peppers and tomatoes

This dish is very easy to make, ideal in summer when the weather is warm and you have little inclination to cook. Peppers and tomatoes are ripe and flavoursome at this time of year too. Serve with a crisp green salad tossed in a herb vinaigrette.

750 g (1 1/2 lb) ripe plum tomatoes
3 large red peppers, total weight about 500 g (1 lb)
4 garlic cloves
4 chicken pieces
2 tablespoons chopped fresh oregano
2 tablespoons olive oil
salt and freshly ground black pepper

Serves 4

Preparation time: 15 minutes
Cooking time: 40–50 minutes

1 Preheat the oven to 190°C (375°F) Gas 5. Halve, core and deseed the tomatoes. Quarter the red peppers lengthways, then remove the cores and seeds. Thickly slice the garlic.

2 Slash the chicken with a sharp knife and place in a large non-stick roasting tin with the tomatoes, red peppers and garlic. Sprinkle with the oregano and oil and season generously with salt and pepper.

3 Roast in the oven for 40–50 minutes or until the chicken is cooked through. The juices should run clear, not pink or red, when the thickest part of the meat is pierced.

To Serve Arrange the chicken pieces on warm plates with the roasted vegetables over and around. Serve hot.

Chef's Tips

Chicken quarters are best for this dish, either wings or legs. The skin of the chicken will help keep the flesh moist during roasting if you leave it on, but if you prefer less fat in the dish, remove it before cooking.

◆

Fresh oregano is not always easy to find, but you can use marjoram if this is easier to get. Oregano is a wild version of marjoram, with a slightly stronger taste. They are both used extensively in Mediterranean cooking and have a special affinity with peppers and tomatoes.

Turkey with a cucumber, cream and herb sauce

Turkey is very low in fat and therefore has a tendency to be a dry meat unless it is cooked carefully. In this recipe it is poached gently in stock, a cooking method which helps make it moist and tasty. Serve with plain boiled rice.

- ½ cucumber
- 2 shallots
- 4 teaspoons olive oil
- 4 turkey steaks, each weighing 150–175 g (5–6 oz)
- 500 ml (18 fl oz) chicken stock
- salt and freshly ground black pepper
- 125 ml (4 fl oz) dry white wine
- 200 ml (7 fl oz) half-fat crème fraîche
- 1 tablespoon snipped fresh chives
- 1 tablespoon finely chopped fresh chervil

Serves 4

Preparation time: 10–15 minutes
Cooking time: about 20 minutes

1 Peel the cucumber and cut it in half lengthways, then scoop out the seeds and slice the flesh crossways. Finely chop the shallots.

2 Heat 3 teaspoons of the oil in a sauté pan, add the turkey steaks and cook for 1–2 minutes on each side until lightly coloured. Add all but 125 ml (4 fl oz) of the stock and bring to the boil, then season to taste and simmer gently until the turkey is tender, 10–12 minutes.

3 Meanwhile, heat the remaining oil in a separate pan and fry the shallots over low heat for a few minutes until softened. Add the remaining stock and the wine, increase the heat and boil until reduced by half. Turn the heat down to low, add the cucumber, crème fraîche and herbs, season well and gently heat through.

To Serve Lift the turkey steaks out of the stock and place them on warm plates. Spoon the sauce over and around and serve immediately.

Chef's Tips

For optimum flavour, use a homemade chicken stock (page 354) or one of the chilled fresh varieties sold in cartons at supermarkets.

◆

Use scissors to snip the chives because they will cut through the delicate stems cleanly. If you use a knife to chop chives they can easily be crushed or bruised.

Poussins with oregano, garlic and red wine

Young, tender-fleshed poussins (baby chickens) make a speedy, low-fat meal for any number of people. This recipe serves two, but the quantities of ingredients can easily be halved, doubled or tripled. The timing remains the same.

4 garlic cloves
2 oven-ready poussins
1 small bunch of fresh oregano
salt and freshly ground black pepper
1 tablespoon olive oil
300 ml (½ pint) red wine

Serves 2

Preparation time: 20 minutes
Cooking time: 50 minutes

Chef's Tip

Poussins are four to six week old chickens, which weigh about 500 g (1 lb), just enough for one serving. Because they are young, the meat is very succulent – and much leaner than older chickens. They are up to 15 per cent lower in fat and 10 per cent lower in calories.

1 Preheat the oven to 180°C (350°F) Gas 4. Cut 2 garlic cloves into slivers and place inside the poussins with two-thirds of the oregano sprigs. Season the birds with salt and pepper. Finely chop the remaining garlic and all but 4 of the oregano sprigs.

2 Heat the oil in a large casserole, add the birds and brown them gently, turning occasionally, until golden all over. Add the wine and enough cold water to come about halfway up the poussins, then sprinkle in the chopped garlic and oregano and bring the liquid to the boil. Quickly transfer the uncovered casserole to the oven.

3 Pot roast the poussins for 50 minutes or until the birds are tender and the sauce has reduced by about half. If the liquid reduces too much before the poussins are cooked, add a little extra water. When the poussins are cooked, remove them from the pan and place them on warm plates. Cover and leave in a warm place for about 5 minutes.

4 Spoon off any excess fat from the surface of the cooking liquid and bring the liquid to the boil on top of the stove. Boil rapidly until reduced further, stirring constantly and loosening any cooking residue from the sides and bottom of the pan with a wooden spoon.

To Serve Pour the sauce over the poussins, garnish with the remaining oregano sprigs and serve immediately.

Partridge in filo with a cardamom sauce

Filo pastry is light because it is paper thin and contains no fat. Here it is doubly useful because it protects the delicate flesh of partridge breasts during roasting. Celeriac Purée (page 368) is the traditional accompaniment for partridge.

8 boneless partridge breasts, each weighing about 60 g (2 oz)
10 sheets of filo pastry
2–3 teaspoons olive oil
4 tablespoons mango chutney
2 tablespoons sherry or red wine vinegar
300 ml (½ pint) chicken stock
3 crushed cardamom pods
salt and freshly ground black pepper

Serves 4

Preparation time: 30 minutes, plus cooling time
Cooking time: 15 minutes

1 Preheat the oven to 200°C (400°F) Gas 6. Heat a non-stick frying pan until hot and cook the partridge breasts for 2–3 minutes on each side until nicely coloured. Remove from the pan and leave until cold.

2 Cut 8 filo sheets in half crossways to make 16 pieces that are almost square. Brush a little oil on one of the pieces of filo, then place another piece directly on top. Place a partridge breast in the centre and spread with 1 teaspoon mango chutney. Brush the edges of the filo with oil and wrap the filo around the partridge to make a neat parcel. Repeat to make 8 parcels in all.

3 Place the parcels on an oiled baking sheet and brush the pastry with oil. Cut each remaining sheet of filo into quarters and scrunch each piece up with your fingers. Place on top of each parcel and brush with oil. Bake for 15 minutes or until the pastry is golden.

4 Meanwhile, deglaze the frying pan with the vinegar and add the remaining mango chutney, the stock and cardamom pods. Simmer until syrupy and reduced by half. Strain and season.

To Serve Arrange 2 filo parcels on each warm plate, drizzle the sauce over and serve immediately.

Chef's Tips

Fresh partridge is available in the winter months, from October onwards. It has a plump breast, so this is the best part of the bird to use. At other times of year or if you can't get partridge, you can use pheasant, duck or chicken breasts instead – allow 1 breast per person and remove the fat and skin before cooking. The flavour of the spiced cardamom sauce tastes good with any of these meats.

To release the aromatic seeds of cardamom, crush the whole pods with a pestle or rolling pin or by pressing with your fist on the flat side of a large chef's knife. The pods can be left in the sauce because it is strained before use.

Stir-fried ginger chicken

Low-fat protein and vegetables are combined in this fresh-tasting stir-fry, making this a quick and well-balanced meal for after work. Serve with boiled noodles or rice, which can be cooked at the same time as the chicken.

500 g (1 lb) skinless boneless chicken breasts
5–6 cm (2–2½ inch) piece of fresh root ginger
2 garlic cloves
175 g (6 oz) broccoli
90 g (3 oz) mangetouts
1 bunch of spring onions
2 tablespoons vegetable oil
2 tablespoons light soy sauce
1 tablespoon rice vinegar
extra soy sauce, to serve (optional)

Marinade
2 teaspoons cornflour
1 egg white
2 tablespoons light soy sauce
1 tablespoon rice vinegar

Serves 4

Preparation time: 15–20 minutes
Cooking time: about 10 minutes

1 Cut the chicken into strips, about 4 x 1 cm (1½ x ½ inch). Lightly whisk the ingredients for the marinade in a bowl, add the chicken and stir well. Cover and set aside.

2 Finely grate the ginger and crush the garlic. Divide the broccoli into tiny sprigs and trim the stalks. Cut the mangetouts in half crossways and cut the spring onions into 5 cm (2 inch) lengths.

3 Heat the oil in a wok or deep sauté pan over moderate to high heat until very hot. Add the ginger and garlic and stir-fry for 1 minute. Add the chicken and stir-fry vigorously for 4–5 minutes, just until it turns white in colour.

4 Add the vegetables, the soy sauce, vinegar and 4 tablespoons cold water. Stir-fry for 2–3 minutes or until the vegetables have softened slightly but still remain crisp.

To Serve Taste the stir-fry and add more soy sauce if you like. Serve immediately.

Chef's Tips

Most supermarkets sell chicken breast meat cut into strips ready for stir-frying. This will save you time if you are in a hurry.

Any vegetable oil can be used for stir-frying, but groundnut (rapeseed) oil is one of the best because it is less likely to scorch when heated to a high temperature.

Chinese rice vinegar comes in two different colours, red and white. The white is the stronger of the two and the most commonly available at supermarkets, but either colour can be used in this recipe.

Thai chicken

Succulent skewered chicken that has been marinated in pungent Thai ingredients makes a delicious summer meal served on a bed of fragrant jasmine rice. If you like, you can do the cooking on the barbecue rather than under the grill.

Serves 4

Preparation time: 15–20 minutes, plus marinating time
Cooking time: 14–20 minutes

60 g (2 oz) fresh coriander
2 garlic cloves
1 cm (1/2 inch) piece of fresh root ginger
1/2 bunch of spring onions
1–2 green chillies, to taste
1/2 stalk of lemon grass
rind and juice of 2 limes
2 tablespoons light soy sauce
125 ml (4 fl oz) coconut milk
8 skinless boneless chicken thighs
lime wedges, to serve

1 In a food processor or blender, finely chop the coriander, garlic, ginger, spring onions, chillies, lemon grass and lime rind with the lime juice, soy sauce and coconut milk.

2 Using a sharp knife, cut 3 diagonal slashes in each piece of chicken. Put the chicken in a non-metallic dish and pour the chopped mixture over them. Cover the dish with cling film and marinate in the refrigerator for several hours or overnight.

3 Preheat the grill to hot. Thread 2 pieces of chicken on each of 4 metal skewers. Put the skewers on the grill pan and grill for 7–10 minutes on each side, turning once.

4 Meanwhile, pour the remaining marinade into a saucepan. Bring to the boil and simmer for 5–10 minutes, stirring often.

To Serve Arrange the skewers on plates and spoon the cooked marinade over them. Serve hot, with lime wedges for squeezing.

Chef's Tips

Coconut milk is an essential Thai ingredient, and cans and cartons are the most convenient way to buy it. The milk is made by steeping coconut flesh in water, then straining off the white liquid. When very thick, this liquid is called coconut cream or creamed coconut. Don't confuse coconut milk with the liquid inside a fresh coconut, this is not used in cooking but as a drink.

◆

Chicken thighs are excellent for marinating and grilling because the flesh is juicier than chicken breast, which tends to toughen when cooked by dry heat.

LATTICE CUT CHICKEN WITH HERBS

Mixed fresh herbs give chicken an intense flavour, and balsamic vinegar gives an exquisite boost at the last minute. Serve hot with new potatoes boiled in their skins and tossed in olive oil, or cold with Potato Salad with a Mustard Dressing (page 223).

- 1 small bunch of fresh chives or flat-leaf parsley
- 1 small bunch of fresh tarragon
- leaves of 2 fresh rosemary sprigs
- 6 spring onions
- 1 garlic clove
- 2 tablespoons olive oil
- 1 tablespoon tarragon vinegar
- 4 skinless boneless chicken breasts
- 4 teaspoons balsamic vinegar

Serves 4

Preparation time: 10 minutes, plus marinating time
Cooking time: 8–10 minutes

1 Set aside a few herb sprigs for the garnish, then finely chop the remaining herbs with the spring onions and garlic. Put half of the oil in a bowl, add the tarragon vinegar and chopped herbs and stir together to form a thick herb paste.

2 Using a sharp knife, cut a criss-cross pattern in the smooth, rounded side of the chicken breasts. Put the chicken in a shallow dish and coat with the herb paste. Cover and leave to marinate in a cool place for at least 30 minutes.

3 Heat a ridged cast iron griddle pan until very hot. Dip a wad of kitchen paper in oil and wipe it over the hot pan. Place the chicken on the pan and chargrill for 4–5 minutes on each side, or until the chicken has cooked through.

To Serve Mix the remaining oil with the balsamic vinegar and drizzle over the hot chicken. Garnish with the reserved herb sprigs and serve hot or cold.

Chef's Tips

You can chop the herb mixture in a food processor. Strip the leaves off the rosemary and tarragon sprigs first, and use the pulse button so the herbs are not overprocessed.

◆

The chicken can be marinated for up to 24 hours. Cover the dish with cling film and refrigerate.

◆

While the chicken is cooking, press it down firmly with a fish slice or spatula so the ridges from the pan make charred stripes on the flesh.

Honey baked chicken

Sweet and tangy, these chicken pieces make really tasty hot or cold finger food for a party, and children love them. They are also good for an informal supper served with a saffron rice pilaf and a salad of crisp and colourful mixed leaves.

3 tablespoons clear or set honey
3 tablespoons Dijon mustard
1 tablespoon medium curry powder
8 chicken pieces
lime or lemon wedges, to serve

Serves 4

Preparation time: 10 minutes
Cooking time: 40–50 minutes

1 Preheat the oven to 180°C (350°F) Gas 4. Gently heat the honey, mustard and curry powder in a saucepan until they have melted together and formed a paste.

2 Remove the skin from the chicken. With a sharp knife, slash the flesh right through to the bone. Put the chicken pieces in a non-stick roasting tin and pour the sauce over them. Turn to coat.

3 Bake the chicken for 40–50 minutes or until cooked through and dark brown in colour. Turn the pieces from time to time during baking and add a few tablespoons of cold water to prevent the chicken from sticking to the pan and burning.

To Serve Arrange the chicken pieces on a platter with the lime or lemon wedges. Serve hot or cold.

Chef's Tips

Dijon mustard is smooth and hot. If you prefer a milder flavour with texture use a grainy mustard, such as the French moutarde de Meaux.

◆

To get 8 neat pieces of chicken, buy 4 whole legs and cut them in half across their central joints to make 4 drumsticks and 4 thighs. If you are planning to serve the chicken as finger food, buy 8 drumsticks.

Pan-fried pigeon with a spiced plum sauce

Pigeon has a strong, gamey flavour and the breasts are plump and meaty, yet low in fat and cholesterol. The sauce in this dish is also highly flavoured and quite spicy, so a plain accompaniment like boiled noodles or rice is called for.

2 teaspoons olive oil
8 pigeon breasts
2 tablespoons sherry vinegar

Plum Sauce
1 x 250 g can plums in syrup
1 tablespoon clear or set honey
1 tablespoon dark soy sauce
1 teaspoon Worcestershire sauce
1/2 teaspoon Tabasco sauce
1/4 teaspoon ground cardamom
salt and freshly ground black pepper

1 First make the sauce. Put all the ingredients, except salt and pepper, in a small saucepan and bring to the boil over moderate heat. Simmer for 5 minutes, then remove from the heat and leave to cool.

2 Once the sauce has cooled, pour it into a food processor or blender and process until completely smooth. Check the seasoning, adding salt and pepper only if necessary, and transfer to a small bowl. Cover and chill in the refrigerator.

3 Heat the oil in a non-stick frying pan and pan-fry the pigeon breasts for 3–4 minutes on each side until tender.

To Serve Slice the pigeon breasts on the diagonal and arrange on warm plates. Quickly deglaze the pan with the vinegar and drizzle it over. Serve hot, with the chilled plum sauce handed separately.

Serves 4

Preparation time: 15 minutes, plus chilling time
Cooking time: about 15 minutes

Chef's Tips

Wood pigeon is the most commonly available pigeon and it is sold all year round. You will most likely have to buy 4 whole birds to get 8 individual breasts, but it is easy to cut the breasts off either side of the breastbone. Use the legs and carcass to make stock.

◆

Check the label before buying canned plums and try to get stoneless ones or you will have the fiddly job of removing the stones.

◆

If you can't get pigeon, use duck breasts, which go well with the Chinese-style plum sauce. They are larger than pigeon breasts, so you will only need 2 to serve 4 people. Cut them in half on the diagonal and remove all the fat and skin before cooking.

Chargrilled chicken with a fruity salsa

The contrast of hot chargrilled chicken and cool refreshing salsa is a real taste sensation. Use as much chilli as you dare to heighten the experience further. Prepare the salsa several hours ahead so that it gets really cold and the flavours mingle.

3 tablespoons olive oil
6 skinless boneless chicken breasts
juice of 1 1/2 limes
4 fresh coriander sprigs, to serve

Salsa
4 tomatoes
2 shallots
1 handful of fresh coriander leaves
1–2 green chillies, to taste
1 mango
juice of 1 lime
salt and freshly ground black pepper

Serves 6

Preparation time: 20 minutes, plus chilling time
Cooking time: 10–15 minutes

1 First make the salsa. Finely dice the tomatoes, removing the cores and seeds, and finely chop the shallots and coriander. Cut the chillies lengthways in half and scrape out the seeds, then dice the flesh very finely. Peel and stone the mango and cut the flesh into small dice. Mix all the diced ingredients in a bowl with the lime juice and salt and pepper to taste. Cover and chill in the refrigerator until ready to serve.

2 Heat a ridged cast iron griddle pan until very hot. Rub the chicken pieces with 2 tablespoons of the oil and season with black pepper. Place the chicken on the pan and chargrill for 10–15 minutes or until cooked through, turning once.

3 Transfer the chicken to warm plates and season well. Add the remaining oil and the lime juice to the pan and stir vigorously with a wooden spoon to mix with any pan juices.

To Serve Pour the juices over the chicken and garnish with coriander sprigs. Serve immediately, with the salsa spooned alongside.

Chef's Tips

There are many types of green chilli. The small thin, pointed ones that are dark green in colour tend to be fiery hot, while the fatter pale green ones are generally milder. If you like your salsa searingly hot, choose habañeros, bird's eye or Scotch bonnet. Milder green chillies are anaheim, fresco and jalapeño, but even these can be quite hot, so always use them with caution.

◆

Mangoes have one of the most delicious flavours of all fruits when they are ripe and at their best, but they are so often spoiled by their stringy flesh. When shopping for mangoes, ask for Alfonso from India or Sindri or Chaunca from Pakistan. These three varieties are among the sweetest and best for flavour, and their smooth juicy flesh literally melts in the mouth.

Paella

An all-in-one dish that is good for an informal midweek supper with friends. Serve with crusty bread and a Spanish-style salad of sliced tomatoes, raw onion rings and chopped garlic with olive oil, lemon juice and salt and pepper.

1 pinch of saffron threads
2 skinless boneless chicken breasts
1 medium onion
1 medium green pepper
1–2 garlic cloves, to taste
12 large fresh mussels
2 tablespoons olive oil

200 g (7 oz) long grain rice
750 ml (1¼ pints) hot chicken stock or water
salt and freshly ground black pepper
3–4 raw tiger king prawns in their shells, thawed if frozen
chopped fresh flat-leaf parsley, to garnish

Serves 3–4

Preparation time: 15 minutes
Cooking time: about 35 minutes

1 Soak the saffron threads in 1 tablespoon hot water. Meanwhile, cut the chicken into 1.25 cm (½ inch) cubes or little-finger-sized strips. Finely slice the onion and green pepper. Crush the garlic. Scrub and rinse the mussels.

2 Heat the oil in a deep sauté pan or flameproof casserole. Add the chicken and toss over moderate to high heat for about 2 minutes until all of the pieces have turned white. Remove to a plate.

3 Add the onion and sauté over low heat until soft and light golden. Add the rice, green pepper and garlic and cook, stirring, for 1 minute until well coated with oil. Add 600 ml (1 pint) of the stock or water, the saffron and its liquid and salt and pepper. Stir until boiling, then cover and cook over low heat for 10 minutes.

4 Add the chicken and remaining stock or water. Stir to mix well. Place the mussels and prawns on top of the rice, cover tightly and cook for a further 10 minutes.

To Serve Uncover the pan and check that all of the mussels have opened. Discard any that are closed. Sprinkle with chopped parsley and serve hot.

Chef's Tip

In Spain, paella is usually made with a short grain rice, which gives a sticky consistency similar to that of risotto. Long grain rice is easier to use because it can be left unattended for longer without sticking. If you like, you can use easy-cook long grain rice. This has polished grains to prevent it from sticking.

CREOLE JAMBALAYA

Spicy and hot, this chicken, rice and prawn dish comes from the Caribbean. It is perfect for midweek entertaining because it can be partially prepared the night before. The flavour improves with standing and reheating.

1 small onion
1 green pepper
4 celery sticks
4 garlic cloves
100 g (3½ oz) butter
1 teaspoon cayenne pepper
1 bay leaf
2 fresh thyme sprigs
1 teaspoon dried oregano
salt and freshly ground black pepper
1 x 700–800 g can whole peeled tomatoes
375 ml (12 fl oz) hot chicken or vegetable stock
8 skinless chicken thighs
175 g (6 oz) long grain rice
250 g (8 oz) cooked and peeled tiger king prawns, thawed if frozen
fresh thyme leaves, to garnish

Serves 4

Preparation time: 10 minutes
Cooking time: about 45 minutes

1 Finely chop the onion, green pepper, celery and garlic, in a food processor if you have one. Melt the butter in a large flameproof casserole and sauté the chopped vegetables over low to moderate heat until soft and lightly coloured.

2 Add the cayenne, herbs and salt and pepper to taste. Stir for 1–2 minutes, then add the tomatoes and stock and simmer for 10 minutes, stirring frequently. Add the chicken, cover and simmer for 20 minutes.

3 Add the rice and stir to mix, then cover and cook for 15 minutes, stirring occasionally. Place the prawns on top of the jambalaya, cover and heat through for 2–3 minutes.

To Serve Taste for seasoning and serve hot, sprinkled with fresh thyme leaves.

Chef's Tips

Chicken thighs are sold in packets in most supermarkets. They have moist, tender meat that is better for casseroles and stews than breast meat, which tends to be dry if cooked too long. Bone-in thighs are the most succulent, but if you prefer you can buy boneless thighs and cut the meat into chunks.

◆

To prepare ahead, cook up to the end of step 2, leave to cool, then refrigerate. About 20 minutes before serving, bring to a simmer, then continue with the recipe.

Chicken breasts with wild mushrooms

This rich and creamy dish is ideal for a quick after-work supper party. Serve it with fresh pasta such as tagliatelle, or boiled basmati rice. Follow with a mixed salad tossed in Vinaigrette (page 360).

250 g (8 oz) mixed wild mushrooms
3 shallots
1–2 garlic cloves
2 tablespoons sunflower oil
15 g (½ oz) butter
salt and freshly ground black pepper
4 skinless boneless chicken breasts, each weighing about 175 g (6 oz)
300 ml (½ pint) hot chicken stock
175 ml (6 fl oz) double cream
fresh chives, chervil or flat-leaf parsley, to garnish

Serves 4

Preparation time: 10–15 minutes
Cooking time: about 30 minutes

1 Slice the mushrooms, finely chop the shallots and crush the garlic. Heat the oil and butter in a frying pan. Season the chicken breasts, place them in the pan and cook them over low to moderate heat until they are lightly golden, about 3 minutes on each side.

2 Remove the chicken breasts to a plate and set aside. Add the shallots to the pan and cook, stirring, for 3–5 minutes until softened but not coloured. Add the mushrooms and garlic and toss over moderate to high heat for 2–3 minutes.

3 Pour in the stock and bring to the boil, stirring. Return the chicken to the pan, together with any juices that have collected on the plate, cover and cook over low heat for 10 minutes. Uncover the pan, remove the chicken to the plate again and keep hot.

4 Cook the sauce for another 8–12 minutes over moderate heat, then season to taste and mix in all but about 4 tablespoons of the cream. Return the chicken and any juices to the pan and simmer for another 1–2 minutes, turning once.

To Serve Transfer the chicken to warm plates and spoon the sauce over so that the mushrooms nestle on top of the chicken. Spoon 1 tablespoon cream over each portion, then garnish with herbs. Serve immediately.

Chef's Tip

A mixture of chanterelles, ceps and horns of plenty is a good choice of mushrooms for this dish, but if these are out of season or otherwise unavailable, a mixture of shiitake, oyster and button mushrooms would be equally good. Many supermarkets now sell boxes of mixed wild mushrooms. These are not only convenient but are also good value.

Chicken tagine

Spicy Moroccan tagine is a good dish for an informal supper party. Here it is made with tangy olives and lemons. Potatoes are included in the stew, so no accompaniment is needed, but a refreshing cucumber or tomato salad would be nice to follow.

2 onions
2 garlic cloves
500 g (1 lb) peeled new potatoes
1 chicken, cut into 8 serving pieces
salt and freshly ground black pepper
3 tablespoons olive oil
1 tablespoon ground cumin
1 teaspoon ground ginger
1 teaspoon paprika
1 large pinch of saffron threads or 1 sachet saffron powder
about 500 ml (16 fl oz) hot chicken stock
2–3 pieces of pickled lemon (optional)
60–90 g (2–3 oz) stoned black olives
chopped fresh coriander or flat-leaf parsley, to garnish

Serves 4

Preparation time: 15 minutes
Cooking time:: about 1¼ hours

1 Finely slice the onions. Crush the garlic. Cut the potatoes into halves or quarters if large. Remove the skin from the chicken and sprinkle the chicken with salt and pepper.

2 Heat the oil in a large flameproof casserole. Place half the chicken pieces in the hot oil and fry until browned on all sides. Remove and repeat with the remaining chicken.

3 Return all the chicken pieces to the pan and add the onions, garlic and spices. Stir until the chicken pieces are well coated, then pour in enough stock to just cover them. Bring to the boil, cover and simmer gently for 30 minutes.

4 Roughly chop the pickled lemon pieces (if using) and add to the tagine with the potatoes and olives. Cover and cook for a further 30 minutes or until both the chicken and potatoes are tender.

To Serve Taste the sauce for seasoning and serve the tagine hot, sprinkled with chopped coriander or parsley.

Chef's Tips

A whole chicken is normally used to make tagine, but pieces are easier to serve. For convenience, ask your butcher to joint the chicken for you, or buy pieces from the supermarket. Legs and thighs are best for stews like this.

◆

Pickled lemons are used in tagines for their sharp and salty citrus tang, but they are not essential. You may find them in a Middle Eastern or North African grocer, or you can make them using the recipe on page 350. An alternative is to buy a bottle of preserved lemon slices in lemon juice. Although not authentic, they do add the required touch of sourness. They are available at most supermarkets.

Thai chicken with peppers

Thai ingredients and French culinary techniques fuse harmoniously in this delicately presented dish. Its flavour is superb and needs no embellishment, so serve it very simply, with jasmine-scented Thai rice.

4 skinless boneless chicken breasts
4–6 tablespoons green Thai curry paste
1 tablespoon English mustard powder
1 large onion
2 peppers (green and red)
2 tablespoons groundnut oil
30 g (1 oz) butter
pinch of salt
200 ml (7 fl oz) hot chicken stock
5 tablespoons warm sesame oil
2 tablespoons peanut butter

Serves 4

Preparation time: 20 minutes, plus marinating
Cooking time: about 30 minutes

1 Make a few diagonal slashes in the chicken breasts, then place them in a glass dish. Mix the green curry paste with the mustard powder and spread over the chicken. Cover and marinate in the refrigerator for at least 2 hours, preferably overnight.

2 Finely slice the onion and cut the peppers into very thin strips. Heat the oil and butter in a frying pan, add the chicken and fry over low to moderate heat for 7 minutes on each side or until lightly coloured and tender. Transfer to a dish with a slotted spoon, cover and keep hot.

3 Add the onion and peppers to the pan and sprinkle with the salt. Cook gently, stirring occasionally, for 10 minutes until soft. Meanwhile, boil the stock until reduced by half, stirring in the warm sesame oil and peanut butter when the stock is simmering well.

To Serve Slice the chicken on the diagonal and arrange on warm plates. Spoon the sauce over the chicken and the pepper mixture alongside. Serve immediately.

Chef's Tip

You can buy small bottles of both green and red Thai curry paste in supermarkets, and sachets or packets of freshly made paste in the chilled sections of oriental shops and some gourmet delicatessens. Alternatively, you can make your own using the recipe on page 351.

Chicken with mushrooms and leeks

Chicken breasts are made succulent with a stuffing of leeks and a mushroom and sherry sauce. Serve with mangetouts and boiled new potatoes tossed in butter and chopped fresh herbs.

- 2 leeks (white part only), weighing about 175 g (6 oz)
- 250 g (8 oz) white button mushrooms
- 1 garlic clove
- 125 g (4 oz) butter
- salt and freshly ground black pepper
- 125 ml (4 fl oz) sunflower oil
- 200 ml (7 fl oz) hot chicken stock
- 4 skinless boneless chicken breasts, each weighing 175–200 g (6–7 oz)
- 4 tablespoons sherry

Serves 4

Preparation time: 30 minutes
Cooking time: 20–25 minutes

1 Cut the leeks into very thin strips, then wash them well in cold water. Leave to soak in fresh cold water for 2 minutes. Slice the mushrooms. Crush the garlic.

2 Melt half the butter in a sauté pan over low heat. Drain the leeks and add them to the hot butter. Cover the pan and cook over low heat until the leeks are soft, about 5 minutes. Transfer to a bowl, season and allow to cool.

3 Heat half the oil in the sauté pan, add the mushrooms, garlic and salt and pepper and sauté over high heat. Drain off any excess liquid, add the stock and leave to simmer until reduced by about half. Remove from the heat.

4 Carefully cut open each chicken breast lengthways to make a pocket in the centre. Fill the pockets with the leeks. Season the chicken. Melt the remaining butter and oil in a frying pan, add the chicken and brown over moderate heat. After about 3 minutes, turn the chicken over and reduce the heat slightly. Cook for a further 5–7 minutes, basting frequently. Transfer the chicken breasts to warm plates, cover and keep hot.

To Serve Deglaze the pan with the sherry, then mix this into the mushrooms and heat through until bubbling and thickened. Taste for seasoning, spoon over and around the chicken and serve immediately.

Chef's Tips

This is an excellent dish for entertaining because the chicken breasts can be prepared and stuffed the day before. Cover them with cling film and keep them in the refrigerator. Make the mushroom sauce and cook the chicken immediately before serving.

◆

If there are too many leeks to fit inside the pockets in the chicken, mix any left over into the mushrooms.

Chicken and cashews

The dark, almost black chillies make a dramatic colour contrast against the whiteness of the chicken in this Chinese stir-fry. Serve it very simply, with boiled egg or buckwheat noodles.

500 g (1 lb) skinless boneless chicken breasts
4–5 cm (1½–2 inch) piece of fresh root ginger
½ teaspoon salt
½ teaspoon freshly ground black pepper
1 teaspoon rice wine or sherry
1 teaspoon sesame oil
2 large egg whites
2 teaspoons cornflour
4 spring onions
4 tablespoons groundnut oil
5 dried chillies
60–90 g (2–3 oz) cashew nuts

Sauce
2 teaspoons cornflour
2 teaspoons rice wine or sherry
2 tablespoons soy sauce
1 teaspoon white vinegar
1–2 tablespoons sugar, to taste
2 teaspoons sesame oil
300 ml (½ pint) chicken stock

Serves 2–3

Preparation time: 15 minutes
Cooking time: about 10 minutes

Chef's Tip

Coating the chicken in egg white and cornflour is a Chinese technique that helps protect the delicate fibres of the meat from the high heat used in stir-frying. It may take a little extra time, but it is well worth it because it ensures a tender, moist result.

1 Cut the chicken into bite-sized pieces and place in a bowl. Grate about one-third of the ginger over the chicken, then add the salt, pepper, rice wine or sherry and sesame oil. Lightly beat the egg whites and mix into the chicken with the cornflour. Cover and set aside while preparing the remaining ingredients.

2 Shred the remaining ginger. Cut the spring onions into 5 cm (2 inch) lengths. Prepare the sauce. In a small bowl, mix the cornflour with 1 tablespoon cold water, then add the remaining sauce ingredients and mix until smooth.

3 Heat the oil in a wok or deep sauté pan over moderate heat. Add the chillies and stir-fry until they begin to darken in colour. Increase the heat to high and continue stirring until the chillies are almost black.

4 Add the chicken and stir-fry until it is white, then add the ginger, spring onions, cashews and the sauce mixture. Stir-fry until all the ingredients are glossy and the sauce has thickened, 3–4 minutes.

To Serve Turn into a warm serving bowl and serve immediately.

Chicken with goat's cheese en papillote

Fresh and light, this main course has a Mediterranean flavour, just perfect for an al fresco summer lunch. The papillotes can be prepared the day before, so all you have to do is pop them in the oven half an hour before serving.

4 large skinless boneless chicken breasts
90 g (3 oz) goat's cheese
salt and freshly ground black pepper
1 large head of fennel
2 medium to large ripe tomatoes
12 black olives
1 tablespoon olive oil
4 tablespoons dry white wine or vermouth

Serves 4

Preparation time: 20 minutes
Cooking time: 25 minutes

1 Preheat the oven to 200°C (400°F) Gas 6. With a sharp pointed knife, make an incision in the rounded side and down the length of each chicken breast, cutting not quite to the ends. Gently open the breast and move the knife to left and right to make a pocket. Divide the cheese into quarters. Using your fingers, stuff one-quarter of the cheese into each chicken pocket. Season with pepper, then close the chicken to conceal the cheese.

2 Trim and finely slice the fennel, saving the feathery tops for the garnish. Peel and slice the tomatoes. Stone and roughly chop the olives. Heat the oil in a pan, add the fennel and sauté for about 5 minutes until softened and lightly coloured.

3 Lightly oil 4 large circles or squares of foil, baking parchment or greaseproof paper. Place the fennel in the middle of each, scatter with the olives and arrange the tomato slices on top. Season. Place the stuffed chicken breasts on top of the tomatoes and spoon 1 tablespoon wine or vermouth over each. Close the parcels and seal tightly to make papillotes. Place in a baking dish and bake for 25 minutes.

To Serve Open the papillotes, taking care to avoid the escaping hot steam. With a fish slice, carefully transfer the chicken and vegetables to warm plates. Arrange a few fennel slices on top of each breast and spoon over any juices. Garnish with the reserved fennel tops and serve immediately.

Chef's Tips

Any type of goat's cheese can be used for the stuffing. If you buy one of the hard kinds, leave it to soften at room temperature before using. This will make it easier to push into the chicken pockets.

◆

If you like, you can wrap each chicken breast in a slice of prosciutto (Parma ham) before sitting it on the vegetables. This will make the chicken more moist.

◆

The chicken will keep hot en papillote for 15–20 minutes, so you can remove it from the oven and let it sit unopened while you are eating the first course.

CHICKEN JALFREZI

This is a fresh and buttery medium-hot curry from India, where the name 'jalfrezi' is used to describe a sauté or stir-fry. Serve it with mango chutney and lime pickle, and a simple Rice Pilaf (page 298).

Serves 4

Preparation time: 15 minutes
Cooking time: about 25 minutes

- 500 g (1 lb) skinless boneless chicken breasts
- 1 medium onion
- 1 garlic clove
- 1 small handful of fresh coriander leaves
- 2.5 cm (1 inch) piece of fresh root ginger
- 60 g (2 oz) butter
- 2 tablespoons sunflower oil
- 1 teaspoon turmeric
- 1 teaspoon chilli powder
- ½ teaspoon salt
- 1 x 400 g can chopped tomatoes
- 1 teaspoon ground cumin
- 1 teaspoon ground coriander
- 1 teaspoon garam masala

1 Cut the chicken into strips or cubes. Finely slice the onion. Chop the garlic and fresh coriander, keeping them separate. Peel and grate the ginger.

2 Melt half the butter with the oil in a large sauté pan, add the onion and stir over low heat for a few minutes until softened. Add the chicken, garlic, turmeric, chilli powder and salt. Increase the heat to moderate and fry for 5 minutes. Stir and scrape the bottom of the pan constantly to ensure the spices do not burn.

3 Add the tomatoes, stir to combine, then cover and simmer for 15 minutes, stirring occasionally. Add the remaining butter, the ground spices, fresh ginger and half the fresh coriander. Stir and simmer for a few minutes until the fat shimmers around the edge of the sauce.

To Serve Taste and add more salt if necessary, turn into a warm serving bowl and sprinkle with the remaining fresh coriander. Serve hot.

Variation

You can use 4 large fresh tomatoes instead of canned tomatoes. Make sure they are ripe and juicy and peel them before chopping them finely. To peel tomatoes quickly, cut a cross in the rounded end of each tomato. Put the tomatoes in a bowl and pour boiling water over them. Lift them out one at a time and immerse in a bowl of cold water – the skins should then peel off easily.

Coq au vin

This is an easy version of the classic bistro recipe that everyone loves. Serve it in true French style with new potatoes tossed in butter and finely chopped flat-leaf parsley, then follow with a green salad dressed with Vinaigrette (page 360).

1 small onion
1 small carrot
1 small celery stick
20 pickling onions
salt and freshly ground black pepper
8 chicken pieces
2 tablespoons sunflower oil
90 g (3 oz) lardons or thickly diced bacon
20 whole button mushrooms
500 ml (16 fl oz) red wine, preferably Burgundy
400 ml (14 fl oz) hot chicken stock
1 bouquet garni
finely chopped fresh fat-leaf parsley, to garnish

Serves 4

Preparation time: 30 minutes
Cooking time: about 1 hour

1 Finely chop the onion, carrot and celery. Peel the pickling onions (see Chef's Tips). Season the chicken. Heat the oil in a flameproof casserole, add the chicken and brown in the hot oil. Remove and set aside. Add the lardons or bacon and cook for 2–3 minutes then add the mushrooms and toss until lightly coloured. With a slotted spoon, remove the lardons or bacon and mushrooms and set aside.

2 Add the chopped vegetables to the pan and cook, stirring, for a few minutes. Add the wine and reduce by about half, then add the stock, whole pickling onions and bouquet garni. Bring to the boil. Return the chicken to the pan, cover and simmer gently for 30–40 minutes until tender.

3 Remove the chicken and pickling onions and keep hot. Discard the bouquet garni. Boil the liquid until reduced and slightly thickened, then add the lardons and mushrooms and stir until hot.

To Serve Taste the sauce for seasoning, return the chicken and onions to the pan and sprinkle with chopped parsley. Serve hot.

Chef's Tips

You can either buy a whole chicken and joint it yourself or buy ready cut pieces from the supermarket. Legs, thighs and wings are a good choice, all with bone in. It is a matter of personal taste whether you leave the skin on or not.

◆

Pickling onions can be fiddly to peel. If you blanch them first you will find the task easier. Put them in a pan, cover with cold water and bring to the boil. Boil for 2–3 minutes, then drain and rinse under cold running water.

Duck breasts with honey coriander sauce

A main course for a special dinner à deux. Its delicate oriental flavour is best complemented with a simple dish of stir-fried egg noodles and vegetables. Spring onions and red pepper are a good choice.

1 large duck breast (magret), weighing at least 250 g (8 oz)
salt and freshly ground black pepper
2 tablespoons coriander seeds
125 ml (4 fl oz) runny honey
4 tablespoons soy sauce
175ml (6 fl oz) hot chicken stock
fresh coriander sprigs, to garnish

Serves 2

Preparation time: 10 minutes
Cooking time: about 10 minutes

1 Trim off any excess fat and skin from the duck to neaten its appearance, then score the fat in a criss-cross pattern and season both sides with salt and pepper.

2 Dry-fry the coriander seeds in a dry non-stick pan until they give off a spicy aroma and are dark in colour, then put them in a mortar and crush with a pestle. Put the honey and soy sauce in a small saucepan and slowly bring to a boil, stirring. Add the stock and crushed coriander seeds and cook at a low boil until reduced, about 10 minutes. Remove from the heat.

3 Put the duck breast, fat-side down, in a frying pan and place over moderate heat. Cook for 10 minutes, pressing the duck frequently with a fish slice to keep it as flat as possible. Pour off the excess fat from the pan, turn the duck over and cook for a further 7 minutes or until done to your liking. Meanwhile, strain the sauce through a sieve into a clean pan and reheat gently.

To Serve Carve the duck on the diagonal into very thin slices and arrange in a fan shape on warm dinner plates. Drizzle the sauce over the slices, garnish each portion with a dainty sprig of coriander and serve immediately.

Chef's Tips

Magrets, boneless duck breasts, originally only came from Barbary ducks, but this is not always the case these days. You will find them at large supermarkets and specialist butchers. The ones imported from France are usually sold in vacuum packs. They are rich and meaty, and in France it is the custom to serve 1 large magret between 2 people, but check the weight when buying – you may need to serve 1 duck breast for each person.

Cajun blackened chicken

Hot spices, herbs, pepper and salt combine together to make a crusty coating for low-fat chicken breasts. Serve with boiled white rice and a cooling tomato salsa or a colourful tossed mixed salad.

4 skinless boneless chicken breasts
2 tablespoons olive oil
lime wedges, to serve

Spice Mixture
1 tablespoon cumin seeds
1 tablespoon dried oregano
1 tablespoon dried basil
1/2 tablespoon sea or rock salt
1/2 tablespoon garlic salt
1 tablespoon ground white pepper
1 tablespoon freshly ground black pepper
1 tablespoon cayenne pepper

Serves 4

Preparation time: 20 minutes
Cooking time: about 10 minutes

Chef's Tips

Cajun food is often cooked in butter to increase the blackened effect, but olive oil is used to here to keep the saturated fat content down.

The chicken can be left to marinate in the refrigerator for several hours or overnight.

1 Make the spice mixture. Using a pestle and mortar, grind the cumin seeds to a powder with the oregano and basil. Mix with both kinds of salt and the three kinds of pepper.

2 Coat the chicken breasts with the spice mixture and set aside for at least 10–15 minutes.

3 Heat the oil in a non-stick frying pan and pan-fry the chicken breasts for about 5 minutes on each side or until cooked through.

To Serve Arrange the chicken breasts on a warm platter with lime wedges for squeezing. Serve hot.

Rabbit in a rich tomato and wine sauce

This Italian-style recipe is similar to the classic chicken dish, pollo alla cacciatore, which is also made with tomatoes, wine and rosemary. It is a hearty, warming casserole for a winter meal. Serve with crusty bread, polenta or Mash (page 367) to mop up the juices.

Serves 4

Preparation time: 20 minutes
Cooking time: 45 minutes

8 skinless boneless rabbit joints
2 red onions
2 garlic cloves
10–12 fresh rosemary sprigs
2 tablespoons olive oil
salt and freshly ground black pepper
750 ml (1 1/4 pints) passata
1 tablespoon tomato purée
150 ml (1/4 pint) dry white wine
150 ml (1/4 pint) chicken stock

1 Preheat the oven to 170°C (325°F) Gas 3. Cut the rabbit into large bite-size pieces. Slice the onions and crush the garlic. Strip the leaves from the rosemary sprigs and chop them finely.

2 Heat the oil in a flameproof casserole and gently fry the garlic with the rabbit pieces until golden brown. Add the onion and rosemary and cook for 2–3 minutes. Season generously.

3 Stir in the passata, tomato purée, wine and stock. Bring to a simmer, stirring occasionally, then cover and cook in the oven for 45 minutes, or until the rabbit is tender.

To Serve Taste for seasoning and serve hot, straight from the casserole.

Chef's Tips

Skinless boneless rabbit joints are sold both fresh and frozen at most large supermarkets. They look and taste very similar to chicken but are slightly darker in colour and stronger in flavour. If you prefer, this recipe can be made with skinless boneless chicken thighs instead of the rabbit.

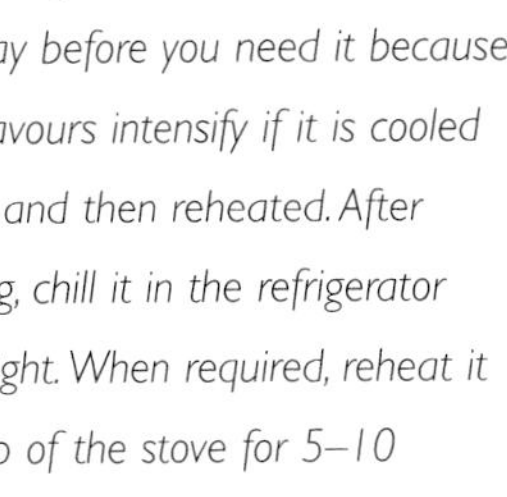

This is a good casserole to make the day before you need it because the flavours intensify if it is cooled down and then reheated. After cooling, chill it in the refrigerator overnight. When required, reheat it on top of the stove for 5–10 minutes until bubbling hot. If the sauce is too thick, add a little more stock, wine or water.

Venison steaks with a redcurrant sauce

Venison is a high-protein meat lower in fat and cholesterol than beef and even skinless chicken, so it is a very good choice for a light diet. This is a dinner party dish, which is quite rich in flavour. Serve it with plain seasonal vegetables.

2 shallots
4 venison steaks, each weighing about 150 g (5 oz)
salt and freshly ground black pepper
90 g (3 oz) fresh redcurrants
1 tablespoon olive oil
300 ml (½ pint) beef stock
4 tablespoons port
1½ tablespoons redcurrant jelly
4 fresh sage sprigs, to serve

Serves 4

Preparation time: 10 minutes
Cooking time: about 15 minutes

Chef's Tip

You can buy venison steaks at large supermarkets and butchers. They are more widely available in the winter, but it is possible to buy them during the summer when fresh redcurrants are also in season. Haunch steaks cut from the leg have lean, prime quality meat and are most reasonably priced. Because the meat is so low in fat, it is best to slightly undercook the steaks as here, then let the meat rest before carving and serving. This will prevent the meat drying out.

1 Finely chop the shallots. Season the steaks well with salt and pepper. Remove the redcurrants from their stalks. Heat the oil in a non-stick sauté pan and cook the steaks over moderate heat for 3–5 minutes on each side, turning once.

2 Remove the steaks from the pan and set them aside to rest in a warm place. Lower the heat, add the shallots and cook gently for a few minutes until softened and browned, then add the stock, port and redcurrant jelly. Stir well, increase the heat and bring to the boil, then simmer until the sauce has reduced by almost half. Add the redcurrants and simmer until the sauce is syrupy.

To Serve Carve the steaks into thin slices on the diagonal and arrange the slices overlapping on warm plates. Spoon the sauce over the steaks and garnish with the sage sprigs. Serve immediately.

Fillet steaks with mushrooms and red wine

This is a classic steak served in true French style with an earthy mix of mushrooms and red wine. It is always popular with meat eaters. Serve with potato wedges (page 210) and a green salad tossed in Vinaigrette Dressing (page 360).

Serves 2

Preparation time: 10 minutes
Cooking time: about 10 minutes

- 2 shallots
- 125 g (4 oz) button mushrooms
- 2 teaspoons olive oil
- 2 fillet steaks, each weighing 125–150 g (4–5 oz)
- salt and freshly ground black pepper
- 1 tablespoon red wine vinegar
- 125 ml (4 fl oz) red wine
- 4 tablespoons hot beef stock

1 Heat a ridged cast iron griddle pan until very hot. Meanwhile, thinly slice the shallots and mushrooms.

2 Dip a wad of kitchen paper in oil and wipe it over the hot pan. Place the steaks on the pan and chargrill for 2–4 minutes on each side, depending on how you like your steak done. Season the steaks with salt and pepper to taste, remove them from the pan and leave them to rest on warm plates.

3 Heat the remaining oil in the pan, add the shallots and mushrooms and stir for 3–5 minutes until the mushrooms are golden and juicy.

4 Add the vinegar and stir to deglaze the pan, then add the wine and simmer for a few minutes until the wine has reduced by about half and is syrupy. Remove the pan from the heat, add the stock and stir to combine. Taste for seasoning.

To Serve Spoon the mushrooooms and sauce over and around the steaks and serve immediately.

Chef's Tip

Fillet steak has the least amount of fat of all the steaks. It is more expensive than rump or sirloin, but there is no waste, it cooks very quickly and is beautifully tender – ideal if you are unused to cooking steak. For rare steak, cook for 2 minutes on each side; for medium, 3 minutes; for well-done, 4 minutes.

VEAL WITH APPLE AND ONION WEDGES

Veal is lean and tender. Ingredients like vinegar, onion and sharp dessert apples give its delicate flavour a boost, and they are all very low in fat. If you prefer you can use slices of pork fillet instead of veal. Pork fillet is also lean and low in fat.

4 veal escalopes, each weighing about 100 g (3½ oz)
salt and freshly ground black pepper
1 red onion
2 red-skinned apples
a little olive oil
2 tablespoons white wine vinegar
150 ml (¼ pint) dry white wine
150 ml (¼ pint) chicken or vegetable stock

Serves 4

Preparation time: 10 minutes
Cooking time: about 10 minutes

1 Heat a ridged cast iron griddle pan until very hot. Meanwhile, season the escalopes with salt and pepper. Slice the onion. Quarter and core the apples, leaving the skin on, then cut each quarter into three.

2 Dip a wad of kitchen paper in oil and wipe it over the hot pan. Place the escalopes on the pan and chargrill for about 3 minutes on each side, turning once. Remove from the heat and keep warm on a serving platter.

3 Add the onion and apples to the pan and cook for 2 minutes on each side or until the onion has softened and the apple wedges are tender with clear griddle marks. Remove them from the pan and place over the veal. Keep warm.

4 Deglaze the pan with the vinegar, then add the wine and stock and stir well. Simmer for about 5 minutes or until the sauce has reduced by about half. Add salt and pepper to taste.

To Serve Spoon the sauce over the escalopes and serve immediately.

Chef's Tips

Veal escalopes are sometimes called schnitzels. They are cut from the fillet end of the leg.

The best kinds of griddle pan have sides and are fairly deep, allowing room to make a sauce in the pan using the sediment and pan juices with additional liquid, as instructed here. If you have a flat griddle without sides, you can deglaze it with a small amount of vinegar, but then you will have to pour the vinegar into a saucepan before adding more liquid.

Saltimbocca

Literally translated, saltimbocca means 'jump in the mouth', and these bite-sized nuggets of veal wrapped around sage and prosciutto seem delicious enough to do just that. Serve them Italian style, with courgettes, broccoli or beans.

4 thin slices of veal escalope, each weighing about 150 g (5 oz)
black pepper
1 small bunch of fresh sage
100 g (3½ oz) prosciutto (Parma ham)
3–4 tablespoons olive oil
250 ml (8 fl oz) dry white wine
salt
fresh sage sprigs, to garnish

1 Put the veal between two layers of cling film and pound with the base of a saucepan until thin. Cut each escalope into small squares or rectangles, making about 30 pieces in all.

2 Grind pepper over the veal, then place 1–2 small sage leaves on top of each piece. Cut the prosciutto into small pieces and arrange over the sage. Roll up each piece of veal and secure with a wooden toothpick.

3 Heat the oil in a large frying pan over moderate to high heat. Add the saltimbocca in batches and cook for no longer than 2–3 minutes, until browned on all sides. Remove and keep hot. Add the wine to the pan and boil until reduced, stirring to loosen any browned bits from the bottom of the pan. Season to taste.

To Serve Remove the toothpicks from the saltimbocca and arrange the veal on a warm serving platter. Pour the sauce over, garnish with fresh sage sprigs and serve immediately.

Serves 4

Preparation time: about 30 minutes
Cooking time: about 10 minutes

Chef's Tips

Although the preparation of the veal rolls may seem long, the cooking time compensates in that it is very short. The rolls can be prepared up to 24 hours in advance and kept, covered, in the refrigerator.

◆

Veal escalope is a delicate and naturally tender meat. Do not overcook it or it will be dry and tough.

KOREAN BEEF WRAPS

These are based on the Korean speciality called bulgogi, sizzling spiced beef traditionally served with kim-chee, a spicy and sour pickled cabbage. Here the beef is wrapped in cool, crisp lettuce leaves with spoonfuls of sweet plum sauce.

500 g (1 lb) sirloin steak
a little olive oil

Marinade
2.5 cm (1 inch) piece of fresh root ginger
3 garlic cloves
1 mild green chilli
2 tablespoons dark soy sauce
1 tablespoon dry sherry
1 tablespoon rice vinegar
1 teaspoon sugar

To Serve
iceberg lettuce leaves
plum sauce
1 tablespoon toasted sesame seeds

Serves 4

Preparation time: 10–15 minutes, plus marinating time
Cooking time: about 10 minutes

1 Make the marinade. Grate the ginger and crush the garlic. Halve, deseed and finely chop the chilli. Put these ingredients in a large bowl and mix in the soy sauce, sherry, rice vinegar and sugar.

2 Trim all the fat off the steak and cut the meat into thin strips, each measuring about 7.5 x 2 cm (3 inches x ¾ inch). Place the strips in the marinade and mix well. Cover and marinate in the refrigerator for 3–4 hours or overnight.

3 Separate, wash and dry the lettuce leaves, then arrange them on a tray or platter, tearing or folding them into neat shapes and cupping them together if they seem thin. Fill 4 small bowls with plum sauce.

4 Heat a ridged cast iron griddle pan until very hot. Dip a wad of kitchen paper in oil and wipe it over the hot pan. Place half the strips of beef on the pan and chargrill for about 5 minutes, turning them frequently with tongs. Remove the strips with tongs and keep warm while chargrilling the remainder.

To Serve Put all the beef in a bowl and sprinkle with the sesame seeds. Let each person put a little plum sauce and a few beef strips on a lettuce leaf, roll up the leaf around them and eat with the hands.

Chef's Tips

To cut steak very thinly, wrap it in cling film and place it in the freezer for a few hours. When it is just frozen, you will find it much easier to slice than when fresh and soft.

◆

To toast sesame seeds, dry-fry them in a non-stick frying pan for a few minutes over low to moderate heat. Shake the pan and keep the sesame seeds on the move to ensure they toast evenly and do not burn.

◆

Plum sauce is sold in bottles in the oriental sections of supermarkets and at Chinese shops. Made from plums, sugar, vinegar, ginger, chillies and salt, it is fruity and sweet with a spicy kick.

SOFT TACOS

The word 'tacos' usually conjures up a picture of crisp, deep-fried shells of corn tortillas, stuffed with chilli, refried beans, grated cheese, guacamole, soured cream and the like. This recipe for a simpler, softer version is Californian in style.

375 g (12 oz) rump steak
1 x 35 g sachet taco seasoning mix
1–2 tablespoons sunflower oil
9–12 flour tortillas

Accompaniments
1 Spanish onion
2–3 ripe tomatoes
90–125 g (3–4 oz) Cheddar or Monterey Jack cheese
150 ml (¼ pint) soured cream
1 x 125 g tub guacamole

Serves 3–4

Preparation time: 20–30 minutes
Cooking time: about 10 minutes

1 Cut the rump steak into thin strips, trimming off excess fat and any sinew. Put the strips in a bowl and sprinkle them with the taco seasoning. Stir the strips to coat them in the seasoning, then set aside.

2 Prepare the accompaniments. Finely chop the onion and tomatoes and grate the cheese. Place in separate small bowls. Spoon the soured cream and guacamole into separate small bowls.

3 Heat the oil in a frying pan until hot. Add the steak strips and fry over moderate to high heat until cooked to your liking, 5–8 minutes. Tip into a serving bowl and keep hot.

4 Dry-fry the tortillas in a non-stick frying pan for a few seconds on each side until they puff up.

To Serve Let each person make their own tacos – the guacamole is usually spread over the tortilla, the beef sprinkled over and topped with onion, tomatoes, cheese and soured cream. Once filled, the tortilla can be rolled up or folded over like an envelope. Tacos are always eaten with the hands.

Chef's Tips

Taco seasoning is sold in the Mexican sections of supermarkets. The spicy mixture is based on chilli powder, paprika, cumin, garlic and oregano.

Flour tortillas are sold in plastic packets in the bread or Mexican sections. Made from ground corn, they are soft and round like thick pancakes, and have a wonderful earthy flavour.

Variation

Make Quesadillas. Sandwich 2 tortillas with grated cheese. chopped jalapeño chillies and stoned black olives. Heat in a hot non-stick frying pan until the cheese starts to melt. Flip the sandwich over and heat the other side.

Chilli

You can make a batch of chilli in 30 minutes, and any leftovers reheat well the next day. In fact, it tastes even better after standing and reheating. Serve it over boiled rice and top with grated Cheddar cheese and soured cream.

1 onion
2 garlic cloves
1 red pepper
2 tablespoons sunflower oil
400 g (14 oz) ground or minced beef
2 teaspoons chilli powder
1 x 400 g can red kidney or pinto beans
1 x 400 g can chopped tomatoes
salt and freshly ground black pepper

Serves 2–3

Preparation time: 5 minutes
Cooking time: about 25 minutes

1 Finely chop the onion and garlic, keeping them separate. Dice the red pepper. Heat the oil in a saucepan, add the onion and cook over low heat until translucent. Add the garlic and red pepper and cook for 1 minute.

2 Add the beef and cook until browned, stirring constantly and pressing with the back of the spoon to remove any lumps. Add the chilli powder and stir for 1–2 minutes.

3 Drain and rinse the beans, then add to the pan with the tomatoes. Stir well, season to taste and simmer for 20 minutes.

To Serve Taste for seasoning and serve hot.

Chef's Tips

There are many types of chilli powder. Most of them are not pure chilli, but a ready mix of the traditional spices and herbs used in chilli con carne – sometimes called chilli seasoning. Check the label for chilli strength before you buy, because some brands are fiery hot. The quantity here is for a medium strength powder, so you may need to add more or less.

◆

The chilli will keep for 3 days in the refrigerator, or it can be frozen for up to 3 months. When you reheat it, add a little hot water to prevent it sticking to the pan, and make sure it is bubbling well for 10 minutes.

Beef with broccoli

An authentic Chinese stir-fry that takes only minutes to cook if you get everything prepared beforehand. Serve with boiled rice or egg noodles for a midweek meal to share with friends.

500–625 g (1–1¼ lb) rump, sirloin or fillet steak
½ teaspoon salt
1 tablespoon rice wine or sherry
3 tablespoons soy sauce
1 tablespoon cornflour

175 g (6 oz) broccoli florets
1 medium yellow or red onion
2 garlic cloves
4 tablespoons groundnut oil
1 tablespoon sugar
2 tablespoons oyster sauce

Serves 3–4

Preparation time: 25 minutes
Cooking time: about 10 minutes

1 Trim the meat of any excess fat or gristle. With the knife at a 45° angle to the cutting board, cut the meat into thin slices. Place the meat in a bowl and add the salt, rice wine or sherry and 1 tablespoon of the soy sauce. Sprinkle with the cornflour and mix everything together well. Cover and set aside for 15 minutes.

2 Meanwhile, divide the broccoli into tiny sprigs and trim the stalks. Cut the onion lengthways into eighths. Crush the garlic.

3 Heat 2 tablespoons of the oil in a wok or deep sauté pan until very hot. Add the beef and stir-fry over high heat for 2–3 minutes. Remove with a slotted spoon and set aside on a plate. Turn the heat down to low, add the remaining oil to the wok, then add the broccoli and 4 tablespoons water. Cover immediately and allow the broccoli to steam for 2 minutes.

4 Uncover, add the onion, garlic and remaining soy sauce and stir-fry over high heat for 1–2 minutes or until the liquid has evaporated. Return the beef to the wok with any juices that have collected on the plate, stir well, then sprinkle with the sugar and oyster sauce. Stir-fry for 1–2 minutes until all the ingredients are well blended.

To Serve Turn into a warm serving bowl and serve immediately.

Chef's Tips

To save preparation time, you can buy ready sliced beef for stir-fries in some supermakets.

◆

Groundnut or peanut oil is often used in stir-fries because it can be heated to a high temperature without burning. Some supermarkets sell bottles of 'stir-fry oil', a mixture of vegetable oil and sesame oil flavoured with ginger and garlic. This would also be ideal for this dish. Never use sesame oil on its own for stir-frying: it has a low smoke point and burns easily.

◆

Variation

Instead of the broccoli, you can use 2 red or orange peppers, cut into thin strips.

Steak with green peppercorn sauce

A classic French bistro-style dish. Serve with pommes allumettes (French fries), which can be cooking in the oven while you are preparing and cooking the steaks. Add a salad garnish if you like.

- 2 small shallots
- 30 g (1 oz) green peppercorns in brine
- 45 g (1½ oz) butter
- 200 ml (7 fl oz) hot beef stock
- 90 ml (3fl oz) double cream
- salt and freshly ground black pepper
- 2 fillet steaks
- 2 teaspoons sunflower oil
- 2 tablespoons brandy (optional)

Serves 2

Preparation time: 7–10 minutes
Cooking time: about 20 minutes

1 Finely chop the shallots. Drain the peppercorns well, then crush them with a fork. In a saucepan, melt 30 g (1 oz) of the butter, add the shallots and cook over low heat for 2–3 minutes. Take care not to let the shallots colour. Add the peppercorns and cook for 2 minutes.

2 Add the stock, bring to the boil and cook for 5–10 minutes or until reduced by about half. Add the cream and simmer for 5 minutes. Add salt to taste and set aside.

3 Heat a frying pan over moderate heat. Season the steaks with salt and pepper. Add the oil and remaining butter to the hot pan and heat them until the butter is foaming. Add the steaks and cook them for 2–4 minutes on each side, according to how you like them. Transfer the steaks to a plate and keep warm.

4 Pour off and discard the fat from the pan, then return the pan to the heat. Add the steaks, then the brandy (if using) and the sauce. Cook for 30 seconds on each side.

To Serve Transfer the steaks to warm plates, spoon the peppercorn sauce over them and serve immediately.

Chef's Tip

Whole green peppercorns are sold in small jars or bottles in delicatessens and supermarkets. Once the jar or bottle has been opened, they will keep in the refrigerator for several months. They are softer than dried peppercorns, but still have quite a crunchy bite to them, so are almost always crushed before use.

BEEF CARBONNADE

A traditional and hearty Flemish casserole for a cold winter's evening. Serve with jacket baked potatoes topped with butter and soured cream, and a fresh green vegetable such as broccoli.

1 large onion
3 tablespoons sunflower oil
1 kg (2 lb) braising steak, cut into thick slices
30 g (1 oz) plain flour
1 x 275 ml can sweet stout
about 750 ml (1¼ pints) hot beef stock
1 bouquet garni
2 juniper berries
1 tablespoon Dijon mustard
2 teaspoons soft brown sugar
salt and freshly ground black pepper

Serves 4–6

Preparation time: 5 minutes
Cooking, time: 1½–2 hours

Chef's Tip

It is traditional to use sliced meat for a carbonnade, but you can cut it into squares if you prefer. Keep them quite large – about 5 cm (2 inches) – or they will cook too quickly and become dry.

1 Preheat the oven to 180°C (350°F) Gas 4. Thinly slice the onion. In a large flame-proof casserole, heat the oil over moderately high heat and brown the sliced beef in batches until nicely coloured on both sides. Once browned, remove and set aside.

2 Lower the heat and cook the onion for 3–5 minutes until lightly coloured, then add the flour. Stir well for 1 minute. Add the stout and allow to simmer for 5 minutes, stirring well. Add the remaining ingredients, season to taste and bring to the boil.

3 Cover the casserole and put it in the oven. Cook for 1¼–1¾ hours or until the meat is tender. Check the level of the cooking liquid from time to time and add more stock if necessary.

To Serve Discard the bouquet garni and taste the sauce for seasoning, Arrange the slices of meat on warm plates and spoon the sauce over them. Serve hot.

Beef pot roast with red wine

The perfect dish for a weekend lunch – all the preparation can be done the day before, then the meat can be slowly simmered in the oven during the morning. Serve with Mashed Potatoes (page 239) and a seasonal vegetable or two.

Serves 4–6

Preparation time: 20 minutes
Cooking time: 2½–3 hours

1 large carrot
1 small onion
1 medium celery stick
2 garlic cloves
2–3 tablespoons sunflower oil
1.5 kg (3 lb) rolled and tied top rump of beef
1 tablespoon plain flour
2 tablespoons tomato purée
1 bouquet garni
salt and freshly ground black pepper
400 ml (14 fl oz) red wine
600 ml (1 pint) hot beef stock

1 Preheat the oven to 170°C (325°F) Gas 3. Finely chop all the vegetables and the garlic, keeping them separate. Heat the oil in a large flameproof casserole and sear the meat over moderately high heat until browned on all sides. Remove and set aside.

2 Pour off any excess fat from the pan and reduce the heat to medium-low. Add the carrot, onion and celery and sauté for 2–3 minutes. Add the flour and tomato purée, stir well and cook for 1 minute, then add the wine, garlic, bouquet garni and salt and pepper to taste.

3 Return the meat to the casserole and simmer until the wine has reduced by about one-third. Add the stock and return to a simmer, then cover the casserole and put it in the oven. Cook for 2–2½ hours or until the meat is very tender.

4 Remove the meat and keep hot. Strain the cooking liquid through a fine sieve, return to the casserole and simmer until reduced to your liking. Taste for seasoning.

To Serve Slice the meat and place on a warm platter. Spoon some of the sauce over the meat and serve immediately, with the remaining sauce handed separately in a sauce boat.

Chef's Tips

Top rump is a good joint for pot roasting. You may not be able to find it ready rolled and tied at the supermarket, but any butcher will do this for you. Less expensive topside, basket and silverside are often sold ready rolled and tied. They can be used, but you may not get such succulent results.

◆

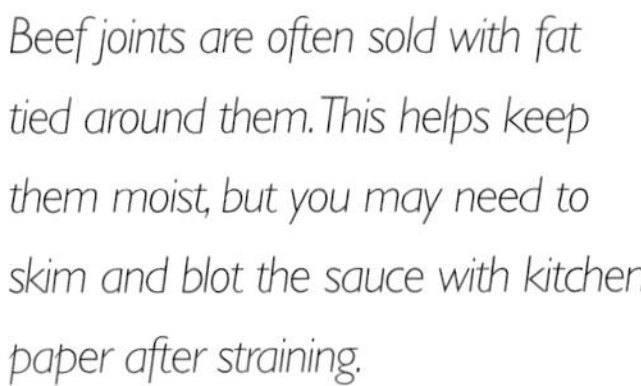

Beef joints are often sold with fat tied around them. This helps keep them moist, but you may need to skim and blot the sauce with kitchen paper after straining.

BEEF STROGANOFF

A good dish for an evening at home when you want to serve something special but haven't much time to spend in the kitchen. Serve with rice and a salad of mixed leaves tossed with Vinaigrette (page 360).

250 g (8 oz) beef fillet (tail end) or good-quality rump or sirloin steak
1 large shallot or 1 small onion
1 small garlic clove
30 g (1 oz) butter
1 rounded teaspoon paprika
2 tablespoons sunflower oil
salt and freshly ground black pepper

To Serve
150 ml (¼ pint) crème fraîche
1 dill or sweet and sour cucumber, cut into julienne
1–2 tablespoons finely chopped fresh flat-leaf parsley

Serves 2

Preparation time: 10–15 minutes
Cooking time: about 10 minutes

1 Trim the meat of any fat and sinew, then cut it into strips about 4 cm (1½ inches) long and 5 mm (¼ inch) thick. Finely chop the shallot or onion. Crush the garlic.

2 Melt the butter in a frying pan, add the shallot or onion and cook over low heat for 5–7 minutes until soft and translucent. Stir in the garlic and paprika. Cook for 1 minute, stirring. Remove the mixture from the pan and set aside.

3 Add the oil to the pan and heat it over high heat. When it sizzles, add the beef and toss for 2–3 minutes until the beef is sealed and lightly browned. Stir in the shallot mixture and salt and pepper to taste and heat through, stirring.

To Serve Swirl in the crème fraîche and serve immediately, topped with the cucumber julienne and the parsley.

Chef's Tip

Be sure to fry the beef over high heat. If the heat is too low, the juices will run out of the meat and result in a stewed appearance and taste.

◆

Variation

If you have some brandy to hand, add 1 tablespoon to the cooked shallot or onion and reduce it down to nothing before adding the garlic and paprika.

Slow cooked lamb

This is a wonderful winter casserole. The dried apricots dissolve into the sauce during cooking and create an intense, rich flavour. Serve with Mash (page 367) or crusty bread and follow with a crisp green salad tossed in Vinaigrette Dressing (page 360).

Serves 4

Preparation time: 20 minutes
Cooking time: 2¼–2¾ hours

- 10 baby onions or small shallots
- 1 large carrot or 2 small ones
- 2 celery sticks
- 2 garlic cloves
- 8 fresh sage sprigs
- 2 teaspoons juniper berries
- 1 tablespoon olive oil
- about 1 kg (2 lb) shoulder of lamb, boned and cut into cubes
- 125 g (4 oz) ready-to-eat dried apricots
- 250 ml (8 fl oz) red wine
- about 900 ml (1½ pints) hot lamb stock
- salt and freshly ground black pepper

1 Preheat the oven to 150°C (300°F) Gas 2. Peel the onions or shallots, leaving them whole and attached at the root end. Dice the carrot and celery. Finely chop the garlic and sage leaves, keeping them separate. Crush the juniper berries with a pestle and mortar.

2 In a flameproof casserole, heat the oil and quickly brown the lamb over moderate to high heat. Add the vegetables, garlic, juniper berries and half the sage, then the apricots, wine and about one-third of the stock. Season generously and bring to the boil.

3 Cover the casserole tightly with the lid, transfer to the oven and cook for 2–2½ hours. Two or three times during cooking, spoon off any excess fat from the surface of the liquid, stir well and add more stock. At the end of the cooking time, the lamb will be very tender and the liquid quite reduced.

To Serve Taste and adjust the seasoning if necessary, then sprinkle with the remaining sage. Serve hot, straight from the casserole.

Chef's Tip

To get about 1 kg (2 lb) boneless lamb, buy a lean shoulder of lamb weighing about 1.5 kg (3 lb) and ask the butcher to bone and cube it for you, removing as much surplus fat as possible. You can use the bones to make a brown stock, following the recipe on page 355.

◆

Variations

Boneless lamb neck fillet can be used instead of shoulder. It is widely available, both at supermarkets and butchers. You will need about 750 g (1½ lb).

◆

Beef can be used instead of lamb. Buy 750 g (1½ lb) boneless beef for stewing or casseroling. The cooking time will be the same as for the lamb.

Orange and rosemary lamb cutlets

The 'eye' of the meat in lamb cutlets is very lean, tender and juicy, but you need to take care to trim off as much visible fat as possible from around the meat and bones before cooking. Serve with new potatoes and a seasonal fresh vegetable.

2 racks of lamb
2 garlic cloves
2 teaspoons olive oil
grated rind and juice of 1 orange
2 tablespoons chopped fresh rosemary
salt and freshly ground black pepper
125 ml (4 fl oz) red wine
1 tablespoon redcurrant jelly
fresh rosemary sprigs, to garnish

Serves 4

Preparation time: 20 minutes
Cooking time: 20–30 minutes

1 Preheat the oven to 200°C (400°F) Gas 6. Trim off as much fat as possible from the lamb. Chop the garlic very finely. Brush the meaty side of each lamb rack with 1 teaspoon oil, then press the garlic, orange rind and rosemary on to the meat with your fingers and season generously with salt and pepper.

2 Place the lamb on a rack in a roasting tin and roast in the oven for 20–30 minutes according to how well done you like your lamb. Transfer the lamb to a board and cover with foil to keep the meat warm and allow it to rest before carving.

3 Put the roasting tin on top of the stove and deglaze with the wine, then stir in the orange juice and redcurrant jelly. Bring to the boil and stir until the jelly has melted. Turn the heat down to very low.

To Serve Carve the lamb into cutlets by inserting the knife between the bones. Arrange the cutlets on warm plates and spoon the sauce over them. Garnish with rosemary sprigs and serve immediately.

Chef's Tip

Racks of lamb from the best end of neck usually have 6–9 bones in them. For 4 people you should buy 2 racks, so that each person will have at least 3 cutlets. Check with your butcher that he has removed the chine bone or you will find the rack difficult to carve. Your butcher should also trim and scrape the bones clean.

◆

Variations

If you like, you can thicken the sauce with 1 teaspoon cornflour mixed to a paste with a little cold water. Add it while the sauce is being stirred and keep stirring to prevent lumps forming.

◆

Try serving the cutlets with Tangy Red Relish (page 358).

Grilled marinated lamb

This lamb is quite spicy hot from the chilli and spring onions, but the mint helps cool it down. Serve on a bed of rice with a side dish of natural yogurt or a simple tzatziki of yogurt mixed with chopped cucumber and fresh mint.

- 1 green chilli
- 1 small bunch of fresh mint
- 1 garlic clove
- ½ bunch of spring onions
- rind and juice of 2 limes or 1 lemon
- salt and freshly ground black pepper
- 500 g (1 lb) lamb fillet, cut into large cubes
- lime or lemon wedges, to serve

Serves 4

Preparation time: 10 minutes, plus marinating time

Cooking time: 8–10 minutes

1 Halve the chilli lengthways and remove the seeds, then finely chop the chilli flesh in a food processor with all but 4 tiny sprigs of mint, the garlic, spring onions and lime or lemon rind.

2 Turn the chopped mixture into a bowl, add the lime or lemon juice and season generously with salt and pepper. Mix well. Add the lamb and thoroughly coat with the mixture, then cover the bowl with cling film and marinate in the refrigerator overnight.

3 Preheat the grill to hot. Thread the cubes of lamb on to 8 small metal skewers and grill the lamb for 8–10 minutes, turning once.

To Serve Arrange the skewers on plates with lime or lemon wedges for squeezing. Garnish with the remaining mint sprigs and serve immediately.

Chef's Tip

Buy lamb neck or leg fillet. Neck is more juicy than leg, because it has a slight marbling of fat; leg is often so lean that it can be dry. Get the butcher to cube the meat for you.

Variations

Add 150 ml (¼ pint) natural yogurt to the chopped mixture in the bowl before adding the lamb. Yogurt will help make the lamb more juicy, which is good if you are using very lean leg meat.

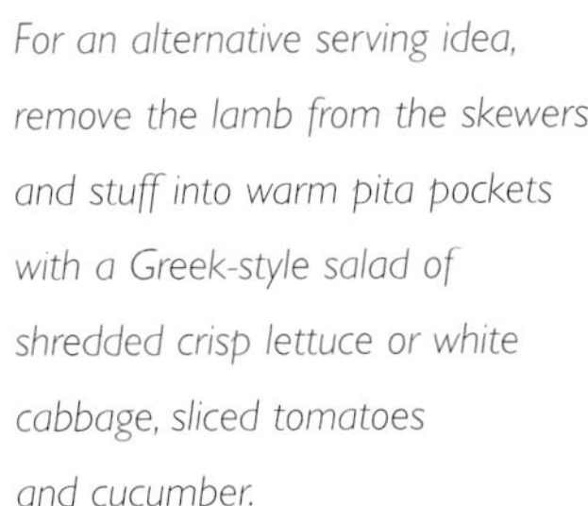

For an alternative serving idea, remove the lamb from the skewers and stuff into warm pita pockets with a Greek-style salad of shredded crisp lettuce or white cabbage, sliced tomatoes and cucumber.

Grilled lamb cutlets with corn and pepper salsa

The combination of sizzling hot cutlets with a cool and refreshing salsa is simply sensational. For a dish that is both colourful and tasty, serve with baby new potatoes tossed in butter and chopped fresh herbs.

6 lamb cutlets (best end of neck)
2 garlic cloves
1 fresh thyme sprig
4 tablespoons olive oil
salt and freshly ground black pepper

Salsa
1 red pepper
1 garlic clove
1 large handful of fresh coriander
1 x 198 g can sweetcorn
4 tablespoons olive oil
1 tablespoon lime juice
pinch of sugar

Serves 2

Preparation time: 20 minutes
Cooking time: 6–8 minutes, or a few minutes longer

1 Trim off any excess fat from the cutlets, then place in a shallow dish. Chop the garlic and thyme leaves, place them in a bowl and mix in the olive oil and pepper to taste. Brush over both sides of the cutlets. Set aside for about 20 minutes.

2 Meanwhile, preheat the grill and make the salsa. Finely dice the red pepper and chop the garlic and coriander. Drain the sweetcorn, place in a bowl and add the red pepper, garlic, coriander, olive oil, lime juice and sugar. Mix well and add salt and pepper to taste.

3 Cook the cutlets under the hot grill for 3–4 minutes on each side or until they are done to your liking.

To Serve Place 3 cutlets on each warm plate and spoon some of the salsa alongside. Serve immediately, with the remaining salsa handed separately.

Chef's Tip

Best end of neck cutlets have a tender and juicy 'eye' of meat, and they cook in next to no time. They are sold in packets in supermarkets, sometimes with the ends of the bones trimmed off. If you like lamb chump chops, these can also be cooked in the same way, allowing a few minutes' extra cooking time.

Lamb couscous

A Tunisian stew with a wonderful aroma and flavour. A meal in itself that needs no accompaniment, it is ideal for informal entertaining. The meat and vegetables taste better when cooked the day before.

1 kg (2 lb) boneless lamb shoulder or neck fillet
2 medium red onions
8–12 baby new potatoes
4 carrots
2 tomatoes, total weight about 150 g (5 oz)
2 garlic cloves
3 tablespoons olive oil
1 teaspoon turmeric
2 tablespoons tomato purée
1 bouquet garni
1 teaspoon sea salt
1 turnip, weighing about 200 g (7 oz)
2 courgettes
1 x 400 g can chickpeas
250 g (8 oz) quick-cooking couscous
½–1 teaspoon harissa, or to taste
chopped fresh coriander, to garnish

Serves 4–6

Preparation time: 15–20 minutes
Cooking time: about 1¼ hours

1 Trim the lamb of any excess fat, then cut the meat into small pieces. Quarter the onions. Halve or quarter the potatoes (there is no need to peel them). Peel the carrots and cut them into large pieces. Chop the tomatoes and crush the garlic.

2 Heat the oil in a large pan and brown the lamb in batches over high heat. Return all of the lamb to the pan and add the onions, potatoes, carrots and turmeric. Stir well, add the tomato purée and stir again. Add the tomatoes and garlic and enough cold water to cover, then add the bouquet garni and salt and bring to a simmer. Cover and cook for 30 minutes.

3 Peel and quarter the turnip. Cut the courgettes into large pieces. Drain and rinse the chickpeas. Add the turnip, courgettes and chickpeas to the pan and cook for 30 minutes or until the lamb is tender. Meanwhile, cook the couscous according to the instructions on the packet.

To Serve Remove the bouquet garni from the stew, then stir in harissa to taste. Pile the couscous in warm dishes or bowls and spoon the stew on top. Sprinkle with fresh coriander and serve.

Chef's Tip

Harissa is a fiery, thick sauce made from chillies, garlic and spices. It is sold in tubes, cans and jars at most supermarkets. The tubes are the most convenient to use. Add it sparingly at first, until you get the degree of heat you like, and serve more in a little bowl at the table for those who like their food extra hot.

LAMB KEBABS WITH TOMATO AND CORIANDER SALSA

Tangy hot kebabs taste sensational with a cool and refreshing salsa. This is a good recipe for a barbecue party because everything can be prepared the day before and the lamb cooked at the last minute. Saffron rice makes a colourful accompaniment.

Serves 4

Preparation time: about 20 minutes, plus marinating
Cooking time: 8–12 minutes

4 large ripe tomatoes
1 handful of fresh coriander
1 small red onion
juice of 1½ lemons
5 tablespoons olive oil
salt and freshly ground black pepper
2 garlic cloves
750 g (1½ lb) boneless lamb shoulder, leg or neck fillet, cut into 2 cm (¾ inch) cubes

1 Dice the tomatoes and remove the seeds, then place in a bowl. Finely chop the coriander and onion. Put one-third of the coriander and onion in the bowl with the tomatoes, add one-third of the lemon juice, 2 tablespoons of the olive oil, and salt and pepper to taste. Toss the salsa well to mix, cover with cling film and refrigerate while preparing and marinating the lamb.

2 Chop the garlic and place in a large bowl with the lamb. Add the remaining coriander, onion, lemon juice and oil. Season with salt and pepper. Toss until the lamb is well coated, cover with cling film and leave to marinate in the refrigerator for at least 4 hours, preferably overnight.

3 Thread the lamb on skewers and cook on the barbecue or under a preheated very hot grill for 8–10 minutes, turning the skewers as necessary.

To Serve Arrange the skewers of lamb on a bed of saffron rice, with the chilled salsa alongside.

Variations

Use chicken instead of lamb, either breast meat or boneless thighs.

◆

Marinate the meat in Spiced Yogurt Marinade (page 351) instead of the marinade given here, and serve with Rice Pilaf (page 298) and Cucumber and Mint Raita (page 369).

Lamb with peppers and tomato

A colourful sauté simply oozing with flavour, good in late summer or early autumn when peppers are at their best. Serve with a plain accompaniment, such as Mashed Potatoes (page 239), boiled polenta or rice.

1 kg (2 lb) boneless lamb shoulder or neck fillet
salt and freshly ground black pepper
3 small peppers (red, yellow and green)
1 onion
4 garlic cloves
3 tablespoons olive oil
½ x 400 g can chopped tomatoes
1 tablespoon sun-dried tomato paste
200 ml (7 fl oz) dry white wine
1 bouquet garni
100 g (3½ oz) prosciutto di Parma (Parma ham) or other cured ham
1 tablespoon chopped fresh flat-leaf parsley
fresh flat-leaf parsley sprigs, to garnish

Serves 4

Preparation time: 20 minutes
Cooking time: about 10 minutes

1 Trim the lamb of any excess fat, then cut the meat into 2.5 cm (1 inch) squares and season with salt and pepper. Slice the the peppers and onion. Chop the garlic.

2 Heat 2 tablespoons of the oil in a large flameproof casserole and brown the lamb in batches over high heat. Remove with a slotted spoon and set aside. Reduce the heat to low and add the peppers and onion. Cook gently until softened, stirring and scraping the sediment from the bottom of the pan.

3 Add the garlic, tomatoes and tomato paste, then return the lamb to the casserole and add the wine and bouquet garni. Bring to the boil, cover and lower the heat to a gentle simmer. Cook for 45 minutes or until the lamb is tender, stirring occasionally. At the end of cooking, discard the bouquet garni and taste the lamb for seasoning.

To Serve Quickly sear the prosciutto in the remaining oil. Place in the bottom of a warm serving dish and spoon the lamb on top. Sprinkle with the chopped parsley and serve immediately, garnished with parsley sprigs.

Chef's Tips

For speed, buy the lamb from the butcher and ask him to cut it into squares for you, trimming off as much fat as possible. At the supermarket, boneless shoulder of lamb is often sold rolled and tied as a joint, but it doesn't take many minutes to undo it and cut it into squares. Neck fillet is usually sold in the piece, rather like pork fillet or tenderloin.

◆

The prosciutto for serving is a professional chef's touch, but it can be omitted.

Roast lamb with garlic and thyme

A simple joint for Sunday lunch, with a superbly flavoured gravy made French chef style. Serve with Roasted Mediterranean Vegetables (page 232) and Mashed Potatoes (page 239) mixed with chopped fresh herbs.

6 garlic cloves
1 small carrot
1 small onion
1 small celery stick
1 boned and rolled joint of lamb (leg or shoulder), weighing about 1.8 kg (3½ lb)
salt and freshly ground black pepper
90 g (3 oz) butter, softened
300 ml (½ pint) dry white wine
500 ml (16 fl oz) hot lamb or beefstock
1 fresh thyme sprig
1 bay leaf

Serves 6

Preparation time: 15 minutes
Cooking time: about 1¼ hours

Chef's Tips

If buying the lamb from a butcher, ask him for the bones from the joint and get him to chop them into small pieces. You can then add them to the roasting tin with the chopped vegetables to make a richer gravy.

◆

The cooking time given here is short, because roast lamb is generally served rare in France. If you prefer it medium, cook for another 10–15 minutes.

1 Preheat the oven to 190°C (375°F) Gas 5. Cut the garlic cloves in half. Roughly chop the carrot, onion and celery. Rub the lamb all over with the cut side of 2 of the garlic clove halves, then rub all over with salt and pepper. Place the lamb in a roasting tin and spread with the butter.

2 Roast the lamb for 30 minutes, then turn the joint over and spread the chopped vegetables and remaining garlic around. Roast for another 30 minutes, or until done to your liking. Remove the lamb, cover with tented foil and keep hot. Turn the oven down to 110°C (225°F) Gas ¼.

3 Tip the contents of the roasting tin into a large sieve and let the fat strain through into a bowl. Discard the fat. Return the vegetables to the roasting tin and place on the hob. Deglaze with the wine, scraping the tin to dissolve the sediment, then simmer, stirring, until the wine has almost evaporated.

4 Add the stock, thyme sprig and bay leaf to the tin. Bring to the boil, stirring, then simmer until reduced by about two-thirds. Meanwhile, carve the lamb, arrange the slices on a warm platter and cover with foil. Reheat in the oven for 3–5 minutes.

To Serve Strain the sauce into a sauce boat and serve with the platter of lamb.

Pork steaks with cider

Pork, cider and apples indicate that this is a dish from Normandy, a region famous for these ingredients and a rich cuisine that uses them to the full. Cream is often used in Normandy too, but in this recipe the sauce is better without it.

4 pork steaks, each weighing about 125 g (4 oz)
1 tablespoon olive oil
12 small shallots
2–3 bay leaves
4 tablespoons cider vinegar
100 ml (3½ fl oz) dry cider
2 large fresh thyme sprigs
salt and freshly ground black pepper
300 ml (½ pint) pork or chicken stock
1 teaspoon clear or thick honey
1 large Bramley apple
2 teaspoons cornflour
fresh thyme sprigs, to serve

Serves 4

Preparation time: 10 minutes
Cooking time: about 45 minutes

1 Trim as much fat as possible off the pork. Heat the oil in a large flameproof casserole and add the pork, shallots and bay leaves. Allow the pork to brown over high heat for 8–10 minutes, turning once.

2 Pour the vinegar and cider into the pan and stir well, then add the thyme and season well with salt and pepper. Add the stock and honey, bring to the boil and stir well, then reduce the heat to a gentle simmer. Cover and cook for about 30 minutes or until the pork is tender when pierced with a skewer.

3 Meanwhile, quarter, core and peel the apple, then cut into 4 cm (1½ inch) chunks. Add to the pork for the last 15 minutes.

4 Remove the meat from the pan and place on warm plates. Cover and keep warm. Mix the cornflour to a paste with 1 tablespoon cold water, pour into the pan and boil for 1–2 minutes, stirring, until the sauce thickens. Taste for seasoning.

To Serve Spoon the sauce over the pork, garnish with thyme and serve immediately.

Chef's Tips

Steaks cut from the leg or shoulder have no outer layer of fat or skin and are a good choice for this recipe. Shoulder is more moist than leg, but it is also fattier. Before buying, check there is only a light marbling of fat through the meat.

◆

Bottles of French dry cider from Normandy are sold at wine merchants and some large supermarkets. Use some for the sauce and serve the rest of the bottle chilled with the meal. It is an excellent drink.

◆

Pork stock cubes are widely available at supermarkets, but if you don't want to buy them especially for this recipe, use chicken stock instead.

◆

If you can't get the pork steaks in the pan in a single layer, fry them in two batches in step 1.

Pork fillet with tomato and sage sauce

Rich, strong flavours are at the heart of the Italian-style sauce that coats slices of tender pork in this hearty main course dish. Serve it in winter with polenta mash. In northern Italy, polenta and rich tomato sauces are traditionally served together.

- 1 onion
- 2 carrots
- 2 celery sticks
- 2 garlic cloves
- 1 small bunch of fresh sage
- 2 whole pork fillets, each weighing about 375 g (3/4 lb)
- 2 tablespoons olive oil
- 2 tablespoons red wine vinegar
- 150 ml (1/4 pint) red wine
- 1 x 400 g can chopped tomatoes
- 1 tablespoon tomato purée
- salt and freshly ground black pepper

Serves 6

Preparation time: 10–15 minutes
Cooking time: 35 minutes, plus standing time

1 Finely chop the onion, carrots, celery and garlic in a food processor. Finely chop the sage with a sharp knife, reserving some small whole sage leaves for the garnish.

2 Trim any fat and membrane from the pork and cut each fillet crossways into 3 pieces. Heat the oil in a heavy-based flameproof casserole, add the pork and brown over moderate to high heat until well coloured on all sides, about 10 minutes. Meanwhile, preheat the oven to 170°C (325°F) Gas 3.

3 Remove the pork from the pan and keep warm. Add the chopped vegetables to the oil in the pan, lower the heat and cook gently for about 5 minutes, stirring frequently until softened. Add the vinegar, wine, tomatoes, tomato purée, chopped sage and salt and pepper to taste. Stir well to mix and bring to the boil, then return the pork to the pan and coat with the sauce.

4 Cover and bake in the oven for 15 minutes, turning the pork over and basting with the sauce halfway. Remove from the oven and leave to stand, without lifting the lid, for 10 minutes.

To Serve Slice the pork on the diagonal and arrange overlapping slices on warm plates. Spoon the tomato sauce over the pork, garnish with the reserved sage leaves and serve immediately.

Chef's Tip

Pork fillet is an excellent meat for light cookery because it is very lean and tender. Sometimes called the tenderloin, it is a prime cut from the centre of the loin – the pork equivalent of fillet steak. Whole fillets are sold at supermarkets and butchers, who often sell them individually in vacuum packs.

Pork with pesto

An ideal dish for last-minute entertaining because it is so quick and easy to prepare and cook. Serve with a julienne of courgettes leeks and carrots or orange pepper. Boiled polenta is another suitable accompaniment.

1 whole pork fillet (tenderloin), weighing about 375 g (12 oz)
1 heaped tablespoon plain flour
salt and freshly ground black pepper
2 tablespoons olive oil
about 3 tablespoons bottled or homemade Basil Pesto (page 349)
125 ml (4 fl oz) medium sherry or Vouvray white wine
fresh basil leaves, to garnish

Serves 2–3

Preparation time: 10 minutes
Cooking time: about 8 minutes

1 Trim the pork fillet, then cut the meat on the diagonal into 2.5 cm (1 inch) slices; you should get about 10 slices. Place the slices on a board and flatten them with the base of a saucepan or a meat mallet until about 1.25 cm (½ inch) thick.

2 Preheat the grill. Spread the flour out on a plate and season well. Put the pork slices on the flour and turn to coat. Heat the oil in a large frying pan and fry the pork slices for 2 minutes on each side.

3 Transfer the slices of pork to the rack of the grill pan. Set the frying pan aside. Spread the top of each pork slice with pesto and grill for 30–60 seconds until bubbling. Transfer to warm plates and keep hot.

4 Add the sherry or wine to the frying pan and stir over moderate heat until well mixed with any sediment and meat juices in the pan. Pour over the pork.

To Serve Garnish with fresh basil and serve immediately.

Chef's Tips

The meat can be sliced and coated in seasoned flour up to 24 hours in advance, then covered and kept in the refrigerator.

◆

Watch the pork closely under the grill and do not grill the pesto for longer than 30–60 seconds or it may burn.

Pork medallions with leeks and mustard sauce

A mingling of French and oriental flavours makes this a very special dish. It goes well with Gratin Dauphinois (page 241), which is baked in the oven, leaving you free to concentrate on cooking the pork on top of the stove.

750 g (1½ lb) pork fillet (tenderloin)
3 garlic cloves
3 tablespoons soy sauce
2 tablespoons rice wine or sherry
a good pinch of sugar
625 g (1¼ lb) small leeks
30 g (1 oz) butter
2–3 tablespoons dry white wine
2 tablespoons sunflower oil
fresh sage leaves, to garnish

Mustard Sauce
3 shallots
1 tablespoon sunflower oil
30 g (1 oz) sugar
3 tablespoons white wine vinegar
4 tablespoons dry vermouth
200 ml (7 fl oz) canned beef consommé
1 tablespoon wholegrain mustard
salt and freshly ground black pepper

Serves 4

Preparation time: 20 minutes
Cooking time: 20–25 minutes

1 Trim the pork and reserve the trimmings for the sauce. Cut the pork into slices on the diagonal about 2.5 cm (1 inch) thick. Finely chop the garlic and mix it in a large bowl with the soy sauce, rice wine or sherry and the sugar. Put the pork in the bowl, stir to coat in the marinade, then set aside. Trim the leeks and cut them on the diagonal into thick slices.

2 Make the mustard sauce. Finely chop the shallots and reserved pork trimmings. Fry them in the oil with the sugar until lightly caramelized. Deglaze the pan with the vinegar, then reduce until syrupy. Add the vermouth and reduce until syrupy. Pour in the consommé and cook for 10–15 minutes. Strain into a clean pan, then add the mustard and seasoning. Cover and keep hot.

3 Melt the butter in a sauté pan and add the leeks, wine and salt and pepper to taste. Cover the pan with a lid and gently steam the leeks. At the same time, heat the oil in a separate sauté pan and sauté the pork slices over moderate to high heat for 3–4 minutes on each side.

To Serve Arrange a bed of leeks on each warm plate and place the pork on top. Drizzle the sauce over the pork and garnish with sage leaves. Serve immediately.

Chef's Tips

The pork and leeks require last-minute cooking, so have all the ingredients prepared and assembled before you start.

◆

You can buy washed and sliced leeks in bags at many supermarkets. They are a little more expensive than whole leeks, but save a lot of time and trouble.

◆

The pork can be sliced and put in the marinade the day before, then left to marinate in the refrigerator overnight. The sauce can also be made and strained the day before, but do not add the mustard at this stage. While the pork is cooking, gently reheat the sauce, then add the mustard.

Pork fillets zingara

Rich and earthy tasting, this is a rustic dish which makes a good main course for an autumn or winter dinner party. Serve it with Mashed Potatoes (page 239) or Polenta (page 296), and follow with a tossed green salad.

750 g (1½ lb) pork fillet (tenderloin)
1 tablespoon paprika
salt and freshly ground black pepper
2 medium to large tomatoes
2 shallots
60 g (2 oz) mushrooms
60 g (2 oz) cooked ham
60 g (2 oz) cooked tongue
30 g (1 oz) butter
2 tablespoons olive oil
4 tablespoons Madeira
300 ml (½ pint) hot chicken stock
finely chopped fresh parsley, to garnish

Serves 4

Preparation time: 20 minutes
Cooking time: about 15 minutes

1 Trim the pork and reserve the trimmings for the sauce. Cut the pork into slices on the diagonal about 2.5 cm (1 inch) thick. Mix the paprika on a plate with salt and pepper to taste, then use to coat the pork. Peel, deseed and finely chop the tomatoes. Finely chop the shallots. Shred the mushrooms, ham and tongue.

2 Melt the butter with 1 tablespoon of the oil in a sauté pan and sauté the pork over moderate to high heat for 3–4 minutes on each side. Remove the pork from the pan with tongs or a slotted spoon and keep hot.

3 Lower the heat under the pan, add the shallots and reserved pork trimmings and stir for 1 minute before adding the Madeira. Increase the heat to moderate and cook until almost dry, then add the tomatoes and stock. Lower the heat and simmer until thickened. Meanwhile, sauté the mushrooms in the remaining oil in a separate pan.

4 Stir the mushrooms, ham and tongue into the sauce, season to taste and heat through.

To Serve Place the pork on warm plates and coat with the sauce. Sprinkle with parsley and serve immediately.

Chef's Tip

Zingara means 'gypsy style' in classic French cuisine, and it is used to describe a dish flavoured with ham, tongue, mushrooms and sometimes truffles. The sauce is traditionally based on Madeira, but if you don't have any, you can use port or red wine instead.

Sausage and mash with onion gravy

An old-fashioned favourite that is always popular, especially on cold winter evenings. This version is rather special, so buy good-quality, pure pork sausages from your butcher or supermarket.

8 large sausages
1 large Spanish onion
2 tablespoons sunflower oil
60 g (2 oz) butter
1 tablespoon plain flour
500 ml (16 fl oz) hot beef stock
salt and freshly ground black pepper
Mashed Potatoes (page 239)
fresh sage sprigs, to garnish

Serves 4

Preparation time: 15 minutes
Cooking time: about 35 minutes

Chef's Tip

Start boiling the potatoes for the mash before frying the sausages, then while the sausages are cooking you will have your hands free to mash the potatoes. You can then reheat the potatoes, adding the hot milk and butter, just before the onion gravy is ready.

1 Prick the sausages. Thinly slice the onion into rings. Heat the oil in a large frying pan, add the sausages and fry gently for about 15 minutes until cooked through and browned on all sides. Remove and keep hot.

2 Add the butter to the pan and heat gently until melted. Add the onion rings and cook over low heat for 3–5 minutes, stirring constantly, then lightly colour them over high heat for 2–3 minutes.

3 Sprinkle in the flour, lower the heat and cook, stirring, for 1–2 minutes. Pour in the hot stock and bring to the boil, stirring. Lower the heat, add salt and pepper to taste and simmer for about 10 minutes.

To Serve Mound the mashed potatoes on warm plates and arrange the sausages on top. Spoon the gravy over and around and serve immediately, garnished with fresh sage.

POULTRY, GAME & MEAT

quick and easy ideas

Chicken breasts

• Pan-fry skinless boneless whole breasts or strips in olive oil or oil and butter. Deglaze pan with 1–2 tablespoons each balsamic vinegar and orange or lemon juice. Drizzle over chicken and sprinkle with chopped fresh sage, rosemary or thyme.

• For a rich sauce, stir a little crème fraîche or double cream into the pan juices.

• For a sweet and sour sauce, add a pinch or two of sugar.

• For a Mediterranean flavour, add a few black olives, stoned and sliced or roughly chopped, or a few thinly sliced sun-dried tomatoes or roasted peppers.

• Split whole breasts lengthways and fill with pesto, then pan-fry in olive oil for 15 minutes, turning once. Deglaze pan with water, wine or Marsala.

• Season skinless boneless whole breasts, wrap in Parma ham and place in an oiled baking dish. Top with slices of cheese and bake at 200°C (400°F) Gas 6 for 20 minutes. If available, wrap 1–2 fresh sage or basil leaves between chicken and ham, or spread top of chicken with pesto or Roasted Garlic flesh (page 348).

• Marinate whole breasts (with skin) or strips in Teryaki Marinade (page 351) for at least 10–20 minutes. Grill whole breasts, brushing frequently with the marinade. Stir-fry strips in a hot wok.

quick and easy ideas

Pork chops and steaks

• Spread with Maître d'Hôtel Butter (page 353) made with sage. Grill on one side. Turn pork over, spread with more butter and continue grilling.

• Serve topped with a cold salsa of finely chopped onion, garlic, tomato, mango or papaya and chilli, tossed with lime juice, chopped fresh coriander and salt and pepper.

• Mix crunchy wholegrain mustard into butter and spread over pork. Grill as above and serve with Corn Salad (page 250).

• Pan-fry pork in sunflower oil and butter. Deglaze pan with pineapple juice, honey, wine vinegar and soy sauce. Pour over pork.

• Or deglaze pan with orange juice, a little marmalade and a pinch of ground coriander or cinnamon.

• Or deglaze with orange juice, wholegrain mustard and brown sugar.

• Add a dash of sherry, Madeira, vermouth or white wine if you have a bottle open.

• Or deglaze pan with cider and add thin slices of unpeeled dessert apple. Soften for a few minutes and pour over pork. The addition of cream or crème fraîche will make it porc à la normande.

quick and easy ideas

Lamb chops and cutlets

• Marinate in Spiced Yogurt Marinade (page 351) for at least 10–20 minutes. Grill and serve with Cucumber and Mint Raita (page 369). Or make an even quicker raita: stir 1-2 tablespoons mint jelly into a carton of Greek yogurt.

• Spread lamb with Snail Butter (page 353). Grill on one side. Turn lamb over, spread with more butter and continue grilling. Or use chutney butter, a classic with lamb. Pound chutney of your choice with a mortar and pestle and mix into softened butter.

• Pan-fry lamb in olive oil. Deglaze pan with white wine, lemon juice and chopped fresh rosemary. Add chopped garlic if you like, and a splash of Pernod if you have some handy.

• Pan-fry lamb in olive oil. Deglaze pan with Madeira, port or sherry, add chopped fresh tarragon, crème fraîche and salt and pepper. Reduce, pour over lamb and top with fresh tarragon. If you like, add a few capers to the sauce.

• Pan-fry lamb. Deglaze pan with red wine, redcurrant jelly and salt and pepper. If you like, add a few crushed juniper berries.

quick and easy ideas

BEEF STEAKS

• Pan-fry seasoned steaks in butter and oil. Remove and keep hot. Deglaze pan with sugar, red wine and garlic, then pour over the steaks.

• Spread steaks with Roasted Red Pepper Butter (page 352). Grill on one side. Turn steaks over, spread with more butter and continue grilling.

• Grill steaks or chargrill them in a ridged cast iron pan. Stir bottled grated horseradish or wasabi (Japanese horseradish) into crème fraîche and serve on the side.

• Or make a simple soubise sauce. Caramelize thinly sliced onions by cooking them for 15 minutes in olive oil with stock, sugar, salt and pepper. Pile on top of grilled steaks.

• Make a simple steak au poivre. Crush black peppercorns coarsely with a mortar and pestle. Brush steaks with oil and press peppercorns all over. Grill to your liking.

4

VEGETABLES & SALADS

Nutritionists recommend that we eat five portions of fruit and vegetables every day. We get vitamins and minerals from vegetables and our bodies cannot store them – hence the need for a daily supply. Fibre and carbohydrate are provided by some vegetables too, and we also need these on a regular basis. For a healthy balanced diet, vegetables and salads are a must.

In this chapter you will find a selection of vegetable side dishes and vegetarian main courses, and some recipes that can double as both. Vegetables are nothing if not versatile, and you will quickly see how easy it is to plan meals around them without a central theme of fish or meat. Many unusual and exotic vegetables are included here to widen your repertoire and add interest to your cooking. You will be surprised how easy these are to get, and preparation and cooking are also simpler than you think. Ring the changes by swapping sweet potatoes for ordinary potatoes, different types of squash for courgettes, Chinese leaves or bok choy for cabbage, and Japanese white mooli for red radish.

The quick and easy ideas on pages 256–259 will give you all the basic information you need to cook and serve most of the popular vegetables, whilst the recipes in the chapter go one step further to bring you some of Le Cordon Bleu's renowned international vegetable dishes.

Spinach, red onion and raspberry salad

This colourful salad has a tangy sweet-and-sour dressing from the raspberries and vinegar. It goes well with plain grilled fish, meat and poultry, and tastes especially good with grilled prawns.

100 g (3½ oz) baby spinach leaves
60 g (2 oz) frisée lettuce
2 red onions
90 g (3 oz) raspberries
3 tablespoons red wine vinegar
2 tablespoons sunflower oil
about ½ teaspoon caster sugar
salt and freshly ground black pepper

Serves 4–6

Preparation time: 10 minutes

1 Wash and dry the spinach and frisée, then tear them in bite-size pieces into a bowl. Thinly slice the onions and add them to the bowl.

2 Purée two-thirds of the raspberries in a blender or food processor with the vinegar, oil, sugar and a little salt and pepper. Taste for seasoning and add a little more sugar if the dressing is too sharp.

To Serve Pour the dressing over the leaves and onions and sprinkle with the remaining whole raspberries. Serve within 2 hours.

Chef's Tip

Frisée is the French name for a slightly bitter tasting salad vegetable, which you may see labelled in English as curly endive. It is a member of the chicory family, hence its bitterness, but it has a loose, blousy head rather than the tightly furled cones which are normally associated with chicory. The leaves are ragged, with attractive frilly edges. It works well in this salad, its bitterness contrasting with the sweetness of the raspberries.

Vegetable curry with cucumber raita

Serve this fresh-tasting curry as a side dish with a spicy Indian grilled chicken dish such as tandoori chicken or chicken tikka. It also makes an excellent vegetarian main course for two people served with rice, chapattis or naan and mango chutney.

Serves 4–6

Preparation time: 15 minutes
Cooking time: 30 minutes

1 onion
2 carrots, total weight about 150 g (5 oz)
1 baking potato, weighing about 250 g (8 oz)
1 courgette, weighing about 200 g (7 oz)
2 large tomatoes
2 tablespoons vegetable oil
1 tablespoon mild curry powder
pinch of chilli powder (optional)
salt and freshly ground black pepper
2 tablespoons chopped fresh coriander, to serve

Raita
½ cucumber
200 g (7 oz) low-fat natural yogurt

1 Thinly slice the onion. Dice the carrots, potato, courgette and tomatoes. Heat the oil in a flameproof casserole until hot, then add the onion, carrots, potato, curry powder and chilli powder (if using). Stir-fry over low heat for 5 minutes.

2 Add the courgette and tomatoes, 250 ml (8 fl oz) cold water and salt and pepper to taste. Bring to the boil, stirring, then cover and simmer over low heat until the vegetables are tender, 20 minutes. Stir and check several times during cooking and add more water if the vegetables are dry.

3 Make the raita while the curry is cooking. Peel, deseed and finely dice the cucumber and mix in a bowl with the yogurt and salt and pepper to taste.

To Serve Taste the curry for seasoning, transfer to a warm dish and sprinkle the chopped coriander over the top. Serve hot, with the bowl of raita alongside.

Chef's Tip

If you can, buy an Indian brand of curry powder. There are very many different ones available, so experiment to find the one you like the best. Most are made with coriander, cumin, mustard and fenugreek seeds, plus turmeric, peppercorns and ginger – and varying amounts of dried red chillies. If you like a fragrant mix, look for ones that contain cinnamon, cloves and nutmeg.

Roasted fennel and aubergine

This is an easy vegetable dish for a dinner party because once it is in the oven it looks after itself. Serve it with something plain and simple like grilled or barbecued chicken or steak because the vegetables and flavourings are quite strong.

- 2 large fennel bulbs
- 300 g (10 oz) baby aubergines or 1 large aubergine
- 2 garlic cloves
- 4 tablespoons olive oil
- juice of 1 lemon
- 1 teaspoon fennel seeds
- salt and freshly ground black pepper
- 2 tablespoons chopped fresh flat-leaf parsley, to serve

Serves 6

Preparation time: 10 minutes
Cooking time: 1 hour

1 Preheat the oven to 170°C (325°F) Gas 3. Remove any tough outer leaves from the fennel and cut each bulb lengthways into about 6 sections. Remove the ends from the baby aubergines. If using a large aubergine, cut it into pieces roughly the same size as the fennel. Place the fennel and aubergines in a large non-stick roasting tin.

2 Crush the garlic and mix it in a bowl with the oil, lemon juice, fennel seeds and salt and pepper to taste. Pour this mixture over the vegetables, then stir to coat.

3 Roast in the oven for 1 hour, turning the vegetables several times.

To Serve Turn into a warm vegetable dish and sprinkle with the parsley. Serve hot or at room temperature.

Chef's Tip

Baby aubergines are in season during the summer. The most common variety has a beautiful glossy purple skin and is shaped like a very large egg, but you may also find pale lilac ones, some streaked with cream stripes, and even pure white, cream and green ones, some of which are pear shaped. Any of these can be used in this recipe, but the dark purple aubergines offer a better colour contrast against the fennel.

Variation

To add more colour, add 1 large red pepper, cored, deseeded and cut into chunks.

Crunchy beansprout and mooli salad

Crunchy and spicy, this oriental salad makes a nutritious side dish to serve with plain grilled chicken, meat or fish. For vegetarians it can be served with other salads, especially those made with grains.

250 g (8 oz) mooli
200 g (7 oz) beansprouts

Dressing
2 tablespoons toasted sesame oil
1 tablespoon rice vinegar
1/2 teaspoon dried crushed chilli flakes
salt

Serves 4

Preparation time: 10 minutes, plus chilling time

1 Peel the mooli, cut it into matchsticks and place in a large bowl. Add the beansprouts and toss the two vegetables together.

2 Put the dressing ingredients in a screw-top jar with a pinch of salt and shake well. Pour over the vegetables and toss through. Cover and refrigerate until well chilled, about 4 hours.

To Serve Taste the salad and add more salt if necessary, then turn into a serving bowl. Serve chilled.

Chef's Tips

Mooli is a Japanese long white radish, also called daikon, which is rich in vitamin C. It is sold in supermarkets, greengrocers and oriental stores. Look for baby mooli for this recipe. They are tender-crisp and sweet, perfect for raw salads.

◆

Beansprouts are sprouted mung beans. Nutritionally they are very good for you, containing protein, a wide variety of B vitamins, vitamin C and amino acids. They are very low in calories.

◆

Variation

To further enhance the sesame flavour of this salad and to boost its nutritional content even further, sprinkle a handful of toasted sesame seeds on top as a garnish just before serving. Sesame seeds are rich in vitamins, minerals, calcium, iron and protein.

Baked beetroot with chive dressing

The cooked beetroot that you buy often tastes very vinegary and sharp, but if you cook it yourself it has a wonderful earthy flavour. Serve these whole beetroot as an accompaniment to chicken and pork, two meats that go especially well with beetroot.

8 fresh uncooked beetroot

Dressing

200 g (7 oz) low-fat natural yogurt
3 tablespoons snipped fresh chives
1/4 teaspoon English mustard powder
salt and freshly ground black pepper

Serves 4

Preparation time: 10 minutes
Cooking time: 3 hours

Chef's Tip

Look for bunches of raw beetroot in supermarkets and greengrocers. If you can only find cooked beetroot, check with the greengrocer – if he boils it himself and sells it freshly cooked, he may not display it uncooked. If you tell him that you need fresh beetroot for baking he will gladly sell it to you.

1 Preheat the oven to 150°C (300°F) Gas 2. Wash the beetroot, taking care not to split or tear the skins, then place them in a casserole. Cover tightly and bake in the oven for 3 hours or until the beetroot are tender when pierced with a fine skewer.

2 Whisk together the ingredients for the dressing, adding salt and pepper to taste.

3 Remove the beetroot from the casserole, cut a deep cross in the top of each one and prise open the four quarters.

To Serve Stand the beetroot on a warm platter and spoon the dressing in the centre of each one. Grind black pepper liberally over the beetroot and and serve immediately.

Warm Three Green Salad

Broccoli, mangetouts and beans are bursting with vitamins and minerals, but so too are the sesame seeds which top them – and they contain protein too. Serve warm as a vegetable, cold as a salad. For a vegetarian main course, serve with rice or another grain.

Serves 4

Preparation time: 10–15 minutes

Cooking time: about 5 minutes

1 head of broccoli
125 g (4 oz) mangetouts
125 g (4 oz) fine green beans
salt and freshly ground black pepper
4 spring onions
2 tablespoons toasted sesame seeds, to serve

Dressing
2.5 cm (1 inch) piece of fresh root ginger
1 garlic clove
75 ml (2½ fl oz) sunflower oil
3 tablespoons rice vinegar

1 First make the dressing. Finely grate the ginger and crush the garlic. Place in a bowl and mix together with the back of a spoon to form a paste. Whisk in the oil and vinegar.

2 Cut the broccoli into small florets. Top and tail the mangetouts and beans. Cook the broccoli in a saucepan of salted boiling water for 4 minutes, the mangetouts and beans in a separate pan of salted boiling water for 2 minutes. Drain well and turn into a bowl.

3 Thinly slice the spring onions on the diagonal, add to the vegetables and pour the dressing over the top. Add salt and pepper to taste and toss gently to mix.

To Serve Turn the vegetables into a serving dish and sprinkle with the sesame seeds. Serve warm.

Chef's Tip

You can use the familiar kind of blue-green broccoli, called calabrese, which has tight, firm florets branching off a thick central stalk, or you can use sprouting broccoli, which is smaller and looser and often has purple heads. Chinese sprouting broccoli, available from oriental stores, is another choice, and it would go well with the Chinese flavourings in this dish.

Potato wedges with chive and yogurt dressing

Served with a salad, these make an excellent vegetarian supper. They are also good for a buffet, arranged on a platter with the dressing in a bowl in the centre for dipping. The celery salt is an inspired flavouring – it makes the potatoes taste similar to parsnips.

Serves 4

Preparation time: 10 minutes
Cooking time: 45 minutes

4 large baking potatoes
3 tablespoons olive oil
1 teaspoon celery salt
½ teaspoon garlic salt
freshly ground black pepper

To Serve
coarse sea or rock salt
200 g (7 oz) low-fat natural yogurt
1 bunch of fresh chives

1 Preheat the oven to 200°C (400°F) Gas 6. Scrub the potatoes, then cut each one lengthways into 6 pieces. Put the wedges in a large non-stick roasting tin, add the oil and toss to coat. Mix together the celery and garlic salts and plenty of pepper, then sprinkle over the potato wedges.

2 Roast the potatoes in the oven for 45 minutes or until crisp and golden, turning them several times to ensure even cooking. Meanwhile, put the yogurt in a bowl, snip in most of the chives and season well. Stir well to mix.

To Serve Turn the potato wedges into a warm bowl and sprinkle with sea or rock salt to taste. Spoon the yogurt into a small serving bowl and snip the remaining chives over the top. Serve immediately.

Chef's Tips

Dry, floury potatoes are best for roasting and baking – you will often see them in supermarkets labelled simply 'baking potatoes'. If not, look for the following: Desirée, King Edward and red Duke of York. All of these have crisp skins and soft, fluffy flesh when roasted or baked.

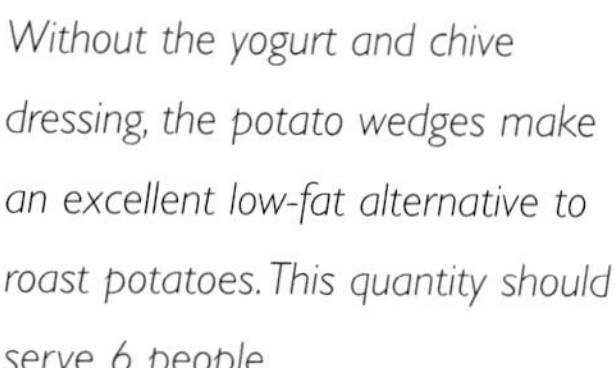

Without the yogurt and chive dressing, the potato wedges make an excellent low-fat alternative to roast potatoes. This quantity should serve 6 people.

Chard, rocket and radish salad

The contrasting colours of this salad make it really eye-catching, and the flavours of the leaves and the orange dressing go well together. It is good with chargrilled, grilled or barbecued meat, especially steak, lamb chops and chicken breasts.

Serves 4

Preparation time: 10–15 minutes

60 g (2 oz) baby spinach leaves
60 g (2 oz) red chard leaves
60 g (2 oz) rocket leaves
90 g (3 oz) radishes

Dressing
juice of 1 orange
1 teaspoon coarsegrain mustard
3 tablespoons extra virgin olive oil
salt and freshly ground black pepper

1 First make the dressing. Whisk the orange juice in a large bowl with the mustard, oil and salt and pepper to taste.

2 Wash and drain the salad leaves. Spin them in a salad spinner or dry them with a clean cloth. Tear the spinach into bite-size pieces if the leaves are large. Slice the radishes very thinly.

3 Add the salad leaves and radishes to the bowl of dressing and toss well until the leaves are evenly coated.

To Serve Transfer the salad to a serving bowl and serve immediately.

Chef's Tip

Red chard, also called ruby chard and rhubarb chard, has small green leaves like baby spinach, but it takes its name from its scarlet stems and veins, which make it look very pretty. Its leaves are very similar to spinach beet, which are actually the tops of a type of beetroot grown specifically for its leaves. You will find bags of red chard in supermarkets and at good greengrocers – it is in season in the summer months.

Honey roasted pumpkin and sweet potato

This makes a good vegetable dish in autumn, when there is a wide variety of different pumpkins and squash available. Sweet potatoes are a great alternative to ordinary roast potatoes, because they have more colour and flavour.

about 750 g (1 1/2 lb) pumpkin
2 sweet potatoes
2 tablespoons olive oil
1 tablespoon clear honey
1–2 teaspoons Cajun spice, to taste
salt and freshly ground black pepper

Serves 4

Preparation time: 10 minutes
Cooking time: 1 hour

1 Preheat the oven to 180°C (350°F) Gas 4. Cut the pumpkin into wedges and remove the peel, seeds and fibres. Peel the sweet potatoes and cut them into similar-size pieces.

2 Put the pumpkin and sweet potatoes in a large non-stick roasting tin and drizzle the oil and honey over them. Sprinkle with the spice and season generously with salt and pepper.

3 Roast in the oven for 1 hour or until golden and tender, turning and basting occasionally,

To Serve Turn into a warm serving dish and serve immediately.

Chef's Tips

Pumpkins grow to enormous sizes, but they are often sold by the piece, so you can buy as much as you need. For a change, you could also use an autumn or winter squash, such as butternut.

You can buy jars of ground Cajun spice, or make your own spice mixture according to the recipe given in Cajun Blackened Chicken (page 156).

Spiced avocado and strawberry salad

Avocados and strawberries make a stunning salad, and balsamic vinegar dressing is a classic with strawberries in Italy. Serve this salad for a summer barbecue party – it looks and tastes sensational.

300 g (10 oz) ripe strawberries
2 large avocados, not too ripe
½ small iceberg or cos lettuce

Dressing
1 teaspoon Sichuan peppercorns
2 tablespoons balsamic vinegar
1 teaspoon caster sugar

Serves 6–8

Preparation time: 10–15 minutes, plus standing time

1 First make the dressing. Crush the peppercorns with a pestle and mortar or the end of a rolling pin, then mix in a small bowl with the vinegar and sugar.

2 Cut the strawberries into halves (or quarters if they are very large) and place them in a large bowl. Halve, peel and stone the avocados. Slice the flesh into wedges and add to the strawberries.

3 Pour the dressing over the strawberries and avocados, turn very gently to coat, then cover and leave to stand for 30 minutes.

To Serve Separate the lettuce leaves and use to line a shallow serving dish. Spoon the avocados and strawberries in the centre. Serve as soon as possible, at room temperature.

Chef's Tips

This salad tastes very good with barbecued food, especially chicken, but it also goes well with goat's cheese and soft cheeses like fromage blanc and cottage cheese.

◆

Avocados are a healthy choice, eaten in moderation. They are rich in vitamins and minerals and they do not contain any cholesterol. Half an avocado contains about the same amount of calories as a handful of dry roasted nuts.

Braised celery in tomato sauce

Celery is often overlooked as a vegetable and used only raw in salads, but it has an excellent flavour when cooked and served hot, and it is very low in calories. This dish is good served with grilled or roast lamb or chicken, or with grilled or chargrilled steak.

3 celery hearts, total weight about 500 g (1 lb)
2 shallots
2 garlic cloves
2 tablespoons olive oil
2 x 400 g cans chopped tomatoes
1 tablespoon chopped fresh thyme
1 tablespoon chopped fresh oregano
salt and freshly ground black pepper

1 Cut each celery heart into 6 lengthways, retaining a little root at the end to keep each section together. Wash well and drain. Finely chop the shallots and crush the garlic.

2 Heat the oil in a sauté pan and cook the shallots over low heat for 2–3 minutes without colouring. Add the celery in a single layer, then add the tomatoes, garlic and chopped herbs. Season with salt and pepper and bring to the boil.

3 Cover the pan, lower the heat and simmer for about 20 minutes or until the celery is tender. If the liquid reduces down and becomes too thick during cooking, add a few tablespoons of cold water.

To Serve Taste the sauce for seasoning. Turn the celery and sauce into a warm serving dish. Serve hot.

Serves 6

Preparation time: 10 minutes
Cooking time: 25–30 minutes

Chef's Tips

You can buy packs of celery hearts in supermarkets. They are the pale, tender central stalks of celery heads.

◆

A wide, deep sauté pan is ideal for cooking the celery and tomatoes, but if you haven't got one, use a wok with a lid.

◆

Variation

This recipe works equally well with fennel instead of the celery hearts, and marjoram instead of the oregano. If you can't get fresh herbs in winter, use 1 teaspoon each dried. Fresh plum tomatoes can be used in the summer. You will need about 750 g (1 1/2 lb).

Chargrilled peppers and sweet potatoes

Using a ridged cast iron pan for chargrilling vegetables is an excellent way to keep fat content down because you only need the smallest amount of oil and yet the flavour is superb. Serve as a side dish, with your favourite grilled meat or fish.

2 red peppers
2 yellow peppers
2 green peppers
1 sweet potato
1–2 tablespoons olive oil

Dressing
1 teaspoon cumin seeds
2 teaspoons clear honey
2 tablespoons balsamic vinegar
1 tablespoon walnut oil
1 tablespoon extra virgin olive oil
salt and freshly ground black pepper

Serves 4–6

Preparation time: 20 minutes
Cooking time: 25–30 minutes

Chef's Tip

The cumin seeds are dry-fried to help release their flavour. If you like, you can crush them with a pestle and mortar after dry-frying.

Variation

Other vegetables, such as sliced courgettes, fennel and aubergines, can be cooked in the same way. Allow 8–10 minutes cooking time for each, turning once.

1 Halve the peppers lengthways and discard the stalks, cores and seeds. Cut each half lengthways into 4 pieces. Peel the sweet potato and slice it into rings about 5 mm (1/4 inch) thick.

2 Make the dressing. In a small non-stick frying pan, dry-fry the cumin seeds over low heat for a few minutes, taking care not to burn them. Place them in a bowl with the honey, vinegar and oils and whisk together. Season with salt and pepper.

3 Heat a ridged cast iron griddle pan until very hot. Place the sweet potato slices on the pan and lightly brush each piece with olive oil. Cook for about 10 minutes, turning the pieces over once, then remove them from the pan and keep warm.

4 Add half the pepper pieces, brush with olive oil and cook for about 8 minutes, turning them over several times. Remove and add to the sweet potatoes, then repeat with the remaining peppers, adding more olive oil if you need it.

To Serve Place the vegetables on a large shallow dish and drizzle the dressing over them. Serve warm.

Salad niçoise

This must be one of the best salads ever. The combination of ingredients is just perfect, and it is impossible to eat it without thinking of the Provençal sun. Serve for an al fresco lunch with a crusty baguette.

250 g (8 oz) small new or salad potatoes
salt and freshly ground black pepper
250 g (8 oz) fine green beans
1 head of round lettuce
100 g (3½ oz) rocket leaves
12 cherry tomatoes
12 black olives
12 hard-boiled quail eggs
1 onion
1 × 200 g can tuna in spring water or brine

Vinaigrette
100 ml (3½ fl oz) extra virgin olive oil
3 tablespoons white wine vinegar

Serves 4

Preparation time: 20 minutes
Cooking time: 20–25 minutes

1 Put the potatoes in a saucepan of salted boiling water, bring back to the boil and cook for 20–25 minutes until just tender. Meanwhile, top and tail the beans and slice them diagonally in half. Bring another pan of water to the boil, add a pinch of salt and then the beans. Cook for about 5 minutes until just tender.

2 Drain the potatoes and beans well. Cut the potatoes into halves or quarters, depending on their size. Make the vinaigrette. Whisk the oil and vinegar together in a jug with salt and pepper to taste. Gently toss the potatoes and beans in half the vinaigrette.

3 Separate the lettuce leaves and wash and dry them with the rocket. Halve the tomatoes and halve and stone the olives. Shell and halve the quail eggs. Slice the onion into thin rings. Drain the tuna and break it into large bite-size flakes.

To Serve Divide the salad leaves between 4 plates and top with the potatoes and beans followed by the remaining ingredients and vinaigrette. Grind pepper over the salad and serve.

Chef's Tips

Two of the best varieties of small potatoes for salads are Nicola and Charlotte. They have waxy yellow flesh which stays in shape when they are sliced after boiling, and they both have a very good flavour. They are widely available, both at supermarkets and greengrocers.

◆

Extra virgin olive oil is from the first cold pressing of the olives. It is the most expensive of the olive oils, but it is worth buying as good a bottle as you can afford to keep for salads like this one. Olive oil from Provençe would be particularly appropriate here, but Italian, Greek and Spanish olive oils are all good, and you should buy according to the colour and flavour you like the most.

Mixed mushroom ragoût

This ragoût is like a vegetarian stroganoff – the mushrooms are so full of flavour and substance that it tastes almost meaty. It can be served as a main course on a bed of boiled or steamed rice, or on its own as a vegetable side dish.

1 onion
about 500 g (1 lb) mixed mushrooms
30 g (1 oz) butter
100 ml (3½ fl oz) vegetable stock
1 tablespoon Madeira
2 tablespoons chopped fresh thyme
salt and freshly ground black pepper

To Serve
2 tablespoons low-fat crème fraîche
1–2 tablespoons chopped fresh parsley

Serves 4–6

Preparation time: 10 minutes
Cooking time: 15 minutes

1 Slice the onion very finely, then slice the mushrooms so they are about the same size as the onion slices but slightly thicker. Melt the butter in a sauté pan, add the onion and cook over low heat for about 5 minutes until soft but not coloured.

2 Add the mushrooms, stir well and cook for 5 minutes. Add the stock and Madeira, cover and simmer gently for about 5 minutes or until the mushrooms are tender. Remove from the heat, add half the thyme and season generously with salt and pepper.

To Serve Swirl the crème fraîche into the mushrooms and turn into a warm dish. Mix the remaining thyme with the parsley, sprinkle over the mushrooms and serve immediately.

Chef's Tips

You can buy inexpensive packs of mixed mushrooms at supermarkets and greengrocers. The contents of the packs vary and some contain wild and cultivated mixed together – these are often labelled 'exotic'. For this dish you can use any variety you like, such as shiitake, blewit, chestnut, portobello, girolles and ceps.

◆

Madeira is a strong, fortified red wine from the island of the same name. Even the small amount used here gives a wonderful depth of flavour to the mushrooms. If you do not have Madeira, you can use port, sherry or brandy instead.

◆

Variation

Add 1–2 garlic cloves, crushed, with the mushrooms in step 2.

Spinach and goat's cheese roulade

The combination of spinach and goat's cheese is hard to beat in a roulade, and this one can be served warm or at room temperature. It makes a delicious lunch dish served with Tangy Red Relish (page 358) and a crusty baguette.

- 250 g (8 oz) frozen leaf spinach, thawed and drained
- 30 g (1 oz) plain flour
- 1/4–1/2 teaspoon freshly grated nutmeg, to taste
- 2 tablespoons snipped fresh chives
- salt and freshly ground black pepper
- 3 eggs, separated

Filling

- 100 g (3 1/2 oz) soft goat's cheese
- 200 g (7 oz) half-fat crème fraîche
- 150 g (5 oz) cucumber

Serves 4–6

Preparation time: 20–30 minutes
Cooking time: 20 minutes

1 Preheat the oven to 180°C (350°F) Gas 4 and line a 33 x 23 cm (13 x 9 inch) Swiss roll tin with non-stick baking parchment.

2 Squeeze as much moisture as possible from the spinach, then put the spinach in a food processor with the flour, nutmeg, chives and plenty of salt and pepper. Process until almost smooth, then turn into a large bowl. Add the egg yolks and beat well to mix.

3 In a separate clean bowl, whisk the egg whites with a pinch of salt until firm. Fold into the spinach, then spread evenly in the tin. Bake for 20 minutes or until firm. Turn the roulade on to a clean sheet of parchment on a wire rack and leave to cool.

4 Mix the goat's cheese and crème fraîche in a bowl and season well. Peel and deseed the cucumber, cut it into small dice and stir into the cheese mixture. When the roulade is completely cool, spread it with the cheese mixture and roll up from one long edge into a roulade, using the parchment paper to help support it.

To Serve Cut the roulade crossways into 8 slices. Arrange the slices slightly overlapping on a warm serving dish and serve immediately.

Chef's Tip

Frozen spinach is convenient and it saves time, but if you want to use fresh spinach you will need 500 g (1 lb). Wash it well and place it in a large saucepan with only the water that clings to the leaves. Cover and cook over low to moderate heat for 5 minutes or until wilted and tender. Drain thoroughly before use.

Potato salad with a mustard dressing

Using low-fat mayonnaise and yogurt gives a light and tangy taste to potato salad, making it far less rich than the classic recipe. The mustard and chives accentuate the tanginess and make it good to serve with cold meats, smoked fish or frankfurters.

1 kg (2 lb) waxy new potatoes
salt and freshly ground black pepper
125 g (4 oz) low-fat natural yogurt
3 tablespoons low-fat or light mayonnaise
1 tablespoon coarsegrain mustard
1 small bunch of fresh chives

Serves 4–6

Preparation time: 10 minutes
Cooking time: 25–30 minutes

1 Put the potatoes in a saucepan of salted boiling water, bring back to the boil and cook for 20–25 minutes until just tender. Drain the potatoes and plunge into a bowl of iced water for 5 minutes to stop them cooking. Drain well and leave to cool.

2 Mix the yogurt, mayonnaise and mustard together in a large bowl and season generously with salt and pepper. Add the potatoes. Using scissors, snip most of the chives over the potatoes. Fold the potatoes in the dressing until evenly coated, then taste for seasoning.

To Serve Transfer the salad to a serving bowl and garnish with the remaining chives, either snipped or as whole stems. If you like, grind black pepper liberally over the top.

Chef's Tips

Try to use the smallest new potatoes you can find because this salad looks most attractive when made with whole potatoes. Many supermarkets sell baby new potatoes, which are about the same size as cherry tomatoes. If you can't get these, cut the potatoes into halves, quarters or slices after cooking and cooling.

The salad can be prepared several hours ahead and kept covered in the refrigerator. Let it come to room temperature about 30 minutes before serving.

Red and green salad

Sweet and tangy with a hint of fresh mint, this stunning salad makes a good accompaniment for roast lamb, grilled lamb chops and cutlets or barbecued kebabs. It also goes well with cheese.

150 g (5 oz) sugarsnap peas or mangetouts
salt and freshly ground black pepper
60 g (2 oz) red chard
60 g (2 oz) radicchio

Dressing
grated rind and juice of ½ lemon
2 tablespoons extra virgin olive oil
1 tablespoon chopped fresh mint
2 teaspoons clear honey

Serves 4–6

Preparation time: 15 minutes
Cooking time: 2 minutes

1 Top and tail the peas and simmer in salted boiling water until just tender but still al dente, about 2 minutes. Drain into a colander and rinse under the cold tap until completely cold. Pat dry, then cut crossways into halves or thirds, depending on their size.

2 Tear the chard and radicchio leaves in bite-size pieces into a large bowl. Add the peas and toss with your hands until the vegetables are evenly combined.

3 Make the dressing. In a small jug, whisk the lemon rind and juice with the oil, mint, honey and salt and pepper to taste. Pour the dressing over the peas and leaves and toss to mix.

To Serve Turn into a salad bowl and serve immediately.

Chef's Tips

Sugarsnap peas are plumper and rounder than mangetouts, which tend to be completely flat in shape, but otherwise they are very similar to one another and can be used interchangeably.

Red chard is a beautiful salad vegetable with dainty, tender green leaves, bright red stems and a mild flavour. It is a variety of Swiss chard, which comes from the same family as beetroot, and is sometimes called ruby chard or rhubarb chard. If you can't get red chard on its own, look for it in bags of ready prepared 'continental' salad at supermarkets. It is often combined with lollo rosso, red oak leaf lettuce and rocket, all of which would be suitable for this salad.

Shredded sprouts and water chestnuts

Except at Christmas, sprouts are often overlooked as a vegetable, but they deserve to be eaten more often because they are a good source of vitamins and minerals. Serve as a side dish, or as a vegetarian main course for two with Thin Egg Pancakes (page 370).

2 shallots
200 g (7 oz) Brussels sprouts
1 x 220 g can water chestnuts
2 spring onions
2 tablespoons sunflower oil
1 tablespoon dark soy sauce
salt and freshly ground black pepper

Serves 4

Preparation time: 10–15 minutes
Cooking time: 10 minutes

1 Chop the shallots. Remove the outer leaves from the sprouts if necessary, then slice the sprouts into very thin ribbons. Drain the water chestnuts and slice each one lengthways into three. Thinly slice the spring onions on the diagonal.

2 Heat the oil in a large non-stick frying pan and sweat the shallots over low heat for about 5 minutes until soft. Add the sprouts, increase the heat and stir-fry for a few minutes until tinged golden brown.

3 Add the water chestnuts, spring onions and soy sauce and heat through, stirring, then taste and add salt and pepper if necessary.

To Serve Turn into a warm dish and serve immediately.

Variations

When fresh sprouts are out of season, use frozen button sprouts. Thaw them, then cut each one lengthways in half. They will take 5 minutes to cook in step 2.

◆

Increase the heat and the oriental flavour of this dish by adding 1 red hot fresh chilli, deseeded and finely chopped, with the shallots.

Spring onion crêpes with chargrilled asparagus

Crêpes made with half vegetable stock and half milk are lighter than those made with all milk, and the fromage frais filling spiked with paprika and orange is also light. Serve for a vegetarian lunch or supper with a crusty baguette or ciabatta.

2 spring onions
crêpe batter (page 315)
1–2 tablespoons olive oil
salt and freshly ground black pepper
200 g (7 oz) fromage frais
1 teaspoon paprika
½ teaspoon grated orange rind
12 young tender asparagus spears
a little extra paprika, for dusting

Serves 4

Preparation time: 25 minutes, plus standing time
Cooking time: 20 minutes

1 Thinly slice the spring onions and add to the crêpe batter with 1 tablespoon oil and salt and pepper to taste. Mix together the fromage frais, paprika and orange rind in a small bowl until smooth. Season to taste.

2 Make 8 crêpes with the batter according to the instructions on page 315, stacking the crêpes on top of each other as they are done (this will keep them warm).

3 Heat a ridged cast iron griddle pan until very hot. Cut each asparagus spear crossways in half. Dip a wad of kitchen paper in oil and wipe it over the hot pan. Place the asparagus on the pan and chargrill for 5–8 minutes or until tender, turning once. Remove from the heat.

4 Spread 1 crêpe with an eighth of the fromage frais mixture, fold in half, then in half again to make a fan shape. Tuck the asparagus inside, allowing the tips to peep out. Repeat with the remaining crêpes, filling and asparagus.

To Serve Place 2 crêpes on each of 4 plates and dust very lightly with paprika. Serve immediately.

Variation

Instead of the asparagus, use 3 small courgettes. Slice them, unpeeled, into lengthways strips about 5 mm (¼ inch) thick. Toss in a little salt and leave in a colander for 30 minutes, then rinse and dry well. Chargrill them as for the asparagus.

SPANISH OMELETTE

A flat omelette made with potato and onion is called tortilla española in Spanish. Traditional tortillas use a lot of olive oil, but this recipe proves that this is not really necessary. Serve with a tangy tomato salad.

2 large potatoes, total weight about 500 g (1 lb)
salt and freshly ground black pepper
1 Spanish onion
6 eggs
2 tablespoons olive oil
1 tablespoon chopped fresh flat-leaf parsley, to serve

Serves 4

Preparation time: 15 minutes
Cooking time: 35–45 minutes

1 Halve or quarter the potatoes, depending on their size, then cook them in salted boiling water for 15–20 minutes or until just tender.

2 Drain the potatoes, leave until cool enough to handle, then cut into dice. Coarsely chop the onion. Beat the eggs in a bowl with salt and pepper to taste.

3 Heat the oil in a deep non-stick frying pan, add the onion and diced potatoes and fry over low heat for 10–15 minutes, stirring frequently, until soft and golden. Meanwhile, preheat the grill.

4 Add the eggs to the pan and draw the edges of the egg into the centre with a fork, letting the runny egg flow to the sides. Cook undisturbed until the eggs are just beginning to set in the centre, about 5 minutes. Slide the omelette under the hot grill and cook for a few minutes until the top is golden brown.

To Serve Slide the omelette out on to a platter and sprinkle with the parsley. Serve warm or cold, cut into wedges.

Chef's Tips

In Spain the potatoes are usually peeled for tortilla, but you may prefer to retain the maximum amount of vitamins and minerals by leaving the skins on.

◆

Wedges of cold tortilla are excellent for packed lunches and picnics.

Frittata

This flat Italian omelette makes a nutritious and satisfying meal served with new potatoes and a crisp salad. It is just as good cold as hot, so any leftovers can be eaten as a snack or lunch next day.

- 100 g (3½ oz) broccoli florets
- salt and freshly ground black pepper
- 100 g (3½ oz) button mushrooms
- 3 spring onions
- 1 garlic clove
- 90 g (3 oz) mature Cheddar cheese
- 8 large eggs
- 3 tablespoons olive oil

Serves 2–3

Preparation time: 10 minutes
Cooking time: about 15 minutes

1 Divide the broccoli into tiny sprigs and trim the stalks, then drop into salted boiling water and bring back to the boil. Drain, refresh immediately in cold water, then drain and leave to dry on kitchen paper. Thinly slice the mushrooms and spring onions and finely chop the garlic. Grate the cheese. Whisk the eggs in a bowl with salt and pepper.

2 Preheat the oven to 200°C (400°F) Gas 6. Heat the oil in a large frying pan (see Chef's Tips) and sauté the mushrooms until lightly coloured. Add the spring onions and garlic. Sauté for 2 minutes, then add the broccoli and stir well to mix. Pour half the eggs over the vegetables and sprinkle with half the cheese. Cook for about 5 minutes until lightly set, then pour in the remaining eggs and sprinkle with the remaining cheese.

3 Cook in the oven for 5 minutes or until the frittata is firm and golden brown.

To Serve Either slice the frittata in the pan and serve on individual plates, or slide out of the pan onto a platter and cut into slices. Serve hot or cold.

Chef's Tips

Make sure the pan handle is ovenproof or removeable; if not, wrap it in a double thickness of foil. If you find it more convenient, you can simply slide the pan under a hot grill to finish cooking.

◆

Cut into thick wedges, cold frittata makes excellent picnic food. It is also good cut into small diamonds or squares to serve as a canapé with drinks.

◆

Variation

This is a good way to use up any leftover vegetables such as peppers (roasted or plain), beans, peas, cauliflower, etc. Slices of cooked chicken, ham, spicy sausage or salami can also be added.

Spinach salad with lardons, croûtons and cheese

A nutritious main course salad for when you crave something crisp and fresh for supper. It is based on fresh ingredients that you can pick up at the supermarket on your way home from work.

150–175 g (5–6 oz) small tender spinach leaves
90 g (3 oz) Cheddar cheese
1 tablespoon sunflower oil
200 g (7 oz) lardons
90 g (3 oz) croûtons

Dressing
2 tablespoons red wine vinegar
salt and freshly ground black pepper
90 ml (3 fl oz) sunflower oil

Serves 2–3

Preparation time: 10 minutes
Cooking time: 7–8 minutes

1 Wash the spinach and remove the stalks. Drain and spin-dry the spinach leaves, then place them in a large bowl. Shred or dice the cheese, add to the bowl and toss to mix.

2 Heat the oil in a non-stick frying pan, add the lardons, bacon or pancetta and fry over moderate to high heat for about 5 minutes until crisp. Toss the lardons and shake the pan constantly. Remove with a slotted spoon and drain on kitchen paper.

3 Make the dressing. Pour the vinegar into the pan, add salt and pepper and stir over moderate heat until the salt has dissolved. Remove from the heat and slowly whisk in the remaining oil.

To Serve Pour the dressing over the salad and toss to mix. Sprinkle the bacon and croûtons on top and serve immediately.

Chef's Tips

This salad can be made very quickly if you buy a bag of ready trimmed and washed baby spinach leaves from the supermarket, plus ready made croûtons and lardons.

◆

If you can't find croûtons, make them yourself from day-old bread. Remove the crusts from 3 slices of sandwich bread, cut the bread into small cubes and shallow-fry in 2 tablespoons very hot oil for about 5 minutes. Drain well on kitchen paper.

◆

Lardons are sold in packets in many supermarkets. If you can't find them, buy bacon chops and dice them. Bacon rashers are a little too thin to make good lardons.

Roasted Mediterranean Vegetables

There is nothing like the chargrilled flavour of roasted vegetables, and yet they are so quick and easy to cook in the oven. They are good served hot as an accompaniment to meat or poultry, or cold as a salad or first course.

2 large peppers (red and yellow)
1 aubergine, weighing about 300 g (10 oz)
2 large courgettes, total weight about 375 g (12 oz)
250 g (8 oz) cherry plum tomatoes
2 large garlic cloves
1–2 fresh thyme sprigs
6 tablespoons olive oil
salt and freshly ground black pepper
extra olive oil and/or balsamic vinegar, to serve (optional)

Serves 4–6

Preparation time: 10 minutes
Cooking time: 40–50 minutes

1 Preheat the oven to 190°C (375°F) Gas 5. Cut the peppers into chunks, removing the seeds and spongy ribs. Cut off the ends of the aubergine and courgettes, then cut these vegetables into chunks. Remove any hulls from the tomatoes. Roughly chop the garlic.

2 Put the prepared vegetables and thyme sprigs in a roasting tin and sprinkle with the garlic, olive oil and salt and pepper. Stir well to mix. Roast for 40–50 minutes until all the vegetables are tender and charred, stirring several times.

To Serve Sprinkle with extra olive oil and/or balsamic vinegar if you like, and serve hot or cold.

Chef's Tips

Roasted vegetables are delicious cold, mixed with chopped fresh herbs such as basil, thyme, rosemary or marjoram. They are also good with chopped stoned black or green olives.

◆

If you want to reheat them, simply pan-fry in a little olive oil. They make a marvellous filling for pitta pockets, with feta cheese.

Aubergines with garlic and rosemary

With its rich Mediterranean flavour, this dish of diced aubergines goes well with roast or barbecued lamb. For a Middle Eastern touch, serve topped with a spoonful of thick Greek yogurt.

2 medium to large aubergines
2–3 garlic cloves
1 fresh rosemary sprig
4 tablespoons olive oil
salt and freshly ground black pepper

Serves 4

Preparation time: 10 minutes
Cooking time: about 12 minutes

1 Trim the aubergines and cut them into small cubes. Finely chop the garlic. Remove the leaves from the rosemary and finely chop them.

2 Heat the olive oil in a sauté pan, add the aubergines and sauté over moderate heat for about 5 minutes. Season with salt and pepper.

3 Add the chopped garlic and sauté for a further 5 minutes, then stir in the rosemary. Remove from the heat and allow to stand for 1 minute.

To Serve Taste for seasoning, then turn into a warm serving bowl. Serve hot.

Variation

Other herbs, such as thyme, flat-leaf parsley or basil, can be used in addition to, or instead of, the rosemary.

Curried cauliflower and potato in coconut milk

Subtly spiced, this is a good accompaniment for Indian meat or fish curries. It also makes a good vegetarian main course for 2 people, served with basmati rice or Indian bread and Cucumber and Mint Raita (page 369).

2 medium potatoes, total weight about 250 g (8 oz)
250 g (8 oz) cauliflower florets
1 small onion
salt and freshly ground black pepper
1 tablespoon sunflower oil
1 tablespoon curry powder or garam masala
1 teaspoon turmeric
1 teaspoon ground ginger
250 ml (8 fl oz) unsweetened coconut milk

To Serve
a little coconut milk
1–2 tablespoons chopped fresh coriander

Serves 4

Preparation time: 10 minutes
Cooking time: 30–35 minutes

Chef's Tip

Buy canned coconut milk. It is much more convenient than blocks of creamed coconut, which need to be dissolved in hot water before use. Any leftover coconut milk will keep in a covered bowl in the refrigerator for several days. If you like, you can use it to make coconut rice – just add it to the water when boiling rice in the usual way.

1 Peel the potatoes, then cut them into 2.5 cm (1 inch) cubes. Divide the cauliflower into small sprigs and trim the stalks. Finely chop the onion.

2 Put the potatoes in a pan of salted cold water, bring to the boil and cook for 5 minutes. Remove with a slotted spoon and set aside. Add the cauliflower to the boiling, water and cook for 2 minutes. Drain and refresh under the cold tap.

3 Heat the oil in a large saucepan over low to moderate heat. Add the onion and cook gently for 3–5 minutes until softened and lightly coloured. Add the ground spices and stir for 1–2 minutes, then add the potatoes and cook for a further 1–2 minutes, stirring until well coated.

4 Add the coconut milk and 150 ml (¼ pint) water, season to taste and bring to a simmer. Cover and cook for 7–10 minutes. Uncover the pan, add the cauliflower and cook for 3 minutes or until the potatoes and cauliflower are just tender.

To Serve Taste for seasoning, then turn into a warm serving bowl. Drizzle a little coconut milk over the top and sprinkle with chopped coriander. Serve hot.

Normandy carrots

A rich vegetable dish, traditionally made with Normandy cider. It is good with plain roast or grilled meat or poultry. Here it is made with sliced carrots, but it can be made equally well with whole baby carrots.

500 g (1 lb) carrots
salt and freshly ground black pepper
200 ml (7 fl oz) dry cider
juice of ½ lemon
20 g (¾ oz) butter
nutmeg
150 ml (¼ pint) double cream
finely chopped fresh flat-leaf parsley, to garnish

Serves 4

Preparation time: 10 minutes
Cooking time: about 15 minutes

1 Peel the carrots and cut them on the diagonal into 5 mm (¼ inch) thick slices. Cook them in salted boiling water for 8 minutes.

2 Drain the carrots and place them in a shallow pan with the cider, lemon juice and butter. Sprinkle with salt and pepper and grate a little nutmeg over them. Bring to a simmer, cover and cook for 5 minutes.

3 Uncover the pan and continue cooking until all the liquid has evaporated and the carrots are covered with a nice glaze. Add the cream and heat through, shaking the pan to coat the carrots with it.

To Serve Taste for seasoning, turn into a warm serving bowl and sprinkle with chopped parsley. Serve immediately.

Chef's Tip

If using old, mature carrots, add a pinch or two of sugar to sweeten them a little.

◆

Variation

For extra flavour, add a finely chopped shallot or small onion to the carrots before adding the cider.

VICHY CARROTS

Named after the spa town of Vichy in the Massif Central, these carrots shine with a sweet, buttery glaze. They are good with plain roast or grilled meat and poultry, and children always seem to love them.

500 g (1 lb) carrots
60 g (2 oz) butter
1–2 teaspoons sugar, to taste
salt and freshly ground black pepper

Serves 4

Preparation time: 10 minutes
Cooking time: about 20 minutes

1 Peel the carrots and cut them into 5 mm (¼ inch) thick slices. Put the slices in a shallow pan with the butter, sugar and salt and pepper to taste. Add just enough water to cover the carrots and bring to the boil. Cover and cook for 10 minutes.

2 Uncover the pan and continue cooking until any remaining liquid has evaporated and the carrots are coated in a nice glaze. Stir occasionally to make sure that the carrots are evenly coated and to keep them from colouring.

To Serve Taste for seasoning, then turn into a warm serving bowl. Serve hot.

Variations

After uncovering the pan in step 2, add 60 g (2 oz) currants that have been soaked in cold water for 30 minutes and drained.

◆

For an oriental flavour, add a sprinkling of ground cumin or cumin seeds after taking the lid off the pan, or some grated fresh root ginger. For a sweeter taste, add finely diced stem ginger

◆

Use young French turnips (navets) instead of carrots.

MASHED POTATOES

Smooth, creamy mash is effortlessly achieved if you follow this recipe. The secret is to use floury potatoes such as King Edward, Desirée or Pentland Squire, purée them with a ricer or food mill, then beat in hot milk.

1 kg (2 lb) potatoes
salt
200 ml (7 fl oz) milk
30–60 g (1–2 oz) butter

Serves 4

Preparation time: 15 minutes
Cooking time: 25–30 minutes

1 Peel the potatoes and cut them lengthways into quarters. Place in a saucepan of salted cold water and bring to the boil, then cover and cook at a medium boil for 15–20 minutes until just tender. Drain and set aside, covered.

2 Bring the milk to the boil and set aside. Mash the potatoes through a ricer or food mill and return them to the saucepan. Beat in the hot milk gradually.

3 Cut the butter into small cubes. Place the puréed potatoes over low heat and stir in the butter cubes using a wooden spoon or spatula. Mix until the butter has completely melted. Taste and add salt if necessary.

To Serve Scoop the mash out of the pan with a large metal spoon (or an ice-cream baller if you like) and serve immediately, while piping hot.

Variations

Make saffron mash. Cook the potatoes in step 1 with a good pinch of saffron threads or powder.

◆

Make garlic mash. Boil 1–2 peeled garlic cloves with the potatoes then mash them with the potatoes as in step 2.

◆

Use single or double cream or crème fraîche instead of some of the milk in step 2.

◆

Use 2–3 tablespoons olive oil instead of the butter in step 3.

Hash browns

Originally from the American South-West, hash browns are now famous all over the world as a brunch dish to serve alongside eggs and bacon. They are also very good with grilled sausages, meat and poultry.

750 g (1½ lb) medium to large floury potatoes
salt and freshly ground black pepper
1 small onion
4 tablespoons sunflower oil
15 g (½ oz) butter

Serves 4

Preparation time: 10 minutes
Cooking time: 35–40 minutes

1 Peel the potatoes and cut them into chunks. Cook in salted boiling water for 15 minutes, then drain and chop. Finely chop the onion.

2 Heat the oil and butter in a shallow non-stick frying pan until hot. Add the onion, stir and cook over low to moderate heat until nicely coloured.

3 Add the chopped potatoes, mix well and shape into a flat cake. Cook over moderate heat until golden brown and crisp underneath, about 15 minutes.

To Serve Invert a warm serving platter over the pan, then turn the platter and pan over so that the golden side of the potato cake is uppermost. Serve immediately, cut into wedges.

Chef's Tip

You can cook the potatoes ahead of time and let them go cold before chopping them.

◆

Variations

Add a chopped green pepper and cook with the onion in step 2.

◆

Add chopped cooked bacon and cook with the potatoes in step 3.

◆

Make corned beef hash. Chop about 125 g (4 oz) corned beef and mix it with the potatoes in step 3.

Gratin dauphinois

This is the perfect potato dish for entertaining because it cooks by itself in the oven while you are busy with other things. Here it is made super speedy by using ready prepared potatoes, a trick often used in France.

500 g (1 lb) thinly sliced potatoes
salt and freshly ground black pepper
15 g (½ oz) butter, softened
125 g (4 oz) Emmenthal, Gruyère or Jarlsberg cheese
1 garlic clove
300 ml (½ pint) double cream

Serves 4

Preparation time: 10 minutes
Cooking time: about 35 minutes

1 Preheat the oven to 190°C (375°F) Gas 5. Toss the potatoes in salt and pepper. Brush the inside of an oven-to-table baking dish with the butter and spread the potatoes out in it. Grate the cheese and set aside.

2 Cut the garlic clove in half and place in a saucepan with the cream. Heat just to boiling point and immediately strain over the potatoes. Sprinkle with the grated cheese and bake for 30 minutes.

To Serve Remove from the oven and leave to stand for 5 minutes. Serve straight from the baking dish.

Chef's Tip

Ready prepared potatoes are sold in vacuum packs or cellophane bags in the fresh chilled sections of most supermarkets. Whole and sliced potatoes are available, and they cook very quickly.

◆

Variation

For potatoes with a beautiful golden glow, add a good pinch of saffron threads or powder to the garlic and cream before scalding.

Mushrooms in garlic cream

The puréed garlic sauce makes these mushrooms wonderfully rich and creamy. They are delicious served with grilled steak or chicken, or tossed with small pasta shapes like penne, farfalle or conchiglie.

Serves 4

Preparation time: 15 minutes
Cooking time: about 30 minutes

- 6–8 garlic cloves, to taste
- 400 ml (14 fl oz) hot vegetable or chicken stock
- 625 g (1¼ lb) button mushrooms
- 30 g (1 oz) butter
- 1 teaspoon lemon juice
- salt and freshly ground black pepper
- 200 ml (7 fl oz) double cream

1 In a small saucepan, gently simmer the whole peeled garlic cloves in the stock until sort, about 18–20 minutes.

2 Meanwhile, finely slice the mushrooms. Melt the butter in a saucepan and add the lemon juice, mushrooms and a pinch of salt. Stir, then cover and simmer over low heat for 10 minutes. Tip the mushrooms into a sieve and reserve the liquid.

3 Put the garlic and stock in a food processor with the mushroom liquid. Blend until smooth. Return to the mushroom pan and boil until reduced and thickened. Add the cream and mushrooms and simmer for 5 minutes, stirring frequently. Season with salt and pepper to taste.

To Serve Turn into a warm serving bowl and serve immediately.

Chef's Tip

For an earthy flavour, use a mixture of cultivated and wild mushrooms. In the autumn when fresh ceps are in season, they are very good cooked in this way.

◆

Variation

For a more intense mushroom flavour, you can add a few dried ceps. These are often sold under their Italian name, porcini. Soak them in warm water for about 20 minutes, then drain them and chop finely. Cook them with the fresh mushrooms in step 2.

SPINACH WITH GARLIC, CREAM AND CORIANDER

Evoke the aroma and flavour of France with this wonderful combination of spinach, garlic and cream. French chefs love to cook spinach this way, without water. It is a very quick and successful method.

500 g (1 lb) young tender spinach leaves
2–4 garlic cloves, to taste
60 g (2 oz) butter
1 teaspoon ground coriander
about 4 tablespoons double cream
salt and freshly ground black pepper

Serves 4

Preparation time: 10 minutes
Cooking time: about 10 minutes

1 Wash the spinach well and remove any stalks. Crush the garlic. Melt the butter in a large saucepan, add the spinach and stir over moderate heat for about 5 minutes until the spinach wilts and has released its liquid.

2 Increase the heat to high and add the garlic and coriander. Stir until all of the liquid has evaporated, then add cream and salt and pepper to taste.

To Serve Turn into a warm serving bowl and serve immediately.

Chef's Tip

Fresh spinach can be very gritty and dirty. Save time by buying it ready prepared and washed in bags from the supermarket. This type of spinach is usually labelled 'baby spinach'. It has small tender leaves that have very little tough stalk on them.

Variation

For an Asian flavour, use canned coconut milk instead of cream.

Rocket with Sautéed Potatoes and Bacon

This is a good way to use up leftover boiled or baked potatoes, but if you don't have any, you can buy vacuum packs of peeled potatoes for convenience. They cook very quickly, and have no additives, preservatives or colourings.

175–250 g (6–8 oz) diced bacon
500 g (1 lb) cold cooked potatoes
1–2 tablespoons olive oil
125 g (4 oz) rocket
125 g (4 oz) oak leaf lettuce, lollo rosso or other salad leaves of your choice
1 quantity Mustard Vinaigrette (page 361)
salt and freshly ground black pepper

Serves 4

Preparation time: 10–15 minutes
Cooking time: about 15 minutes

Chef's Tip

Diced streaky bacon can be found in packets in most supermarkets. It saves preparation time and is well worth buying. If you see diced pancetta, an Italian dry-cured ham, this is worth trying as an alternative. It tastes a little stronger and saltier than bacon.

1 Put the diced bacon in a non-stick frying pan and cook, stirring frequently, over moderate heat for 5–8 minutes until browned and quite crisp. Meanwhile, slice or dice the cold potatoes.

2 Remove the bacon from the pan with a slotted spoon. Add olive oil to the pan (the amount needed will depend on how fatty the bacon was) and heat until hot. Add the potatoes and sauté for 8–10 minutes until nicely coloured and crisp. Return the bacon to the pan and toss with the potatoes.

3 Put the rocket and other salad leaves in a bowl with the potatoes and bacon. Pour in the vinaigrette, add seasoning to taste and toss to mix.

To Serve Divide the salad equally between 2 plates and serve immediately.

Asparagus with Soy and Wasabi Dressing

An excellent salad for an early summer barbecue party. The distinctive flavour of Japanese wasabi, which is usually served with sushi and sashimi, goes particularly well with barbecued fish.

2 bunches of green asparagus, each weighing about 375 g (12 oz)
salt
1 bunch of spring onions
1–2 tablespoons toasted sesame seeds, to garnish (optional)

Dressing
5 cm (2 inch) piece of fresh root ginger
4 tablespoons soy sauce
juice of 1 lemon
½–1 teaspoon wasabi, to taste
90 ml (3 fl oz) soya oil or other vegetable oil

Serves 6–8

Preparation time: 30–40 minutes
Cooking time: 5 minutes

1 Trim off the woody ends of the asparagus, then scrape or peel the bottom of the spears. Cut each spear into 3 equal pieces, each about 4 cm (1½ inches) long, separating the tips from the stems.

2 Cook the stems in salted boiling water for 3–5 minutes until tender. Remove with a slotted spoon to a colander and refresh under the cold tap. Drain, then leave to dry on kitchen paper. Add the tips to the boiling water and cook for 2 minutes, then drain, refresh and dry as for the stems.

3 Make the dressing. Peel the ginger, grate it into a bowl and add the soy sauce, lemon juice and ½ teaspoon wasabi. Whisk well together, then whisk in the oil a little at a time. Taste and add more wasabi if you like.

4 Thinly slice the spring onions on the diagonal and toss them into the dressing. Add the asparagus stems and turn gently to coat.

To Serve Spoon the asparagus stems in the centre of a serving platter and arrange the tips around the outside. Drizzle some of the dressing from the bowl over the tips. Sprinkle with sesame seeds, if you like. Serve at room temperature.

Chef's Tips

Wasabi is the Japanese version of horseradish, and the mustard-like condiment made from it is available in powder and paste form in Japanese stores and the oriental sections of some supermarkets. The bright green paste sold in tubes is the most convenient form of wasabi; the powder needs to be mixed with water.

Wasabi is at its most powerful when first mixed, but will gradually lose its strength the longer it is exposed to the air.

Courgettes hongroise

This colourful dish has a piquant flavour. Serve it with plain grilled or roast meat or poultry. It also makes a very good omelette filling or topping, and can be tossed with pasta for a quick vegetarian supper.

2–3 medium courgettes, total weight about 375 g (12 oz)
½ small onion or 1 shallot
1 small garlic clove
2 tablespoons olive oil
2 teaspoons sweet Hungarian paprika
1 tablespoon tomato purée
300 ml (½ pint) hot vegetable stock or water
salt and freshly ground black pepper

Serves 4

Preparation time: 10 minutes
Cooking time: about 25 minutes

Chef's Tip

You can make the sauce several hours in advance. When you are ready to cook the courgettes, bring the sauce to the boil first.

1 Top and tail the courgettes, then cut them into 1.25 cm (½ inch) thick slices. Chop the onion or shallot. Crush the garlic. Heat the oil in a medium saucepan, add the onion and cook over low heat until soft and translucent.

2 Sprinkle in the paprika and cook, stirring, for 30 seconds. Stir in the tomato purée and garlic and cook for 1 minute, then pour in the stock or water, season and bring to the boil, stirring. Cover, then simmer gently for 10 minutes.

3 Add the courgettes and stir to coat in the sauce, then cover and cook over low heat for 10 minutes, stirring 2–3 times to cook and flavour evenly.

To Serve Taste for seasoning, then turn into a warm serving bowl. Serve hot.

Green beans with leeks and tomatoes

A special vegetable dish to serve with plainly cooked meat or poultry. It goes especially well with roast chicken, and because the beans are coated in sauce there is no need to make gravy.

1 leek (white part only)
2 tablespoons olive oil
1 x 400 g can chopped tomatoes
100 ml (3½ fl oz) dry white wine or water
1 bay leaf
2–3 fresh thyme sprigs
salt and freshly ground black pepper
200 g (7 oz) green beans

Serves 4

Preparation time: 10 minutes
Cooking time: about 30 minutes

Chef's Tip

You can make the sauce up to 3 days ahead of time and keep it in a covered bowl in the refrigerator. Before you serve the sauce, reheat it until bubbling, then blanch and add the beans.

1 Thinly slice the leek and wash thoroughly in a colander or sieve. Drain well. Heat the oil in a shallow pan over low heat, add the leek and cook slowly until soft, about 5 minutes. Add the tomatoes, wine or water, bay leaf, thyme and seasoning to taste. Simmer for 15 minutes.

2 Meanwhile, top and tail the beans and blanch them in salted boiling water for 2 minutes. Drain and refresh under cold running water.

3 Add the beans to the tomato sauce and simmer for 3–5 minutes until the beans are tender and the sauce has reduced and is thick. Discard the bay leaf and thyme.

To Serve Taste for seasoning, then turn into a warm serving bowl. Serve hot.

Corn salad

A tasty accompaniment with a Mexican flavour that goes well with plain roast or grilled meat or poultry. It's ideal with barbecued food, such as spicy chargrilled drumsticks, steaks, chops or burgers.

- 1 large red pepper
- 1 large garlic clove
- 1 x 340 g can sweetcorn
- 1 heaped tablespoon chopped fresh coriander
- 4 tablespoons Balsamic Vinaigrette (page 360), or to taste

Serves 2–3

Preparation time: 10 minutes
Cooking time: 40–50 minutes

1 Preheat the oven to 190°C (375°F) Gas 5. Cut the pepper lengthways into quarters and remove the cores, seeds and spongy ribs. Roast the pepper in the oven for 40–50 minutes until blistered and charred. Place in a plastic bag and set aside to cool, then peel off the skin and dice the flesh. Crush the garlic.

2 Drain the sweetcorn and place in a bowl with the diced roasted pepper, crushed garlic, chopped coriander and vinaigrette. Stir well to mix, then taste and add more vinaigrette if you like.

To Serve Turn into a serving bowl and serve at room temperature.

Chef's Tip

To save time, you can buy ready roasted peppers, either in a jar or loose at the delicatessen. Or, for a crunchier texture and less smoky flavour, simply use fresh unroasted pepper, which will also save time.

◆

Variations

Drain and flake 1 x 200 g can tuna and fold gently into the salad.

◆

Boil and drain 125 g (4 oz) small pasta shapes, then mix with the vinaigrette while hot. Leave to cool, then add the remaining ingredients. To make a main course salad, you can add canned tuna as suggested above.

Celeriac salad

A winter salad that goes well with cooked and smoked meats, especially smoked duck (page 29). In France it is often served as part of an hors d'oeuvre. It also makes a tasty first course served with grated carrots in Vinaigrette (page 360).

Serves 4–6

Preparation time: 10 minutes

1 small celeriac
juice of 1 lemon
salt and freshly ground black pepper
150 ml (¼ pint) mayonnaise

1 Quarter and peel the celeriac, then cut it into pieces that will fit inside the feeder tube of a food processor.

2 Fit the medium or fine grating blade in the processor and grate the celeriac. Place in a bowl and add the lemon juice and salt and pepper to taste. Toss well to mix, add the mayonnaise and toss again.

To Serve Taste for seasoning, then turn into a serving bowl. Cover tightly with cling film and serve as soon as possible or the celeriac may discolour.

Variations

In France, where this salad is called rémoulade, it often has raisins added. Soak about 60 g (2 oz) raisins in cold water for about 30 minutes, then drain and add to the salad at the same time as the mayonnaise.

◆

For a more piquant flavour, add 1–2 teaspoons Dijon or coarse-grained mustard.

THAI VEGETABLE STIR-FRY

Fresh and colourful, this tasty stir-fry makes a good vegetarian supper when served with boiled rice or noodles. The ginger gives the dish a wonderful flavour, and the aroma is quite tantalizing.

1 onion
1 fresh red or green chilli
2 garlic cloves
175–200 g (6–7 oz) broccoli florets
1 red pepper
5 cm (2 inch) piece of fresh root ginger
250 g (8 oz) fresh shiitake or oyster mushrooms
1 x 150 g can baby corn in brine
3 tablespoons sunflower oil
a good pinch of sugar, or more to taste
2–3 tablespoons fish sauce, or to taste
2–3 tablespoons soy sauce, or to taste
250 g (8 oz) bean sprouts

Serves 2

Preparation time: 15 minutes
Cooking time: about 10 minutes

1 Thinly slice the onion. Thinly slice the chilli at an angle. Crush the garlic. Divide the broccoli into tiny sprigs and trim the stalks. Cut the red pepper into thin strips. Peel and grate the ginger. Thinly slice the mushrooms. Drain the corn.

2 Heat the oil in a wok or deep sauté pan, add the onion and stir-fry over low to moderate heat for a few minutes until lightly coloured. Sprinkle in the chilli, garlic and sugar, then add the broccoli and increase the heat to moderately high. Stir-fry for 3 minutes.

3 Add the red pepper, ginger and mushrooms and stir-fry for about 3 minutes, then add the fish sauce and soy sauce and stir well. Add the corn and bean sprouts and toss over high heat until all the vegetables have heated through and are well mixed.

To Serve Taste and add more sugar, fish sauce or soy sauce. Serve immediately, with extra fish sauce or soy sauce at the table.

Chef's Tips

If you keep fresh root ginger in the freezer you will find it very easy to peel and grate.

◆

For a very hot stir-fry, leave the seeds in the chilli when slicing it. For a milder flavour scrape the seeds out and discard them.

◆

If you can't find canned baby corn, use fresh corn and boil it for 8 minutes before adding it to the stir-fry.

Caramelized onion tartlets

These tartlets look spectacular and taste delicious – crisp, light filo cases and a gooey melt-in-the-mouth filling. Serve them for a vegetarian main course followed by a large mixed salad and one or two of your favourite cheeses.

500 g (1 lb) red and Spanish onions
2 garlic cloves
a few sprigs of fresh thyme
4–5 tablespoons olive oil
8 rectangular sheets of filo pastry (see Chef's Tip)
4 small fresh thyme sprigs, to serve

Serves 4

Preparation time: 15–20 minutes
Cooking time: 40–50 minutes

1 Thinly slice the onions. Finely chop the garlic and thyme leaves. Heat 2 tablespoons oil in a non-stick frying pan, add the onions, garlic and thyme and cook over low heat until caramelized and golden, 35–40 minutes. Stir often during this time, to prevent sticking.

2 Meanwhile, preheat the oven to 190°C (375°F) Gas 5 and put a large baking sheet in the oven to heat at the same time. Brush the insides of four 10–12.5 cm (4–5 inch) tart tins lightly with oil.

3 Cut the filo into sixteen 18 cm (7 inch) squares. Brush 1 square lightly with oil and place it in one of the tins, tucking the pastry into the inside edge. Brush another square with oil and place it on top of the first, arranging it so that the points are at different angles from the first and tucking it well in at the inside edge. Repeat with a third and fourth square, then prick the base of the filo all over with a fork, then fill with crumpled foil. Repeat with the remaining 3 tart tins.

4 Put the tart tins on the hot baking sheet and bake blind for 5 minutes. Remove the foil, return the tins to the oven and bake for a further 2 minutes or until the pastry is golden brown. Remove the tartlets from the oven and set them aside to cool a little in the tins.

To Serve Transfer the filo cases to plates, then spoon in the onion mixture and garnish each tartlet with a sprig of thyme. Serve warm.

Chef's Tip

Filo pastry is available frozen in boxes at most supermarkets and Middle Eastern stores. Most boxes contain rectangular sheets in a roll, which must be thawed before they can be unrolled. Sizes vary according to manufacturer, so you may need more or less sheets than the number given here, which is based on the sheets being 30 x 18 cm (12 x 7 inches). Filo pastry is very fragile and it dries out very quickly when it is exposed to air. Always keep the pieces you are not actually working with covered with cling film or a damp cloth.

Asparagus with hazelnut dressing

Fresh young homegrown asparagus appears in the shops in May and June. This simple way of cooking and serving it is one of the best – the flavours in the dressing complement the asparagus perfectly without masking its natural flavour.

- 500 g (1 lb) slender asparagus spears
- 2 tablespoons lemon juice
- 2 tablespoons finely chopped fresh flat-leaf parsley
- 2 tablespoons hazelnut oil
- freshly ground black pepper
- 1 teaspoon sea or rock salt

Serves 4

Preparation time: 10 minutes
Cooking time: about 4 minutes

1 Wash the asparagus spears and trim off any thick or woody ends. Pour water into a large sauté pan to come 5–7.5 cm (2–3 inches) up the sides. Bring the water to simmering point and lower in the asparagus. Simmer until just tender, about 4 minutes, depending on the thickness of the stalks.

2 Meanwhile, put the lemon juice in a jug with the parsley, oil and pepper to taste and whisk together with a fork.

3 Drain the asparagus, spread out on a clean cloth and pat dry.

To Serve Transfer the asparagus to a platter and sprinkle with the sea salt. Whisk the dressing again and spoon it carefully over the asparagus so that each stalk has some dressing on it. Serve warm or at room temperature.

Chef's Tip

The asparagus can be left to soak in the dressing several hours ahead of serving, so it makes an ideal first course for a dinner party. Made in larger quantities, it is also good for a summer buffet or barbecue.

Variations

If you prefer, you can chargrill the asparagus rather than boiling it. Heat a little olive oil on a ridged cast iron griddle pan, add the asparagus and cook for 5–8 minutes, turning once.

For a change, use shredded basil instead of parsley.

VEGETABLES

quick and easy ideas

Asparagus

• Place asparagus spears lying down in a sauté pan of salted boiling water. Simmer for 5–10 minutes until tender. Drain and serve with warm melted butter. Finely grated lemon rind can be added to the butter, or some very finely chopped fresh dill.

• Brush asparagus spears with olive oil and place on a hot ridged cast iron pan. Chargrill for about 5 minutes, turning once. Serve drizzled with a little extra-virgin olive oil and balsamic vinegar and topped with shavings of Parmesan cheese.

Aubergines

• Pan-fry aubergine slices in very hot olive oil. Drain on kitchen paper and sprinkle with salt. Serve with a bowl of Greek yogurt.

• Make Aubergine Parmigiana, an excellent main course for vegetarians. Layer pan-fried aubergine slices in a baking dish with homemade tomato sauce. Top with sliced mozzarella and grated Parmesan cheese. Bake at 190°C (375°F) Gas 5 for about 30 minutes.

Beans

• Cook trimmed French beans in salted boiling water for 6 minutes. Sweat finely chopped shallots in butter. When the beans are tender, drain thoroughly and toss in the shallot butter. Season with salt and pepper.

• Sprinkle drained cooked beans with crispy bacon bits before serving.

• Toss drained cooked beans in homemade tomato sauce, adding shredded fresh basil leaves and plenty of freshly ground black pepper at the last moment.

quick and easy ideas

Broccoli

• Cook trimmed broccoli florets in salted boiling water for 4 minutes. Drain well and toss with toasted almonds or pine nuts, a knob of butter and salt and pepper.

• Add a few chopped canned anchovies and a little grated lemon rind to cooked broccoli. Toss to combine.

• Stir-fry broccoli florets in sunflower oil with red pepper strips. Sprinkle with sesame oil before serving.

Cabbage

• Cook shredded greens in salted boiling water for 3 minutes. Drain and toss with butter and wholegrain mustard, caraway or cumin seeds.

• Blanch shredded cabbage for 1–2 minutes, drain and stir-fry in a mixture of sunflower and sesame oil. Finish with a dash of soy or chilli sauce.

Carrots

• Cook whole baby carrots or batons in salted boiling water with a pinch of sugar. Allow 6 minutes for whole carrots, 3–4 minutes for batons. Drain, return to pan and glaze with butter and cream or crème fraîche. Sprinkle with black pepper before serving.

Courgettes

• Gently pan-fry courgette slices in olive oil with chopped garlic. Sprinkle with dried breadcrumbs, salt and pepper, and fry over high heat until crispy.

VEGETABLES

quick and easy ideas

Mushrooms

• Sauté sliced mushrooms in olive oil with finely chopped garlic, ½–1 teaspoon dried herbes de Provence and salt and freshly ground black pepper. Serve sprinkled with lots of finely chopped fresh parsley. If you have any crème fraîche or cream, stir in a few tablespoons.

Parsnips

• Cook peeled chunks of parsnip in salted boiling water for 15–20 minutes until tender. Drain and mash like potatoes with hot milk, butter and seasoning.

• Pare parsnips into ribbons with a vegetable peeler. Stir-fry in hot oil with ribbons of carrot and grated fresh root ginger. Sprinkle with rice wine or balsamic vinegar.

Potatoes

• Cook new potatoes in salted boiling water with a few sprigs of fresh mint for 15–20 minutes until tender. Drain and return to pan with a good knob of butter. Shake to coat the potatoes in the melting butter, then sprinkle with chopped fresh mint.

• Put small chunks of unpeeled potatoes in a roasting tin with olive oil and whole unpeeled garlic cloves. Roast at 200°C (400°F) Gas 6 for 45 minutes to 1 hour, shaking the tin and turning the potatoes once.

• Cook unpeeled potatoes in salted boiling water for about 20 minutes until tender. Drain, peel off skins and slice potatoes quite thickly. Arrange slices in a baking dish. Sweat finely chopped shallots in butter, add chopped parsley and seasoning and pour over potatoes. Heat through in a hot oven for 5 minutes.

quick and easy ideas

Peas

• Make petits pois à la française. Cook frozen petits pois or peas for 5 minutes in a minimum of salted boiling water with a few letttuce leaves, a knob of butter and a pinch of sugar. Drain and sprinkle with pepper.

• Make petits pois au jambon. Cook frozen petits pois or peas in salted boiling water for 5 minutes, drain and toss with butter and shredded ham.

Peppers

• Roast and peel whole red, orange and yellow peppers (page 348). Cut lengthways into slivers. Arrange in a serving dish and dress with olive oil, lemon juice, crushed garlic and black pepper. Serve cold.

• Quarter red, green and yellow peppers lengthways and deseed. Fill each quarter with a spoonful of pesto and roast at 190°C (375°F) Gas 5 for 30 minutes. Serve hot, topped with shavings of Parmesan cheese.

Spinach

• Wash spinach and cook in a large pan with only the water that clings to the leaves. Allow about 5 minutes until wilted, drain and return to pan. Toss over high heat with butter, salt and freshly ground black pepper. Grate fresh nutmeg over the top just before serving.

• Toss drained cooked spinach in a wok with soy sauce, crushed garlic and sesame oil. For a fiery touch, add a little deseeded and chopped fresh chilli.

5

PULSES, GRAINS & PASTA

Necessity is the mother of invention, and there are thousands of wonderful recipes using pasta, pulses and grains. Without much taste of their own, they readily take on the flavours of other ingredients – as the recipes in this chapter illustrate so well. The pungency of spices, tastiness of garlic and onions, the freshness of herbs, sweetness of fruits and the heat of chillies are just a few examples of the flavours they marry well with. Be adventurous – serve polenta instead of potatoes, and couscous or bulgar in place of rice or pasta. All are quick and easy to cook, so there is no extra time or trouble involved.

The Mediterranean diet makes full use of pulses, grains and pasta. These, together with fresh fruit, vegetables and fish and a moderate amount of meat, make people in this region some of the healthiest in the world. Natural partners in a vegetarian diet, pulses and grains come together to provide a protein that is just as good as that found in fish or meat – a nutritional miracle that has long been recognized in the poorer parts of the world.

Tabbouleh

This Middle Eastern dish made from bulgar is full of flavour, and a favourite salad with vegetarians. It is usually made with lots of fresh herbs and is very green, but you can use less if you prefer. Serve with warm pitta or other Middle Eastern bread.

250 g (8 oz) bulgar wheat
1 x 400 g can chopped tomatoes
2 shallots
15–30 g (½–1 oz) fresh mint
30–60 g (1–2 oz) fresh flat-leaf parsley
15–30 g (½–1 oz) fresh coriander
grated rind and juice of 1 lemon
2 tablespoons extra virgin olive oil

Serves 4–6

Preparation time: 20 minutes, plus standing time

1 Rinse the wheat in a sieve under cold running water. Squeeze out the excess water and place the wheat in a bowl.

2 Bring the chopped tomatoes to the boil in a saucepan, pour them over the wheat and stir well with a fork. Leave to stand for 1 hour, stirring occasionally, until the wheat has absorbed the tomato juices and softened.

3 Reserve a few whole mint sprigs for the garnish. Finely chop the remaining mint leaves with the shallots. Mix into the wheat with the remaining ingredients. Season well and set aside at room temperature for at least 15–20 minutes.

To Serve Taste for seasoning, turn into a serving bowl and garnish with the reserved whole mint sprigs. Serve at room temperature.

Chef's Tips

Bulgar, also called bulgur and burghul, is boiled and dried wheat. You can buy it in supermarkets, health food shops and Middle Eastern stores. It does not need to be cooked, but it does need soaking so that it becomes soft enough to eat. Hot water is generally used, but this recipe uses hot tomatoes and their juice for flavour and colour.

◆

Tightly covered with cling film, tabbouleh will keep in the refrigerator for up to 24 hours, but remember to let it come to room temperature before serving. If it is too cold, it will lack flavour.

Fragrant chickpea pilaf

Cinnamon and toasted cumin give this simple pilaf a subtle spicy fragrance and flavour. It makes a nutritious vegetarian main course served with natural yogurt, or it can be served as a side dish with meat. It goes really well with lamb kebabs.

2 teaspoons cumin seeds
2 onions
2 celery stalks
1 tablespoon olive oil
2 cinnamon sticks
250 g (8 oz) white long-grain rice
1 litre (1¾ pints) hot vegetable stock
1 x 400 g can chickpeas
salt and freshly ground black pepper
chopped fresh coriander, to serve

Serves 4–6

Preparation time: 10–15 minutes
Cooking time: 35 minutes

1 Dry-fry the cumin seeds in a non-stick frying pan over low heat for a few minutes, stirring them constantly until they are lightly browned. Remove them from the pan and crush with a pestle and mortar. Finely chop the onions and celery.

2 Heat the oil in a large non-stick sauté pan and sauté the onions, celery, cinnamon sticks and cumin for about 10 minutes or until the onions are tinged golden brown. Add the rice and stir for 2 minutes.

3 Pour in the hot stock and let it sizzle, then lower the heat, cover the pan and simmer gently until the rice is al dente, about 20 minutes.

4 Add the chickpeas, season well and heat through.

To Serve Turn into a warm serving dish, remove the cinnamon sticks if you like, and sprinkle with chopped coriander. Serve hot.

Chef's Tip

This pilaf needs a flavoursome stock. Buy chilled fresh vegetable stock, available at supermarkets.

Variation

Colour the rice yellow by sprinkling a pinch of saffron threads into the stock in step 3. Stir well before covering the pan.

Mushroom and Pearl Barley Risotto

Pearl barley makes a creamy risotto with a nutty bite. It can be served Italian style as a first course for six people, or English style as a vegetarian main course for four, with a tossed green salad and a selection of cheeses to follow.

Serves 4–6

Preparation time: 10–15 minutes
Cooking time: 45 minutes

- 250 g (8 oz) pearl barley
- 1 litre (1¾ pints) vegetable stock
- 2 bay leaves
- salt and freshly ground black pepper
- 2 shallots
- 2 garlic cloves
- 250 g (8 oz) button mushrooms
- 30 g (1 oz) butter
- 2 tablespoons half-fat crème fraîche
- 4 tablespoons chopped fresh flat-leaf parsley

1 Put the barley in a large saucepan and cover with cold water. Bring to the boil, drain and rinse under the cold tap. Drain again, then return to the rinsed pan. Add the stock, bay leaves and salt and pepper to taste. Bring slowly to the boil, then half cover and simmer for 20 minutes.

2 Meanwhile, finely chop the shallots and garlic. Quarter or halve the mushrooms, depending on their size. Melt the butter in a wide, deep sauté pan and stir-fry the shallots for 2 minutes. Add the mushrooms and garlic and stir-fry for 4–5 minutes until tinged brown.

3 Add the mushroom mixture to the pearl barley, season and stir well, then continue to simmer for 20 minutes or until the barley is al dente. Most of the liquid should be absorbed, but the risotto should have a creamy, soupy consistency.

4 Remove from the heat, cover and leave to stand for 5 minutes, then remove the bay leaves and gently stir in the crème fraîche and about half the parsley. Taste for seasoning.

To Serve Divide the risotto between warm soup plates and sprinkle with the remaining parsley. Serve immediately.

Chef's Tip

Pearl barley is barley grain that has been hulled and polished – or 'pearled'. It has a special affinity with mushrooms and lamb and is often used in soups and stews as a thickener. Look for it in the supermarket or health food shop next to the rice and other grains.

Variation

If you like, top with coarsely grated Italian Parmesan or pecorino cheese, or the hard, salty ricotta salata. You could also use the Spanish manchego.

Green lentil salad

This is a colourful salad that can be made all year round, but it is especially good for picnics and other al fresco meals, served with cold chicken or cooked meats. It is also good on its own, with wholemeal or granary bread, and with cheese.

250 g (8 oz) green lentils
salt and freshly ground black pepper
1 red pepper
1 orange pepper
6 spring onions
1 lemon
½ green dessert apple
2 tablespoons hazelnut, walnut or sesame oil

Serves 4–6

Preparation time: 20 minutes
Cooking time: 35–45 minutes

Chef's Tip

Green lentils hold their shape during cooking and are excellent in salads. Look for them in Middle Eastern stores and health food shops as well as in supermarkets. If you can get the French Puy lentils, these are considered the finest. They are smaller than other green lentils and tinged grey-black.

1 Rinse the lentils in a sieve under cold running water. Place them in a saucepan, cover generously with cold water and add a pinch of salt. Bring to the boil and remove any scum, then simmer until tender, 30–40 minutes. If necessary, add more water if it becomes absorbed by the lentils during this time.

2 While the lentils are cooking, core, deseed and dice the peppers. Thinly slice the spring onions. Grate the lemon rind and squeeze the juice. Core and dice the apple, place in a large bowl and immediately toss in the lemon juice. Add the lemon rind, peppers and spring onions and toss well to mix.

3 Drain the lentils into a sieve and rinse with hot water from the kettle, then mix with the other ingredients while still hot. Add the oil and plenty of salt and pepper and stir well.

To Serve Taste for seasoning and transfer to a serving bowl. Serve warm or at room temperature.

Red rice salad

Charred sweetcorn gives this colourful vegetable and rice salad a smoky flavour, and it goes really well with barbecued chicken or meat. If you like, you can cook the corn on the barbecue too.

125–150 g (4–5 oz) red rice
salt and freshly ground black pepper
1 corn-on-the-cob
1 red pepper
1–2 red chillies
4 ripe plum tomatoes
15 cm (6 inch) piece of cucumber
4 spring onions
30 g (1 oz) fresh flat-leaf parsley
3 tablespoons extra virgin olive oil
2 tablespoons red wine vinegar

Serves 4

Preparation time: 20 minutes
Cooking time: 45 minutes

1 Preheat the grill to hot. Place the rice in a medium saucepan of salted water and bring to the boil. Simmer gently, uncovered, for about 30 minutes or until the rice is just tender. Remove from the heat, cover the pan and leave to stand.

2 Remove the husk and silks from the outside of the corn and place under the hot grill for about 15 minutes, turning several times until the corn is charred on all sides. Leave until cool enough to handle, then stand the corn upright on a chopping board and cut off the kernels using a downward action with a sharp knife.

3 Turn the rice into a sieve and rinse under the cold tap until cool. Set aside to drain well. Halve, core and deseed the red pepper and chillies, then finely dice them. Finely dice the tomatoes, cucumber and spring onions. Finely chop the parsley.

4 Mix the drained rice with the corn and vegetables. Whisk the oil and vinegar together in a jug, pour over the salad and fork through. Add seasoning to taste.

To Serve Turn the salad into a serving bowl and serve at room temperature.

Chef's Tips

Red rice comes from the Camargue in southern France. It is quite easy to get in supermarkets and delicatessens, but you can use brown rice instead – they both have a similar nutty flavour.

If you leave the seeds in the chillies, the salad will be spicy hot. When you taste it for seasoning before serving, add a drop or two of Tabasco if you want a hotter flavour.

Spiced fruity couscous

Dried fruit and cumin seeds give couscous a sweet and spicy flavour. Serve as a vegetarian main course with a raita of yogurt, cucumber and mint, or as a side dish with grilled or barbecued meat.

Serves 4–6

Preparation time: 15 minutes
Cooking time: 10 minutes, plus standing time

- 2 teaspoons cumin seeds
- 500 ml (18 fl oz) vegetable stock
- 200 g (7 oz) couscous
- 90 g (3 oz) ready-to-eat prunes
- 90 g (3 oz) ready-to-eat dried apricots
- 2 tablespoons extra virgin olive oil
- 2 tablespoons chopped fresh coriander
- salt and freshly ground black pepper

1 Dry-fry the cumin seeds over low heat in a non-stick frying pan for a few minutes, stirring constantly. Crush the seeds finely with a pestle and mortar and set aside.

2 Bring the stock to the boil in a large saucepan, add the couscous and stir well. Turn off the heat, cover the pan tightly with the lid and leave to stand for 10 minutes.

3 Fork the couscous through. Using scissors, snip the dried fruit into the couscous, then add the cumin seeds, oil, half the coriander and salt and pepper to taste. Fork through until evenly mixed.

To Serve Turn the couscous into a serving bowl and sprinkle with the remaining coriander. Serve hot or at room temperature.

Chef's Tip

The couscous you buy in packets at supermarkets and health food shops is precooked and only needs soaking in hot liquid or very short cooking to become light and fluffy. It is made from steamed and dried semolina grains, and is part of the staple diet of North Africa, where it is most often steamed over meat and vegetable stews.

LEMON, PARSLEY AND PINE NUT PASTA

Quick and easy, this is one of the new-style pasta dishes. A handful of raw ingredients is simply tosssed with hot pasta and dressing to make a high energy meal that is literally bursting with fresh flavour. Serve it for a first or main course, topped with thin shavings of Parmesan or pecorino if you like.

Serves 4–6

Preparation time: 15 minutes
Cooking time: 10 minutes

375 g (3/4 lb) dried pasta twists
salt and freshly ground black pepper
30 g (1 oz) fresh flat-leaf parsley
1 lemon
6 tablespoons extra virgin olive oil
2 tablespoons balsamic vinegar
60 g (2 oz) pine nuts, toasted

1 Cook the pasta in salted boiling water for 10 minutes or according to packet instructions.

2 Meanwhile, finely chop the parsley, then grate the lemon rind and squeeze the juice. Place in a large bowl with the oil, vinegar and salt and pepper to taste and stir well to mix.

3 Drain the pasta, add to the dressing with about half the pine nuts and toss well to mix.

To Serve Taste for seasoning and sprinkle with the remaining pine nuts. Serve immediately.

Chef's Tips

Balsamic vinegar comes from Modena in northern Italy. Genuine aceto balsamico tradizionale di Modena is controlled by Italian law and is aged in wooden barrels for at least 10–12 years. It has an exquisite aroma and flavour, but it is very expensive. For everyday use, simply buy the best you can afford. Look for Italian brands with aceto balsamico di Modena on the label.

◆

Creamy coloured, waxy textured pine nuts are frequently used in Italian cooking, especially in Liguria where they are included in the famous pesto sauce. To toast them, dry-fry over low heat in a non-stick frying pan for a few minutes, shaking the pan and stirring the nuts constantly to prevent them from burning.

Spiced dhal

Served with rice, lentil dhal makes a most nutritious meal. The combination of pulse and grain makes protein that is just as good as the protein we get from meat or fish. Natural yogurt is the traditional, healthy accompaniment.

375 g (3/4 lb) red lentils
salt and freshly ground black pepper
2 onions
3 garlic cloves
2 tablespoons vegetable oil
1 teaspoon ground coriander
1/2 teaspoon fennel seeds
2 red chillies
1 tablespoon chopped fresh coriander

Serves 4–6

Preparation time: 15 minutes
Cooking time: 25–30 minutes

1 Rinse the lentils in a sieve under cold running water. Place them in a saucepan, cover generously with cold water and add a pinch of salt. Bring to the boil and remove any scum, then simmer until tender, about 20 minutes. If necessary, add more water if it becomes absorbed by the lentils during this time.

2 Meanwhile, finely chop the onions and garlic. Heat half the oil in a non-stick frying pan until hot. Add the onions, garlic, ground coriander and fennel seeds and stir-fry over low to moderate heat until the onions are soft and caramelized, about 10 minutes.

3 Add the onion mixture to the lentils, season generously and fork through until evenly mixed. Turn off the heat under the pan, cover tightly and leave to stand.

4 Thinly slice the chillies, including the seeds if you like their heat. Heat the remaining oil in the frying pan and stir-fry the chillies quickly for 1–2 minutes over high heat.

To Serve Turn the dhal into a warm serving dish and top with the chillies and oil and the chopped coriander. Serve hot.

Chef's Tip

The chilli and oil topping for this dhal is called tarka in Indian cookery. A tarka is usually made with ghee (clarified butter) and often has onions and aromatic spices as well as chillies.

Variation

Red lentils cook down to a rough purée and are good for making dhal, but you can use brown or green lentils if you prefer. They take 30–40 minutes to cook and hold their shape better than red lentils.

WILD RICE WITH RASPBERRIES

Wild rice is the seed of a wild aquatic grass, not a rice at all, but it looks like very long grains of rice. It is a dramatic dark brown, almost black, colour. Here it is teamed with a sweet raspberry and orange dressing and the result is sensational.

- 3 strips of pared orange rind
- 1 teaspoon coarsely crushed black peppercorns
- 1 bay leaf
- salt and freshly ground black pepper
- 60 g (2 oz) wild rice
- 100 g (3½ oz) long-grain white rice
- 150 g (5 oz) raspberries
- 4 tablespoons extra virgin olive oil
- 2 tablespoons orange juice
- a few orange slices, to serve

Serves 4

Preparation time: 10–15 minutes

Cooking time: 50–55 minutes

Chef's Tip

Wild rice is expensive and it is often cooked with other rice to make it go further. For convenience and economy, you can buy packets of wild rice and long-grain white rice mixed together. For this recipe you will need 175 g (6 oz). Cook for the length of time given on the packet.

1 Place the orange rind in a large pan with the pepper and bay leaf. Add 1 litre (1¾ pints) cold water and a good pinch of salt to taste and bring to the boil. Add the wild rice and simmer for 30 minutes. Add the white rice, stir and simmer for another 15–20 minutes or until both types of rice are tender.

2 Meanwhile, purée 100 g (3½ oz) of the raspberries in a food processor or blender, then work through a sieve into a large bowl. Discard the raspberry seeds. Add the oil and orange juice to the purée and whisk to make a dressing.

3 Drain the rice into a large sieve and discard the orange rind and bay leaf. Turn the rice into the bowl of dressing and fork through gently. Taste and add salt and pepper if necessary.

To Serve Turn into a warm serving bowl and garnish with the orange slices and remaining raspberries. Serve hot.

Pasticcio with Roasted Vegetables

Pasticcio is the Italian word for a pasta pie that is baked in the oven. Italian cooks don't need a recipe, they simply make it with whatever ingredients they have on the day. It makes a substantial supper.

Serves 4–6

Preparation time: 20 minutes
Cooking time: 45–60 minutes, plus standing time

- 1 red pepper
- 1 yellow pepper
- 1 aubergine
- 1 large courgette
- 2 garlic cloves
- 1 teaspoon dried mixed herbs
- 2 tablespoons olive oil
- salt and freshly ground black pepper
- 250 g (8 oz) short pasta
- 1 quantity Chunky Tomato Sauce (page 357)
- 200 ml (7 fl oz) vegetable stock
- 2 x 150 g packets half-fat mozzarella
- 1 small handful of fresh basil leaves, to serve

1 Preheat the oven to 200°C (400°F) Gas 6. Halve, core and deseed the peppers, then cut them into chunks. Top and tail the aubergine and courgette and cut them into chunks like the peppers. Crush the garlic.

2 Place the vegetables in a large non-stick roasting tin and mix in the garlic, dried herbs, oil and salt and pepper to taste. Roast in the oven for 30–40 minutes or until lightly charred, stirring occasionally.

3 Meanwhile, cook the pasta in salted boiling water according to packet instructions until al dente. Drain well. In a separate pan, heat the tomato sauce with the stock. Drain and dice the mozzarella.

4 Place the vegetables and pasta in a large baking dish and mix well. Pour the tomato sauce over and mix in, then put the mozzarella cubes on top. Bake for 15–20 minutes or until melted and golden. Leave to stand for 5–10 minutes before serving.

To Serve Scatter the basil leaves over the top of the pasticcio and serve hot.

Chef's Tip

You can use any shape of pasta you like, either fresh or dried, although you will find there is far more choice with dried shapes than fresh. Rigatoni, penne, conchiglie, fusilli and garganelli are some of the shapes that are available fresh, and they all work well in baked dishes like this one.

FELAFELS

Little patties made of chickpeas, felafels come from the Middle East, where they are traditionally fried in oil and served in pitta bread pockets. Here they are baked, then topped with a yogurt dressing. Served with a salad and pitta bread, they make a delicious lunch.

2 x 400 g cans chickpeas
1/4 onion
2 garlic cloves
about 15 g (1/2 oz) fresh flat-leaf parsley leaves
about 15 g (1/2 oz) fresh coriander leaves
1 teaspoon ground cumin
1 tablespoon lemon juice
salt and freshly ground black pepper
1/2 beaten egg
1–2 tablespoons olive oil
fresh flat-leaf parsley, coriander or mint sprigs, to serve

Dressing
1 small handful of fresh mint
1 garlic clove
1 x 200 g carton 0% fat Greek yogurt

Serves 4–6

Preparation time: 20 minutes, plus chilling time
Cooking time: 20 minutes

Variation

Felafels make good cocktail appetizers. Shape the mixture into 40 small patties and bake for the same length of time as the larger felafels in the main recipe. Before serving, top each one with a small spoonful of yogurt dressing and a tiny mint sprig.

1 Drain and rinse the chickpeas, then work them in a food processor or blender with the remaining ingredients except the egg and oil. Turn the mixture into a bowl and beat in the egg, then cover and chill in the refrigerator for 30–60 minutes, or longer if more convenient. Meanwhile, preheat the oven to 180°C (350°F) Gas 4.

2 With wet hands, shape the mixture into 20 equal-size balls. Place the felafels on an oiled baking sheet and flatten them slightly, then brush them with more oil. Bake for 20 minutes, turning them over halfway.

3 Meanwhile, make the dressing. Work the mint, garlic and yogurt in the food processor or blender, turn into a bowl and add salt and pepper to taste.

To Serve Place the felafels on a serving platter and spoon the dressing over them. Serve hot, garnished with parsley, coriander or mint.

TAGLIATELLE WITH FENNEL, PEPPER AND TOMATO SAUCE

This pasta dish is full of Mediterranean flavour – from the fennel, peppers and tomatoes. Serve it for a vegetarian main course with warm olive focaccia or ciabatta and a tossed green salad.

Serves 4

Preparation time: 20 minutes
Cooking time: 30 minutes

- 2 fennel bulbs
- 1 red pepper
- 1 small onion
- 2 garlic cloves
- 1–2 tablespoons olive oil
- 1 x 400 g can chopped tomatoes
- salt and freshly ground black pepper
- 500 g (1 lb) fresh tagliatelle
- grated Parmesan or pecorino cheese, to serve (optional)

1 Trim and halve the fennel bulbs, then cut the fennel into strips about 2 cm (3/4 inch) wide. Halve the red pepper and remove the core and seeds. Thinly slice the onion. Crush the garlic.

2 Preheat the grill. Heat the oil in a medium saucepan, add the onion and garlic and fry gently for 5 minutes or until softened but not coloured. Add the tomatoes and season generously with salt and pepper, then cover and simmer gently for 20 minutes.

3 Meanwhile, put the red pepper in the grill pan and place under the grill for 5–8 minutes until the skin is charred and blistered. Remove and place in a plastic bag to cool slightly. Grill the strips of fennel for 5 minutes or until they are golden brown.

4 Peel off the pepper skin and slice the flesh into strips. Add to the tomato sauce with the fennel.

5 Cook the tagliatelle in salted boiling water for 2–3 minutes or according to packet instructions. Drain well and tip into a warm large bowl. Add the tomato sauce and toss to coat.

To Serve Divide the pasta and sauce between warm soup plates and serve immediately, with grated cheese if you like.

Variations

Use 2 large red, orange or yellow peppers instead of the fennel.

◆

Use another pasta shape instead of the tagliatelle. The sauce is chunky and robust, best suited to a wide ribbon noodle like pappardelle, or short shapes like penne (quills) or penne rigate (ridged quills).

Smoky courgette and pecorino pasta

The strong, summery flavours of chargrilled courgettes and basil go well with salty pecorino and tangy lime. Serve for a quick, midweek supper with chunky Italian bread like focaccia or ciabatta.

Serves 4

Preparation time: 15 minutes
Cooking time: 15–20 minutes

2 small courgettes
90 g (3 oz) pecorino cheese
4 tablespoons extra virgin olive oil, or more to taste
juice of 1 lime
salt and freshly ground black pepper
375 g (3/4 lb) fresh or dried pappardelle
3 tablespoons fresh basil leaves

1 Heat a ridged cast iron griddle pan until very hot. Meanwhile, top and tail the courgettes, then slice them along their length into thin strips. Shave the cheese into ribbons with a potato peeler.

2 Brush about 1 tablespoon olive oil over the courgette strips, then place them on the pan in batches and chargrill for 1–2 minutes each batch. Turn them with tongs until they are tender and lightly charred on all sides, then transfer them to a bowl.

3 Mix another tablespoon of oil with the lime juice and plenty of seasoning. Drizzle over the courgettes, cover and set aside.

4 Cook the pasta in salted boiling water according to packet instructions until al dente. Drain and turn into a warm large serving bowl. Add the courgette ribbons and marinade and three-quarters of the basil leaves. Toss gently to mix, then add more oil and seasoning according to taste.

To Serve Top with the pecorino cheese and the remaining basil leaves and serve immediately.

Chef's Tips

Pecorino is a hard Italian cheese similar to Parmesan, but with a slightly sharper, saltier flavour. It is made from sheep's milk.

◆

Pappardelle are a wide, flat ribbon pasta which originated in Tuscany. Traditional pappardelle have wavy edges, but nowadays they are often made with straight edges. You can get them fresh and dried, and they are usually made with egg.

◆

Variation

If you prefer, use lemon instead of lime. It tastes slightly less sharp.

Mushroom risotto cakes

These make a very tasty vegetarian lunch served with a salad. Made into balls half the size, they are also good for a first course served with a salsa or dip. Tiny balls can be served on cocktail sticks with drinks.

125 g (4 oz) button or chestnut mushrooms
60 g (2 oz) leek
1 garlic clove
10–12 fresh thyme sprigs
2 tablespoons olive oil
150 g (5 oz) risotto rice
600 ml (1 pint) hot vegetable stock
salt and freshly ground black pepper
1 egg, beaten
about 125 g (4 oz) fresh wholemeal breadcrumbs
lemon wedges and fresh thyme sprigs, to serve

Serves 4

Preparation time: 15 minutes, plus cooling time
Cooking time: 50 minutes

1 Finely chop the mushrooms, leek and garlic. Strip the leaves from the sprigs of thyme and chop them finely.

2 Heat the oil in a non-stick frying pan and gently fry the chopped mushrooms, leek and garlic until soft. Add the rice and stir over low to moderate heat for 1–2 minutes, then pour in about one-third of the stock and stir well. Season to taste, then simmer uncovered until the stock is absorbed, stirring frequently. Add the remaining stock in two stages and continue to simmer and stir until all the liquid has been absorbed and the rice is tender and quite dry, 15–20 minutes.

3 Remove the pan from the heat and stir in the thyme. Taste for seasoning. Turn the risotto out on to a large plate or tray and spread it out flat. Leave to cool slightly, 20–30 minutes. Meanwhile, preheat the oven to 180°C (350°F) Gas 4.

4 With wet hands, divide the risotto into 8–12 equal-size balls, squeezing them so that the rice compresses together. Flatten each one slightly, then dip into the beaten egg and then the breadcrumbs.

5 Put the risotto cakes on an oiled baking tray and bake in the oven for 20 minutes or until crisp and golden in colour.

To Serve Transfer the risotto cakes to individual plates, garnish with lemon and thyme and serve warm.

Chef's Tips

Risotto rice has short, round grains which absorb liquid slowly to become plump and soft with a nutty bite. You will find it at the supermarket labelled as risotto, arborio or carnaroli rice. At Italian delicatessens you may get even more of a choice – ask the shopkeeper for advice.

◆

Chop the vegetables and thyme in a food processor. Not only to save time, but to get the very fine texture that is best for these cakes.

◆

These are best served warm. They can be prepared ahead up to the end of step 4.

Smoked salmon and asparagus linguine

A lemony light hollandaise sauce is used to coat thin strands of linguine pasta. Combined with smoked salmon and fresh asparagus, it makes the perfect dish for a Spring lunch or supper.

150 g (5 oz) fine asparagus
175 g (6 oz) smoked salmon trimmings
salt and freshly ground black pepper
2 eggs
juice of $^1/_2$ lemon
2 tablespoons chopped fresh dill
300 g (10 oz) fresh linguine

Serves 3–4

Preparation time: 15–20 minutes
Cooking time: 15 minutes

1 Trim any tough ends off the asparagus, then cut the asparagus into 5 cm (2 inch) lengths. Cut the salmon into thin strips.

2 Cook the asparagus in salted boiling water until just tender to the tip of a knife. This will take 2–5 minutes, depending on thickness. Remove the asparagus with a slotted spoon and drain on kitchen paper. Keep the water hot in the pan.

3 Place the eggs and lemon juice in a round-bottomed bowl. Set the bowl over a pan of hot water, making sure the bottom of the bowl does not touch the water. Whisk the eggs until warmed, pale and very frothy. Season and stir in half the dill, then remove the bowl from the pan and set aside in a warm place.

4 Top up the asparagus water with boiling water and bring back to the boil, then add the linguine. Boil for 2–3 minutes or according to packet instructions until al dente.

5 Drain the linguine, reserving the water, then return the linguine to the pan. Add the asparagus and salmon with 1 ladleful of the water and the lemon sauce. Toss and add more water if necessary.

To Serve Transfer the linguine to warm bowls and sprinkle with the remaining dill. Serve immediately.

Chef's Tips

Smoked salmon trimmings, sometimes called 'cocktail salmon', are much cheaper than thinly sliced salmon, yet they are perfectly good enough for cooking. You can buy them in packets at supermarkets, delicatessens and fishmongers.

◆

Take care not to let the hollandaise get too hot or the eggs may scramble or curdle. They need to be just warm enough to thicken. Vigorous whisking is essential.

◆

Variation

For a special treat, whisk 1–2 tablespoons crème fraîche or whipping cream into the hollandaise after removing it from the heat.

Penne with honey roast squash

The bright orange, sweet flesh of butternut squash looks and tastes so good when roasted with honey, orange juice and mustard – and it mingles well with pasta and mature manchego cheese. Serve for a vegetarian main course.

1 butternut squash, weighing about 625 g (1 1/4 lb)
2 small courgettes
leaves of 1 fresh rosemary sprig
salt and freshly ground black pepper
1 tablespoon clear honey
1 tablespoon coarsegrain mustard
2 tablespoons orange juice
60 g (2 oz) manchego cheese
375 g (3/4 lb) fresh penne
100 ml (3 1/2 fl oz) hot vegetable stock
1 tablespoon extra virgin olive oil

Serves 4

Preparation time: 20 minutes
Cooking time: 40–50 minutes

1 Preheat the oven to 200°C (400°F) Gas 6. Cut the butternut squash into 2 cm (3/4 inch) chunks and remove the peel, seeds and fibres. Cut the courgettes into similar-size pieces. Place the vegetables in a large non-stick roasting tin. Scatter the rosemary leaves over the vegetables, then sprinkle with a little salt.

2 Mix the honey, mustard and orange juice in a small bowl. Pour over the vegetables and bake in the oven until the vegetables are tender in the centre and crisp around the edges, 40–50 minutes. Turn them gently once or twice during roasting so they colour evenly.

3 Meanwhile, thinly slice the cheese with a vegetable peeler. Cook the pasta in salted boiling water according to packet instructions until al dente.

4 Turn the roasted vegetables into a warm bowl and deglaze the roasting tin with the stock.

5 Drain the pasta and add to the vegetables with the deglazed pan juices. Toss well to mix, then taste for seasoning.

To Serve Transfer to warm bowls and sprinkle the oil and cheese over the top. Serve immediately.

Chef's Tips

Butternut squash is a pear-shaped squash with hard green skin and bright orange flesh. It is a winter vegetable, although it can be found at other times of year. Pumpkin can be used instead.

Manchego is a creamy yellow sheep's milk cheese from Spain with a mild, buttery flavour. You can buy it young and fresh, but for this recipe a mature, ripe manchego is most suitable. You could use Gruyère or Emmental instead, both of which also melt well over hot pasta.

Fresh herb risotto

This is a versatile risotto, delicious in spring or summer when soft and leafy fresh herbs have their best flavour, but it can also be made in winter with a change of herbs. Serve it as a first course for 6 people, or as a main course for four.

Serves 4–6

Preparation time: 10 minutes
Cooking time: 25–30 minutes

1 onion
2 garlic cloves
1 tablespoon olive oil
250 g (8 oz) risotto rice
125 ml (4 fl oz) dry white wine
900 ml (1½ pints) hot vegetable stock
salt and freshly ground black pepper
3 tablespoons chopped mixed fresh herbs
grated rind of 1 lemon

1 Finely chop the onion and garlic. Heat the oil in a medium saucepan and gently cook the onion and garlic until soft. Add the rice and stir over low to moderate heat for 1–2 minutes, then pour in the wine and let it sizzle.

2 Pour in one-third of the stock and stir well. Season to taste, then simmer until the stock is absorbed, stirring frequently. Add the remaining stock in two stages and continue to simmer and stir until all the liquid has been absorbed and the rice is tender, 15–20 minutes.

3 Remove from the heat and stir in 2 tablespoons of the fresh herbs and the lemon rind. Season well.

To Serve Divide the risotto equally between warm soup plates and sprinkle with the remaining herbs. Serve immediately.

Chef's Tip

Summer herbs, such as basil, oregano, marjoram and parsley, are all good choices and you can use just one or two of them or a mixture. In the winter, you could use parsley, sage or thyme, but take care not to use too much sage because it has a strong flavour.

Summer pea and sage risotto

Risottos make ideal summer food because they are quick to make. Freshly shelled peas are sweet at the beginning of the season, so make this risotto in early summer as soon as you see them in the shops.

500 g (1 lb) young fresh peas, unshelled weight
3 fresh sage sprigs
6 white peppercorns
salt and freshly ground black pepper
1 white onion
1 teaspoon pink peppercorns
2 tablespoons olive oil
300 g (10 oz) risotto rice
100 ml (3½ fl oz) dry white wine
4 tablespoons low-fat crème fraîche or soured cream, to serve

Serves 4

Preparation time: 10 minutes
Cooking time: 30 minutes

1 Shell the peas. Wash the pea pods and place them in a large saucepan. Add 1.5 litres (2½ pints) cold water, 2 whole sage sprigs, the white peppercorns and a pinch of salt. Bring to the boil and simmer for 5 minutes, then strain the stock into another saucepan. Discard the pea pods and flavourings and keep the stock hot.

2 Finely chop the onion. Crush the pink peppercorns. Strip the leaves off the remaining sage sprig and set aside some small whole leaves for the garnish. Finely chop the rest.

3 Heat the oil in a heavy saucepan and sweat the onion over low heat for about 5 minutes without colouring. Add the rice and stir for about 2 minutes. Add the wine and simmer until evaporated. Stir in the peppercorns, chopped sage and salt and pepper to taste.

4 Begin to add the hot stock to the rice a ladleful at a time, stirring between each addition until the rice has absorbed the liquid. Add the peas after about 10 minutes, then continue adding stock and stirring for another 10 minutes or until the rice is al dente and the consistency of the risotto is creamy. You may not need all of the liquid.

To Serve Taste the risotto for seasoning, then divide between warm soup plates. Top each serving with a spoonful of crème fraîche and a few sage leaves. Serve immediately.

Variation

To make a light main course meal for 4 people, top each serving with a poached egg. Bring a wide sauté pan of water to the boil and stir in 1 tablespoon white wine vinegar. Gently break 4 eggs into the water. Remove from the heat, cover and leave to stand for 3–4 minutes until the eggs are softly poached.

Wild rice and tomato salad

The contrasting colours of the black, red and green ingredients in this simple salad make it look dramatic. Serve it as a side dish to hot chargrilled or barbecued meat – it goes well with chicken or steak.

90 g (3 oz) wild rice
salt and freshly ground black pepper
6–8 sun-dried tomatoes
125 g (4 oz) cherry tomatoes
about 125 g (4 oz) lamb's lettuce, to serve

Dressing
2 teaspoons honey
2 tablespoons balsamic vinegar
1 tablespoon walnut oil
1 tablespoon olive oil

Serves 4

Preparation time: 15 minutes
Cooking time: 45–50 minutes

1 Cook the wild rice in plenty of salted boiling water for about 45–50 minutes or until tender. Drain into a sieve and rinse under the cold tap until the rice is cold. Allow to drain thoroughly.

2 Slice the sun-dried tomatoes and halve the cherry tomatoes. Put them in a large bowl, add the wild rice and toss to mix.

3 Make the dressing. In a small bowl, mix together the honey, vinegar and oils with salt and pepper to taste.

To Serve Line a shallow serving dish with the lamb's lettuce, pile the rice and tomato salad in the centre and drizzle the dressing over. Serve at room temperature.

Chef's Tips

Wild rice is not a rice at all, but an aquatic grass which looks like brown-black grains of rice. It can be used instead of rice whenever you want a change of colour, but it takes longer to cook – and it costs more. Its nutty flavour and striking good looks make it well worth the extra expense.

◆

Lamb's lettuce is also called mâche. It has pretty little leaves and a delicate flavour, and is often sold in small bunches at greengrocers. Some supermarkets sell it ready trimmed and washed in small plastic boxes or packets.

CHICKPEA, RED ONION AND CORIANDER SALAD

Chickpeas are a favourite pulse with vegetarians because they have a crunchy bite and a nutty flavour that goes well with so many different ingredients. This simple salad is bursting with zingy flavours. Serve it with warm wholemeal pitta bread.

250 g (8 oz) chickpeas, soaked in cold water overnight
4 tablespoons extra virgin olive oil
juice of 1 lemon
salt and freshly ground black pepper
1 red onion
1 bunch of fresh coriander
2 garlic cloves

Serves 4

Preparation time: 20 minutes, plus soaking time
Cooking time: about 2 hours

1 Drain and rinse the chickpeas, place them in a saucepan of fresh cold water and bring to the boil. Skim off any scum, then half cover and simmer for 1½–2 hours or until tender, stirring and topping up the water level as needed.

2 Drain the chickpeas and place them in a large bowl. Add the oil, lemon juice and salt and pepper to taste and toss well.

3 Cut a few thin rings from the onion and set aside. Roughly chop the rest. Roughly chop the coriander and garlic. Add the chopped onion, garlic and coriander to the chickpeas, toss to mix thoroughly, then taste for seasoning.

To Serve Turn the salad into a large serving bowl and garnish with the reserved red onion rings. Serve as soon as possible.

Chef's Tip

Serve with wedges of your favourite cheese for a vegetarian main course, or with canned tuna for non-vegetarians.

Variation

Use two 400 g cans chickpeas instead of dried peas. Drain and rinse them well, then heat them through in the olive oil, lemon juice and seasoning before adding the remaining ingredients.

Butter beans with broccoli and tomato

Sweet juicy plum tomatoes are roasted with garlic and fresh herbs, then tossed with creamy butter beans and tender-crisp broccoli florets to make a tasty vegetarian main course. Serve with nutty brown rice for a nutritious meal.

125 ml (4 fl oz) olive oil
250 g (8 oz) dried butter beans, soaked in cold water overnight
500 g (1 lb) ripe plum tomatoes
2 garlic cloves
1 tablespoon fresh thyme leaves
2 teaspoons fresh marjoram leaves
salt and freshly ground black pepper
juice of 1/2 lemon
250–300 g (8–10 oz) broccoli florets

Serves 6

Preparation time: 20 minutes, plus soaking time
Cooking time: about 1 1/2 hours

1 Preheat the oven 180°C (350°F) Gas 4. Brush a non-stick roasting tin lightly with oil. Drain and rinse the butter beans, place them in a saucepan of fresh cold water and bring to the boil. Skim off any scum, then half cover and simmer for 1 1/4 hours or until tender, stirring and topping up the water level as needed.

2 While the beans are cooking, halve the tomatoes lengthways and scoop out the seeds. Place them cut side uppermost in the roasting tin. Roughly chop the garlic and herbs and sprinkle them evenly over the tomatoes with salt and pepper to taste. Drizzle with half the remaining oil, then roast for 1 hour.

3 Drain the beans and place them in a large bowl with the lemon juice, the remaining oil and plenty of salt and pepper. Turn the beans in the dressing until evenly coated. Add the tomatoes and toss to mix thoroughly.

4 Plunge the broccoli florets into a saucepan of salted boiling water and boil for 3 minutes until cooked but still quite crisp. Drain thoroughly and pat dry with kitchen paper or a cloth, then add to the beans and tomatoes and toss gently to mix.

To Serve Taste for seasoning, then transfer to a warm serving dish. Serve warm.

Variations

Use two 400 g cans butter beans instead of dried beans. Drain and rinse them well, then heat them through in the lemon juice and olive oil before tossing them with the roasted tomatoes.

As an alternative to butter beans, dried white kidney or haricot beans can be used, or two 400 g cans cannellini beans.

Vegetable paella

Fennel, shallots and tomatoes replace the usual chicken and shellfish in this vegetarian version of paella, which is subtly spiced with coriander. Serve it as a main course for lunch or dinner, with crusty farmhouse bread and a leafy green side salad.

- 3 tablespoons olive oil
- 2 small fennel bulbs
- 200–250 g (7–8 oz) cherry tomatoes
- 2 teaspoons coriander seeds
- salt and freshly ground black pepper
- 900 ml (1½ pints) hot vegetable stock
- 100 g (3½ oz) wild rice
- 200 g (7 oz) long-grain white rice
- 2 tablespoons chopped fresh coriander
- juice of ½–1 lemon, to taste

Serves 4

Preparation time: 15 minutes

Cooking time: 50–55 minutes

Variation

Use all white rice instead of the mixture of wild and white rice, and colour it yellow by adding a good pinch of saffron threads to the water at the beginning of boiling.

1 Preheat the oven to 200°C (400°F) Gas 6. Brush a non-stick roasting tin lightly with oil. Cut each fennel bulb lengthways into eighths, leaving a little trimmed stalk attached to the base of each section to hold it together. Peel the shallots and halve them lengthways, or quarter them if they are large. Halve the tomatoes. Lightly crush the coriander seeds.

2 Place the vegetables in the roasting tin and sprinkle the coriander seeds and salt and pepper to taste over them. Roast the vegetables, turning them once or twice, for about 40 minutes or until tender.

3 Meanwhile, bring the stock to the boil in a large saucepan. Add the wild rice and simmer for 30 minutes, then add the white rice and continue to cook for 15–20 minutes or until both types of rice are tender. Drain, retaining a little moisture.

To Serve Turn the rice and roasted vegetables into a large bowl and toss to mix. Add the chopped coriander and the juice of ½ lemon, then taste for seasoning and add more lemon juice if you like. Serve hot.

Pasta alla diavola

Alla diavola means 'devilled', a name sometimes used to describe dishes containing chillies. Often such dishes come from southern Italy and Sicily, a legacy from the days when the Arabs settled there.

250 g (8 oz) spaghetti or other pasta of your choice
salt and freshly ground black pepper
flesh from a few cloves of Roasted Garlic (page 348)
8 tablespoons olive oil
¼–½ teaspoon crushed dried chillies, or to taste
freshly grated Parmesan cheese, to serve

Serves 2

Preparation time: 5 minutes, plus time to make the roasted garlic
Cooking time: 10–12 minutes

1 Cook the pasta in salted boiling water according to packet instructions.

2 Meanwhile, put the roasted garlic flesh in a bowl with the olive oil and mash with a fork.

3 Drain the pasta. Heat the garlic oil in the pan in which the pasta was cooked. Add the pasta and chillies and quickly toss together. Taste for seasoning.

To Serve Divide the pasta equally between 2 warm bowls and serve immediately, topped with Parmesan.

Chef's Tip

This simple pasta dish should be made with a good quality, cold-pressed virgin olive oil. There are very few other ingredients, so the fruity flavour of the oil can be fully appreciated.

Pasta with Italian Sausage and Aubergines

This hearty pasta dish comes from northern Italy, where robustly flavoured meat sauces are very popular. If you are a vegetarian, just omit the sausages – the sauce tastes good with or without them.

Serves 3–4

Preparation time: 10 minutes
Cooking time: about 30 minutes

1 small onion
2 garlic cloves
1 aubergine, weighing about 150 g (5 oz)
3 tablespoons olive oil
about 175 g (6 oz) Italian sausages
salt and freshly ground black pepper
1 x 400 g can chopped tomatoes
1 tablespoon tomato purée
250–375 g (8–12 oz) pasta
freshly grated Parmesan cheese, to serve

1 Finely chop the onion and garlic, keeping them separate. Halve and dice the aubergine. Heat 1 tablespoon of the oil in a sauté pan and brown the sausages in it. Remove them with a slotted spoon and set aside on kitchen paper.

2 Heat the remaining oil in the pan, add the onion and cook over low heat until softened, then add the aubergine and garlic with a good pinch of salt. Stir over moderate heat until the aubergine begins to soften and colour.

3 Add the tomatoes, tomato purée and 175 ml (6 fl oz) water. Bring to a simmer and cook for 10 minutes, stirring occasionally. Meanwhile, cook the pasta in salted boiling water according to packet instructions.

4 Cut the sausages into thick slices and add to the sauce. Cook for 5–10 minutes more, then season to taste.

To Serve Drain the pasta and turn it into a warm bowl. Pour the sauce over the pasta and toss to mix. Serve immediately, with Parmesan cheese.

Chef's Tip

Italian sausages can be found in some large supermarkets, but for the best choice go to an Italian delicatessen and ask for salsiccia puro suino – fresh pure pork sausage. It comes in many different shapes and sizes, and can be mild or spicy. Luganega is a popular variety that is easy to find. You can of course use other sausages if you prefer.

Pasta alle vongole

Many traditional Italian recipes use fresh clams. For speed and convenience, bottled clams are used here – a handy storecupboard item that Italian cooks tend to rely on a lot.

250 g (8 oz) pasta
salt and freshly ground black pepper
2–3 garlic cloves
1 x 200 g can or jar clams in brine
6 tablespoons olive oil
3–4 tablespoons finely chopped fresh flat-leaf parsley, to serve

Serves 2

Preparation time: 5 minutes
Cooking time: 10–12 minutes

1 Cook the pasta in salted boiling, water according to packet instructions.

2 Meanwhile, finely chop the garlic and drain and roughly chop the clams. Heat the oil in a saucepan, add the garlic and cook over very low heat for 1–2 minutes. Stir constantly and watch carefully so that the garlic does not brown.

3 Add the chopped clams, stir and season well.

To Serve Drain the pasta and return it to the pan. Add the clam sauce and chopped parsley and toss to mix. Serve immediately, in warm bowls.

Chef's Tips

In Italy, clam sauce is usually served with a long thin pasta such as linguine, spaghetti or spaghettini, but you can use any pasta shape you like.

◆

Take care not to boil the clams or they may become rubbery. They are already cooked, and only need heating through.

◆

Variation

If you like tomato sauce with clams, add 1 x 400 g can chopped tomatoes after softening the garlic and cook for about 10 minutes. A splash of dry white wine can also be added, whether you use tomatoes or not.

Risotto with Peas and Prosciutto

A risotto is the ideal dish for a midweek evening meal because it is so quick to prepare and cook. If you have friends round, serve it with crusty ciabatta, some Italian cheese and a tossed green salad – and a bottle of Italian wine of course.

Serves 2–3

Preparation time: 10 minutes
Cooking time: 20–25 minutes

1 small onion
125 g (4 oz) prosciutto (Parma ham)
800–900 ml (1⅓–1½ pints) hot chicken or vegetable stock
1 fresh thyme sprig
1 bay leaf
90 g (3 oz) butter
200 g (7 oz) short grain risotto rice (arborio or carnaroli)
125 ml (4 fl oz) dry white wine
125 g (4 oz) frozen peas
salt and freshly ground black pepper
fresh Parmesan cheese shavings, to serve

1 Finely chop the onion. Cut the prosciutto into thin strips. Bring the stock to the boil in a saucepan with the thyme and bay leaf and keep at simmering point.

2 Melt the butter in a heavy flameproof casserole, add the onion and cook over moderate heat until soft. Add the rice and stir for 1–2 minutes until the grains are coated in butter.

3 Add the wine. Stir until the liquid has been absorbed completely, then begin adding the simmering stock a ladleful at a time, allowing the rice to absorb the stock before adding more. Once half the stock has been absorbed, add the frozen peas, then continue cooking and adding more stock until the rice is al dente. The consistency should be moist and creamy, but not too runny.

To Serve Stir in the prosciutto and seasoning to taste. Remove from the heat and allow to rest for about 2 minutes. Serve topped with Parmesan cheese shavings.

Variation

Substitute 2 Italian sausages for the prosciutto and 1 red and 1 green pepper for the peas. Remove the casings from the sausages and dice the peppers. Fry the meat from the sausages with the onion until browned, add the peppers and continue as described in the recipe. Stir in 2 tablespoons shredded fresh basil just before serving.

Polenta

Rings of fried polenta make an excellent accompaniment to saucy stews and casseroles, or a tasty side dish to eggs and bacon for brunch. For a first course or snack, they taste superb with a rich tomato sauce.

- 125 g (4 oz) instant polenta
- 1 tablespoon grated Parmesan cheese
- 15 g (½ oz) butter
- salt and freshly ground black pepper
- olive oil, for frying

Serves 4

Preparation time: 5 minutes plus cooling and chilling
Cooking time: about 3 minutes

1 Cook the polenta according to the instructions on the packet. Once cooked, mix in the Parmesan and butter, then season to taste. Turn the polenta out onto a sheet of cling film, leave until just cool enough to handle, then roll it into a tight log and twist the ends. Allow to cool completely, then chill in the refrigerator until firm.

2 Unwrap the chilled polenta roll and cut it into 1.25 cm (½ inch) thick slices. Fry in hot olive oil in a non-stick frying pan until golden brown on both sides, turning once. The polenta should be firm and crisp on the outside but moist on the inside.

To Serve Remove from the pan with a fish slice, drain on kitchen paper, then arrange on a warm platter. Serve immediately.

Chef's Tip

Double-check the packet of polenta before buying – instant or pre-cooked polenta cooks in about 3 minutes and is virtually foolproof. Other types can take up to 20 minutes and are diffcult to get smooth if you are not used to cooking polenta regularly. The usual amount of water is 500 ml (16 fl oz) to 125 g (4 oz) polenta, but always read the instructions on the packet before you start.

Variation

Top the rings of polenta with sliced goat's cheese or grated Parmesan, Gruyère or Emmenthal, and melt under the grill.

Rice pilaf

Basmati rice is given extra flavour and texture with the addition of onion, pistachio nuts and raisins. An ideal accompaniment for Indian curries and other dishes that are cooked in a sauce, it is also good with kebabs and grilled chicken.

1 small onion
90 g (3 oz) shelled pistachio nuts
2 tablespoons olive oil
250 g (8 oz) basmati rice
500 ml (16 fl oz) hot vegetable or chicken stock
salt and freshly ground black pepper
15 g (½ oz) butter
90 g (3 oz) raisins or currants

Serves 4

Preparation time: 5 minutes
Cooking time: about 30 minutes

1 Finely chop the onion. Shred the pistachios. Heat the oil in a saucepan, add the onion and cook over low heat for 3–5 minutes until softened and lightly coloured.

2 Add the rice and stir for 2–3 minutes until mixed with the onion. Slowly pour in the stock, stir to mix, then bring to the boil. Cover the pan and simmer gently for 20 minutes without lifting the lid.

3 Lift the lid and fork the rice through. Add the butter, pistachios and raisins or currants and fork through until evenly mixed. Season to taste.

To Serve Turn into a warm serving bowl and serve hot.

Chef's Tips

Before cooking basmati rice, read the instructions on the packet. Some varieties need to be rinsed in a sieve under cold running water until the water runs clear. This helps to keep the grains separate.

◆

If you are cooking other things on the top of the stove, you may find it easier to cook the pilaf in the oven. Make it in a flameproof casserole, cover with the lid and cook at 190°C (375°F) Gas 5 for 20 minutes.

◆

Variation

For a touch of colour and spice, add a pinch or two of turmeric or saffron threads or powder after pouring in the stock in step 2.

Pasta salad with Mediterranean vegetables

This tasty salad is perfect for picnics and other al fresco meals. It is best made the day before, to allow time for the different flavours to mingle and mellow, and will keep for 2–3 days in an airtight container in the refrigerator.

Serves 4–6

Preparation time: 20 minutes
plus chilling
Cooking time: 40– 50 minutes

- 1 aubergine, weighing about 250 g (8 oz)
- 1 large courgette, weighing about 250 g (8 oz)
- 2 large peppers (red and yellow)
- 2 garlic cloves
- 4 tablespoons olive oil
- 125 g (4 oz) dried pasta shapes
- 1 large handful of fresh basil
- 2 tablespoons bottled or homemade red pesto
- 2 tablespoons balsamic vinegar
- salt and freshly ground black pepper
- 100 ml (3½ fl oz) olive oil

1 Preheat the oven to 190°C (375°F) Gas 5. Cut the vegetables into large chunks, discarding the cores, seeds and spongy ribs from the peppers. Roughly chop the garlic. Place the vegetables in a roasting tin, add the garlic and olive oil and toss to combine. Roast for 40–50 minutes, turning the vegetables several times.

2 Meanwhile, cook the pasta according to the instructions on the packet. Make the dressing. Place the pesto in a large bowl with the vinegar and 1 tablespoon cold water. Whisk to mix, season to taste with salt and pepper, then whisk in the olive oil.

3 Drain the pasta well, then add it to the bowl of dressing while it is still hot. Toss lightly but thoroughly until all the pasta shapes are coated.

4 When the vegetables are cooked, add them to the pasta and dressing and toss to combine. Set aside until cool, then cover the bowl with cling film and refrigerate for at least 4 hours, preferably overnight.

To Serve Let stand at room temperature for about 1 hour, then mix the salad well to redistribute the dressing. Taste for seasoning. Shred or tear the basil and add to the salad at the last moment. Serve as a side salad, or as a vegetarian first or main course with hot garlic bread.

Chef's Tip

Red pesto is made from sun-dried tomatoes. You can make it yourself as on page 349, or buy it at most supermarkets and delicatessens. It usually comes in a 190 g jar. After opening and using, cover the top of the pesto with a thin film of olive oil, seal the jar and keep it in the refrigerator. Red pesto is excellent tossed with hot cheese-stuffed ravioli for a quick meal, or spread on toasted bread, topped with sliced or grated cheese and popped under the grill.

Couscous salad with prawns

A main course salad that is both colourful and full of flavour. Serve with crusty bread for a summer al fresco meal. For vegetarians or to serve as a side salad, simply omit the prawns.

Serves 6

Preparation time: about 30 minutes

- 200 g (7 oz) quick-cooking couscous
- 2–3 firm tomatoes, total weight about 250 g (8 oz)
- 2 peppers (red and yellow), each weighing about 150 g (5 oz)
- 1–2 garlic cloves, to taste
- 250 g (8 oz) peeled cooked prawns, thawed if frozen
- juice of 2 limes
- salt and freshly ground black pepper
- 150 ml (¼ pint) extra-virgin olive oil
- 1 large handful of fresh coriander or mint

1 Put the couscous in a large bowl and pour boiling water over to cover the grains by about 2.5 cm (1 inch). Leave to soak for about 20 minutes, fluffing up the grains with a fork halfway through.

2 Meanwhile, core, deseed and dice the tomatoes. Place them in a sieve to drain off excess liquid. Deseed the peppers and dice to the same size as the tomatoes. Crush the garlic. Dry the prawns thoroughly on kitchen paper.

3 Make the dressing. Whisk together the lime juice, garlic and salt and pepper until the salt has dissolved. Gradually whisk in the oil until it emulsifies. Finely chop about one-third of the coriander or mint and whisk into the dressing.

4 Roughly chop about three-quarters of the prawns and add to the couscous with the vegetables and dressing. Mix everything together well. Set aside one sprig of the remaining coriander or mint for the garnish, then coarsely chop the rest and mix it into the salad. Chill until serving time.

To Serve Stir the salad well and taste for seasoning, then turn into a serving bowl. Arrange the remaining whole prawns and the reserved herb sprig on top. Serve chilled or at room temperature.

Variations

Use bulgar wheat instead of couscous, preparing it according to the instructions on the packet.

◆

Roasted Peppers (page 348) can be used instead of fresh peppers.

◆

The prawns can be replaced with drained and flaked canned tuna.

◆

Fresh raw scallops or fish can be marinated in the dressing for up to 4 hours, then mixed into the salad instead of the prawns.

6

Desserts

Everyone loves dessert, even if they won't admit it. Chocolate, ice-cream, fresh fruit, pies and tarts, old-fashioned 'nursery' puddings, cheesecakes, crêpes and crumbles – who can resist? So even when you're very busy, take just a little time to plan dessert.

Fresh fruit is hard to beat because it is so refreshing, especially in summer when there is a wide choice in season. A platter of plump, ripe fruits looks sensational, and if they are locally grown they will probably have the flavour to match. The recipes in this chapter concentrate on fruit because it is so good for you, but there are lots of other recipes here also. For really quick and easy ideas, turn to pages 340–343 for desserts that you can put together in moments. If you choose to make a full-scale dessert, you will find many of the recipes can be made in advance and kept in the refrigerator until serving time – a bonus if you are entertaining. Offering two desserts is a nice touch if it is a special celebration or you are serving a crowd. Guests appreciate a choice and the possibility of a second helping, helping to bring the meal to a relaxed end.

With all foods, but particularly with desserts, presentation is key. A few fresh fruits look beautiful when arranged on a pretty plate or served in a fine glass bowl and a dusting of icing or caster sugar will lift even the plainest of puddings. Finishing touches add style to your presentation – try fresh herbs, strawberries with their hulls on or a single swirl of cream – these are all tricks used to dramatize desserts.

Lime cheeses with green fruit salad

The beauty of this dessert is that it looks and tastes cool and refreshing. The lime cheeses are exquisitely light, and the fruit salad a striking contrast. Serve for a dinner party in summer when galia melons are sweet and ripe.

1 x 250 g carton fromage frais
grated rind and juice of 2 limes
200 ml (7 fl oz) whipping cream
30–45 g (1–1½ oz) icing sugar, to taste
4 fresh mint sprigs, to serve

Fruit Salad
3 ripe kiwi fruit
1 small ripe galia melon

Serves 4

Preparation time: 20–30 minutes, plus chilling time

Variations

If galia melon is difficult to get, use another green-fleshed melon such as an ogen.

◆

In winter, use seedless green grapes or green-skinned apples instead of the melon.

1 Line four 150 ml (¼ pint) ramekins with cling film or dampened muslin, letting it hang over the edges.

2 Put the fromage frais and lime rind and juice in a bowl and beat well until smooth. Whip the cream until it just holds its shape and fold it into the cheese. Sift in icing sugar to taste.

3 Spoon the mixture into the ramekins, cover with the overhanging cling film or muslin and chill for up to 8 hours, preferably overnight.

4 A few hours before serving, prepare the fruit over a bowl to catch the juice. Peel the kiwi fruit and slice them into rounds or wedges. Halve the melon and scoop out the seeds, then scoop the flesh into balls with a melon baller or cut it into small chunks with a knife. Gently combine the fruit in a bowl with the juice, then cover and chill until serving time.

To Serve Unfold the cling film or muslin and place an inverted chilled plate on top of each ramekin. Turn the cheeses out on to the plates and remove the cling film. Spoon the fruit around, then top each serving with a sprig of mint. Serve chilled.

Wild strawberry creams

Wild strawberries go by the pretty French name of fraises des bois. They are tiny with an intense flavour, but they are only in season for a very short time in the summer. If you can't get them, use very small strawberries and slice them, or use raspberries.

4 tablespoons grenadine
4 eggs
60 g (2 oz) caster sugar
1/2 teaspoon vanilla extract
400 ml (14 fl oz) milk
90 g (3 oz) fraises des bois

To Serve
about 200 g (7 oz) fraises des bois
4 tablespoons grenadine
2 tablespoons caster sugar, or to taste

Serves 4

Preparation time: 20–30 minutes, plus cooling and chilling time
Cooking time: 30–40 minutes

1 Preheat the oven to 150°C (300°F) Gas 2. Pour 1 tablespoon grenadine into each of four 200 ml (7 fl oz) moulds.

2 Beat the eggs and sugar in a bowl with the vanilla extract. Scald the milk in a saucepan and slowly stir it into the egg mixture. Strain into a jug, then pour into the moulds. The grenadine will mix into the milk, but then sink back to the bottom. Hull the fraises des bois and divide them between the moulds. They will float.

3 Place the moulds gently in a bain marie of hot water and bake in the oven until just set, about 30–40 minutes. Leave to cool, then cover and chill in the refrigerator for at least 4 hours.

4 A few hours before serving, set aside 4 of the prettiest fraises des bois for the decoration. Hull the rest and place them in a bowl. Sprinkle with the grenadine and sugar to taste, cover and chill in the refrigerator until serving time.

To Serve Loosen the top of each set cream with your fingers or by running a knife around the edge. Invert a chilled plate over each mould, then turn the cream out on to the plate. Spoon the fraises des bois and juices over and around the creams and decorate the tops with reserved unhulled fraises des bois. Serve chilled.

Chef's Tips

Grenadine is a scarlet-red fruit syrup. It takes its name from the island of Grenada in the Caribbean, where it was originally made from pomegranate juice, but nowadays it is also made with other fruit juices. Check the label because sometimes it is alcoholic and sometimes not. You can use either. It is generally available at wine merchants and supermarkets, but if you can't get it you can use blackcurrant syrup or the blackcurrant liqueur, crème de cassis, instead.

◆

Dariole moulds or individual pudding basins are the best moulds to use because they have rounded bottoms, but ramekins or soufflé dishes can also be used.

Warm spiced pears

This is a classic winter dessert that never fails to please. It is simple, but it tastes superb. If you like, sprinkle the pears with a few toasted flaked almonds for a crunchy contrast in textures, and serve with chilled low-fat crème fraîche or natural yogurt.

250 g (8 oz) granulated sugar
250 ml (8 fl oz) red wine
1 cinnamon stick
5 cloves
pared rind of 1 orange
pared rind of 1 lemon
8 pears
juice of 1/2 lemon

Serves 4

Preparation time: 20–30 minutes
Cooking time: 50–55 minutes

1 Put the sugar in a saucepan and add 250 ml (8 fl oz) cold water. Heat gently until the sugar has dissolved, then increase the heat and boil for 1 minute. Add the wine, spices and citrus rinds and simmer for about 10 minutes.

2 Peel the pears. With a small, pointed vegetable peeler, remove the cores from the bottoms of the pears, leaving the stalks intact at the top. Immediately brush the pears with lemon juice, then lower them into the wine mixture. Cover with a circle of greaseproof paper and cook gently until tender, about 30–35 minutes. Remove from the heat and leave to cool until lukewarm.

3 Lift the pears carefully out of the spiced wine and place in serving bowls. Strain the cooking liquid into a clean pan and boil rapidly until reduced by about half.

To Serve Pour the spiced wine sauce over and around the pears and serve warm or cold.

Chef's Tips

One of the best varieties of pears for poaching is Conference. They are fairly small, with firm flesh that holds its shape well.

◆

If you like, serve the pears in bowls with wide rims and sift cocoa powder lightly over the edges.

ICED MINTED BLACKCURRANT SOUFFLÉS

The flavours of mint and blackcurrant go so well together in these tangy, creamy soufflés. They taste rich and delicious – like iced fruit mousses. Make them in high summer, when fresh blackcurrants are in season, and serve with crisp, sweet biscuits.

300 g (10 oz) blackcurrants
60 g (2 oz) granulated sugar
4 egg whites
175 g (6 oz) caster sugar
200 ml (7 fl oz) whipping cream
200 g (7 oz) natural bio yogurt or Greek yogurt
3 tablespoons crème de menthe
edible flowers and leaves, to decorate (optional)

Serves 8

Preparation time: 20–30 minutes, plus freezing time

1 Tie greaseproof paper collars around eight 100 ml (3½ fl oz) glass dishes or ramekins to come about 2.5 cm (1 inch) above the rims. Top and tail the blackcurrants.

2 Dissolve the granulated sugar in a saucepan in 100 ml (3½ fl oz) water. Add the blackcurrants and simmer for 3–4 minutes, then pour into a food processor or blender. Work to a purée, then pour through a sieve into a bowl to remove the skins and seeds.

3 Whisk the egg whites until stiff, then whisk in the caster sugar a little at a time to make a shiny meringue. Half whip the cream in a separate large bowl, then fold together with the blackcurrant purée, yogurt and liqueur. Fold in the meringue.

4 Pour into the prepared dishes or ramekins, level the surface and freeze until firm, at least 4 hours.

To Serve Untie and remove the paper collars, then decorate the tops of the soufflés with edible flowers and leaves if you like. Serve immediately.

Chef's Tip

Crème de menthe is a sweet, mint-flavoured liqueur, which may be green or white. You can use either, although the white crème de menthe is best because it will not alter the colour of the mixture.

Variation

Blackberries can be used instead of blackcurrants.

Peach and apricot terrine with muscat

Fruit jelly made with muscat wine is an excellent way to suspend pieces of fruit in a terrine. The flavour is pleasantly sweet and musky. Almonds provide a little crunch, which contrasts with the softness of the jelly, but they can be omitted if you prefer.

1 x 400 g can peaches in natural juice
1 x 400 g can apricots in natural juice
60 g (2 oz) whole blanched almonds
½ vanilla pod, split lengthways
250 ml (8 fl oz) sweet muscat wine
15 g (½ oz) gelatine powder
nasturtium flowers, to decorate

Serves 6

Preparation time: 30 minutes, plus cooling and chilling time

Chef's Tip

Muscat wine is a sweet dessert wine made from muscat grapes. Its colour varies but it is usually golden yellow or amber. Muscat de Beaumes-de-Venise and Rivesaltes are two well known muscat wines that are suitable for this recipe.

◆

Variation

Canned pears in natural juice can be used instead of either the peaches or apricots.

1 Drain the peaches and apricots into a sieve over a bowl to catch the juice. Cut the fruit into slices, not too small. Coarsely chop the almonds. Arrange half the fruit in a 1 kg (2 lb) non-stick loaf tin. Place the almonds on top and then the remaining fruit.

2 Pour the wine and 150 ml (¼ pint) of the reserved fruit juice into a saucepan and add the vanilla pod. Bring to the boil and simmer for about 5 minutes, then remove from the heat and leave to cool a little.

3 Sprinkle the gelatine powder over 100 ml (3½ fl oz) cold water in a small heatproof bowl. Leave for 5 minutes until spongy, then place the bowl in a saucepan of gently simmering water for a few minutes until the gelatine has dissolved.

4 Remove the vanilla pod from the cool wine, then pour in the dissolved gelatine. Stir to mix. Leave until just cold, then slowly pour it over the fruit. Cover and chill in the refrigerator overnight.

To Serve Invert a chilled plate over the loaf tin, then warm the loaf tin by covering it with a hot damp cloth. This will help release the jelly. Turn the jelly out on to the plate and slice with a hot knife. Arrange slices on dessert plates, decorate with nasturtium flowers and serve chilled.

Lemon and yogurt ice

This refreshing, tangy iced dessert is simplicity itself to make. It is good served plain, with dainty sweet biscuits, or you can top it with thinly sliced stem ginger or toasted shredded coconut.

200 ml (7 fl oz) whipping cream
500 g (1 lb) low-fat natural yogurt
125 g (4 oz) lemon curd

Serves 4

Preparation time: 10 minutes, plus freezing time

1 In a large bowl, half whip the cream until it just holds its shape. Add the yogurt and fold the two together until smooth. Streak through the lemon curd.

2 Pour the mixture into a freezer container, cover and freeze until firm, at least 4 hours.

To Serve Transfer the freezer container to the refrigerator for 10–15 minutes, then scoop into stemmed glasses. Serve immediately.

Chef's Tips

Greek yogurt is smooth and creamy, and there are many different types. One variety is 0% fat. Another good yogurt to use is bio yogurt.

◆

Use a good-quality, tangy lemon curd. Homemade is best.

Hot rum and citrus salad

The Caribbean meets the Far East in this spiced fruit salad, which combines citrus fruit with exotic mangoes and is subtly flavoured with star anise. Served warm with crisp, thin wafers, it is a very useful all-year-round recipe.

5 oranges
3 ruby or pink grapefruit
1 lemon
2 mangoes, slightly under ripe
100 g (3½ oz) soft brown sugar
100 ml (3½ fl oz) orange juice
4 tablespoons dark rum
4 star anise, plus extra to serve if liked

Serves 6–8

Preparation time: 20–30 minutes, plus infusing time

1 Peel and segment the oranges, grapefruit and lemon. Peel and stone the mangoes, then cut the flesh into pieces of a similar size to the citrus fruit. Put all of the fruit in a heatproof serving bowl.

2 Put the sugar in a saucepan, add 100 ml (3½ fl oz) cold water and heat gently until the sugar has dissolved. Add the orange juice, rum and star anise. Simmer for 10 minutes, then remove from the heat, cover and leave to infuse for 30 minutes.

To Serve Pour the syrup over the fruit. Decorate the top with star anise if you like (you can use the ones from the syrup) and serve warm.

Chef's Tip

To segment citrus fruit neatly, cut a thick slice off the top and bottom of the fruit, then cut off the peel all around so that no white pith remains on the fruit. With a small sharp knife, cut vertically between the flesh and the membranes, working all round the fruit until every segment has been released and you are left with just the core and membranes joined together.

Baked apples and figs

This is a versatile dessert, which can be made in summer or winter. Apples are in season all year round, fresh figs in the summer, so you can make it with both fruits when they are available – or with just one or the other.

4 small dessert apples
4 large fresh figs, not over ripe
60 g (2 oz) marzipan
1 tablespoon whole blanched almonds
1 small piece of stem ginger
1 tablespoon syrup from ginger jar

Amaretti Cream
10 amaretti biscuits
1 x 250 g carton low-fat fromage frais
1 tablespoon sifted icing sugar
1 tablespoon amaretto liqueur (optional)

Serves 4

Preparation time: 20–30 minutes
Cooking time: about 45 minutes

Chef's Tips

Golden Delicious are good dessert apples to use because they hold their shape well during baking.

Stem ginger is sold in small bottles in the baking sections of supermarkets and in delicatessens. It is sometimes labelled as 'preserved ginger in syrup'.

1 Preheat the oven to 180°C (350°F) Gas 4. Core the apples and score horizontally around their middles with the point of a sharp knife. Cut the figs lengthways almost through into quarters, leaving them intact at the base.

2 Finely chop the almonds. Very finely chop the ginger. Mix the marzipan, almonds, ginger and syrup until smooth and roll into 8 cylinders or balls. Place in the centre of each fruit.

3 Place the apples in a baking dish with 3 tablespoons cold water and bake for 30 minutes. Add the figs to the tray and bake for another 10–15 minutes or until both types of fruit are tender.

4 Meanwhile, roughly crush the amaretti biscuits and mix with the remaining ingredients for the amaretti cream.

To Serve Put 1 apple and 1 fig on each plate and top with a little of the cream. Serve hot, with the remaining cream handed separately.

Black cherry crêpes

Don't deny yourself treats like crêpes when you're eating light. If you make them with semi-skimmed milk and use a fruity, low-fat filling, they are healthy and light. This recipe makes 8 filled crêpes, which can serve 4–8 people.

375 g (3/4 lb) black cherries
1–2 tablespoons icing sugar, to taste
150 g (5 oz) low-fat natural yogurt or 0% fat Greek yogurt
2 teaspoons vegetable oil

Crêpe Batter
125 g (4 oz) plain flour
1 egg
about 300 ml (1/2 pint) semi-skimmed milk

Makes 8

Preparation time: 20 minutes, plus standing time
Cooking time: 20–35 minutes

1 First make the crêpe batter. Whisk together the flour, egg and 300 ml (1/2 pint) milk until smooth. Cover and set aside for 30 minutes.

2 Meanwhile, prepare the filling. Pit the cherries and halve or quarter them if they are large. Stir icing sugar to taste into the yogurt.

3 Brush a 15 cm (7 inch) non-stick crêpe pan very lightly with oil and heat until hot. Whisk the batter well, and thin it with a little milk if it is too thick. Pour one-eighth of the batter into the hot pan and swirl it around to cover the base. Cook for 1–2 minutes until golden underneath, then turn over and cook the other side. Turn the crêpe out of the pan, first side facing down, and keep warm. Repeat with the remaining mixture to make 8 crêpes altogether, adding more oil as necessary and stacking the crêpes on top of each other as they are done.

To Serve Place a spoonful of sweetened yogurt in the centre of each crêpe and top with a spoonful of cherries. Fold the crêpes into quarters and dust with a little icing sugar. Serve warm.

Chef's Tip

For a lump-free crêpe batter, use an electric mixer for whisking.

Variation

Fresh cherries have a very short season in June and July. When they are not available, use bottled cherries, preferably ones that have been macerated in kirsch.

Exotic fruit pavlovas

Pavlovas are incredibly simple to make and great for preparing ahead for a dinner party. Here, the tangy yogurt topping makes a refreshing alternative to the more traditional sweetened double cream, and the fresh fruit is juicy and luscious.

6 egg whites
375 g (3/4 lb) caster sugar
1 1/2 teaspoons white wine vinegar
2 pinches of cream of tartar

Topping
150 g (5 oz) ripe pineapple
1 large ripe mango
2 ripe peaches
1 x 200 g carton 0% fat Greek yogurt
2 teaspoons clear honey
1/2–1 teaspoon vanilla extract
1 ripe banana
juice of 1/4–1/2 lemon
2 passion fruit

Makes 12

Preparation time: 30 minutes
Cooking time: 45–60 minutes

1 First make the pavlovas. Preheat the oven to 150°C (300°F) Gas 2 and line a large baking sheet with non-stick baking parchment. Whisk the egg whites with an electric mixer until stiff, then gradually add the sugar and continue whisking until the meringue is shiny. Whisk in the vinegar and cream of tartar with the last amount of sugar.

2 Mound the meringue in 12 large egg shapes on the parchment. Bake for 45–60 minutes until crisp on the outside but still soft inside. Transfer the pavlovas to a wire rack and leave to cool.

3 Make the topping. Peel and stone the fruit as necessary and cut the flesh into small slices or cubes. If the pineapple has a fresh leafy top, reserve a few of the smaller leaves for decoration. Place the fruit in a bowl and stir gently to combine. In a separate bowl, mix together the yogurt, honey and vanilla extract. Peel and chop the banana and toss in a little lemon juice. Fold into the yogurt.

To Serve Spoon the yogurt mixture over the pavlovas, then the exotic fruit. Halve the passion fruit and scrape the seeds over the top. Decorate with pineapple leaves, if you have any.

Chef's Tips

To cube a mango, cut it lengthways into three, avoiding the central stone. Score the flesh of both stoneless sections in a lattice pattern, then push the peel inside out and cut off the cubes.

The pavlovas and yogurt topping can be prepared the day before required and kept in the refrigerator where they will go pleasantly squidgy and chewy. Top with the fruit 1–2 hours before serving.

Chilled fruit soup with Bandol wine

On a hot summer's day, chilled seasonal fruits steeped in sweetened wine are very refreshing, and they look sensational in a glass bowl. Serve with a jug of chilled low-fat crème fraîche, and some dainty crisp biscuits if you like.

1 x 75 cl bottle of Bandol wine
100 g (3½ oz) sugar
250 g (8 oz) cherries
375 g (¾ lb) strawberries
2 white peaches
few drops of lemon juice
125 g (4 oz) raspberries
finely shredded fresh mint leaves, to serve

Serves 4

Preparation time: 30 minutes, plus chilling time

Chef's Tip

Bandol wine comes from Provence. You can use red or rosé for this recipe, although you are most likely to find the rosé easiest to get. If you can't get Bandol, or you would prefer to use a less expensive wine, you can use any other rosé.

1 Pour the wine into a saucepan. Add the sugar and heat gently, stirring occasionally, until dissolved, then boil without stirring until reduced by half. Pour into a large bowl and leave to cool.

2 Cut the cherries in half and remove the stones. Hull the strawberries and cut them in half lengthways. Blanch the white peaches in boiling water for 15 seconds, then lift them out with a slotted spoon and peel off the skin. Cut the peaches in half and remove the stones, then slice the flesh.

3 Stir the lemon juice into the cold wine, then add the prepared fruit and the whole raspberries. Cover and chill in the refrigerator for at least 4 hours.

To Serve Transfer to a serving bowl and scatter finely shredded mint over the top. Serve well chilled.

Champagne granita

A granita is grainy as its name suggests. Like a water ice or slush, it is cool and very refreshing, just perfect for a hot summer's day. This one is very special, ideal as a dessert at the end of a celebration meal.

100 g (3½ oz) sugar
200 ml (7 fl oz) water
400 ml (14 fl oz) pink champagne

Serves 4

Preparation time: 20 minutes, plus freezing time

1 Put the sugar and water in a heavy saucepan and heat gently, stirring occasionally, until the sugar has dissolved, then boil without stirring until a light sugar syrup is formed (105°C on a sugar thermometer). Remove from the heat and leave to cool.

2 Open the bottle of champagne and pour it into a measuring jug, letting the bubbles subside until the liquid comes up to the 400 ml (14 fl oz) mark. Mix the champagne and sugar syrup together, pour into a freezerproof container and freeze overnight until firm.

To Serve Flake the granita into glasses and serve immediately.

Chef's Tip

If you have an ice-cream machine churn the granita in it until frozen, according to the manufacturer's instructions.

◆

Variation

Use a sparkling rosé wine instead of champagne – it is much less expensive.

Icebox cake

An American dessert, so called because 'icebox' was the original word for refrigerator. It needs to chill for at least 8 hours before serving, so it is the perfect dessert to make the day before a dinner party.

- 1 x 250 g (8 oz) punnet ripe strawberries
- 450 ml (¾ pint) double cream
- 1 x 250 g (8 oz) tub fresh mango slices
- 1 x 125 g (4 oz) punnet ripe raspberries
- 8 trifle sponges
- 4 tablespoons kirsch or brandy

Serves 6–8

Preparation time: 30 minutes plus chilling

1 Brush a 23 x 12.5 cm (9 x 5 inch) loaf tin very lightly with oil, then line with cling film, letting it overhang the sides. Set aside 6–8 whole strawberries and about 4 tablespoons of the cream for the decoration.

2 Hull and finely chop the remaining strawberries. Drain and finely chop the mango slices. Put the whole raspberries in a bowl, add the chopped fruit and stir to mix. Whip the remaining cream until thick but not buttery.

3 Place 4 trifle sponges side by side in the bottom of the loaf tin and sprinkle with half the kirsch or brandy. Cover with half the fruit mixture, then spread half the whipped cream over the fruit.

4 Repeat the layers, then cover with the overhanging cling film. Chill in the refrigerator for at least 8 hours, preferably overnight.

To Serve Run a palette knife between the cling film and the loaf tin, then unfold the cling film on the top and invert the cake onto a plate. Remove the tin and cling film. Whip the reserved cream and spread it over the top of the cake. Halve the reserved strawberries lengthways and place them cut-side down on the cream.

Chef's Tip

If you can't find ready prepared mango slices, you will need 1 medium mango to give 250 g (8 oz) flesh without the skin and stone.

◆

Variation

Use sponge fingers (boudoir biscuits) instead of trifle sponges. You will need 18–20, depending on the shape of your loaf tin – some tins are not straight-sided.

ETON MESS

What could be more English than strawberries and cream? This is a variation that was supposedly created at Eton, when the strawberries were overripe and too soft to serve whole.

2 x 250 g (8 oz) punnets ripe strawberries
2 tablespoons Cointreau
300 ml (½ pint) double or whipping cream
60 g (2 oz) ready made meringue

Serves 6

Preparation time: 15 minutes

1 Wash the strawberries and set aside the 6 best ones for decoration. Hull the rest of the strawberries and put them in a large bowl. Add the Cointreau and crush the strawberries lightly with a fork.

2 Whip the cream until it is thick enough to leave a ribbon trail. Fold it into the crushed strawberry and Cointreau mixture.

3 With your hands, lightly crush two-thirds of the meringue over the strawberry and cream mixture. Gently fold the meringue in with a rubber spatula or large metal spoon until it is evenly mixed.

To Serve Pile into 6 glass dishes or wine glasses and crush the remaining meringue over the top. Serve decorated with the reserved strawberries, using them whole, halved or fanned out.

Chef's Tips

This dessert was created for strawberries that are past their best, so only use really ripe fruit. It is intended to be eaten straight after making, but can be kept in the refrigerator for several hours before serving.

◆

You can buy ready made individual meringue nests, large meringue baskets and pavlova shells in boxes in supermarkets. They are all equally suitable for this recipe, but try to get the best quality. Some bought meringues, especially the snowy white ones, are too sugary sweet.

◆

Variation

Ripe raspberries can be used instead of strawberries. They do not need to be crushed.

CHOCOLATE VACHERIN

This simple trick of artful assembly is bound to impress your guests, and it takes no time at all to do. For an extra touch of luxury, pipe melted dark chocolate onto each plate before serving, as shown in the photograph.

1 litre (1¾ pints) chocolate ice-cream
2 x 90 g packets meringue nests
1 heaped teaspoon cocoa powder, to finish

Serves 8

Preparation time:
10–15 minutes

1 Allow the ice-cream to soften slightly at room temperature. Roughly crush the meringues with your hands.

2 Place about one-third of the meringue in a layer over the bottom of a 23 cm (9 inch) springform cake tin. Spread with half the ice-cream, pressing it down well with the back of a metal spoon or a small palette knife.

3 Cover with another layer of meringue, then spread with the remaining ice-cream. Top with the remaining meringue and freeze until ready to serve.

To Serve Run a palette knife between the vacherin and the tin, then unclip the side of the tin and lift off. Sift cocoa powder over the top layer of meringue. then transfer the vacherin to a cake stand or serving plate. Serve at once, in generous slices.

Chef's Tips

You can use any ice-cream or sorbet you like. If you use a fruit flavour, dust the top of the vacherin with icing sugar rather than cocoa powder.

◆

Buy ready made meringues from a good retailer or you will be disappointed with the result. Cheap meringues tend to be snowy white and very hard, and can taste quite synthetic.

Lemon cheesecake

The perfect cheesecake – rich and creamy, with a tangy kick from the lemon rind and juice. You can serve it plain, with thick pouring cream, or top it with seasonal fruits. It looks and tastes especially good with soft summer berries.

6 digestive biscuits
3 tablespoons caster sugar
30 g (1 oz) butter, melted
500 g (1 lb) cream cheese
150 g (5 oz) caster sugar
2 large eggs
grated rind and juice of 1 lemon
icing sugar, to serve

Serves 6–8

Preparation time: 20 minutes, plus chilling
Cooking time: 40 minutes

1 Preheat the oven to 170°C (325°F) Gas 3. Butter the inside of a 20 cm (8 inch) springform cake tin. Crush the biscuits finely in a food processor, mix in the sugar, then the melted butter. Press the mixture firmly into the bottom of the tin. Set aside.

2 Make the filling. Beat the cream cheese with an electric whisk to soften it, then add the sugar and beat well. Add the eggs one at a time and finally add the lemon rind and juice. Beat well to combine.

3 Pour the filling into the prepared tin, level the surface and bake for 40 minutes. Remove from the oven and allow to cool completely, then refrigerate for at least 4 hours, preferably longer.

To Serve Unclip the side of the tin and remove. Slide a palette knife between the bottom of the cheesecake and the tin and carefully lift the cheesecake off the metal base onto a serving plate. Sift icing sugar over the top just before serving.

Variation

Use lime or orange instead of lemon and, if using orange, add 4 tablespoons finely ground toasted hazelnuts. Gingersnaps or chocolate chip cookies can be used instead of digestive biscuits, or you can reduce the amount of digestive biscuits and make up the weight with chopped nuts. If making a chocolate crust, melt 60 g (2 oz) unsweetened chocolate and add it to the filling with 4 tablespoons Frangelico or Amaretto liqueur. For a fruity filling, mix about 175 g (6 oz) frozen blueberries into the filling before baking. For a marbled filling, flavour one-third of the mixture with chocolate or coffee and swirl it in.

White chocolate and cream cheese tart

A sensational-looking dessert that is unbelievably simple to make, especially if you use ready rolled frozen pastry. The combination of cream cheese and white chocolate is wonderful, but your guests will find it difficult to guess what it is.

1 sheet frozen shortcrust pastry, about 28 cm (11 inches) in diameter, thawed
400 g (14 oz) cream cheese
125 g (4 oz) caster sugar
1 x 150 g (5 oz) bar good-quality white chocolate

To Serve
about 90 g (3 oz) ripe berries
a little caster sugar

1 Preheat the oven to 190°C (375°F) Gas 5. Put a baking sheet in the oven to heat. Line a 24.5 cm (9½ inch) loose-bottomed metal tart tin with the sheet of pastry and trim the edge. Line the pastry with foil and fill with baking beans. Place on the hot baking sheet and bake blind for 10 minutes. Remove the beans and foil and bake the empty tart shell for 5 minutes. Remove the tart shell from the oven and set it aside to cool in its tin on a wire rack.

2 Meanwhile, beat the cream cheese and sugar together until light and fluffy. Break the chocolate into pieces and place in a heatproof bowl. Set over a saucepan of hot water until melted. Stir into the cream cheese.

3 Spread the cream cheese mixture evenly in the pastry case and leave in a cool place until set, about 1 hour.

To Serve Top with berries, sift caster sugar over and serve immediately.

Serves 6–8

Preparation time: 15 minutes plus setting
Cooking time: 15 minutes

Chef's Tips

If you prefer to make your own sweet shortcrust pastry, there is a recipe on page 373.

◆

You can make the tart up to 24 hours in advance and keep it loosely covered in a cold place. Add the berries just before serving or juice may weep into the filling and spoil its appearance. Halved small strawberries look good arranged cut side down in a regular pattern, or you can simply toss together smaller fruit like raspberries and blueberries and pile them on top of the tart.

Chocolate cups

These dainty little tartlets look sensational. They make very good petits fours to serve with coffee after dinner. Using ready made chocolate cups means that they can be assembled in minutes – perfect for last-minute entertaining.

200 g (7 oz) good-quality dark chocolate
100 ml (3½ fl oz) double cream
8 dark chocolate dessert cups

To Serve
150 g (5 oz) ripe raspberries
1–2 teaspoons icing sugar

Serves 8

Preparation time: about 30 minutes including setting

Chef's Tips

Chocolate dessert cups can be bought in boxes at many supermarkets and delicatessens. Made from good-quality dark chocolate, they are not too sweet.

◆

Instead of the chocolate ganache filling used here, you can fill the cups with fresh cream, chocolate mousse, crème pâtissière (pastry cream) or ice-cream.

1 Make the ganache filling. Break or chop the chocolate into pieces and melt gently in a heatproof bowl over a pan of barely simmering water. Take care not to let the base of the bowl touch the water or the chocolate will scorch. Remove the bowl from the pan.

2 Heat the cream in a small pan until hot, then pour onto the melted chocolate. Stir until evenly mixed, smooth and glossy.

3 Spoon the ganache filling into the chocolate cups and leave to set. This will take 15–20 minutes, depending on the room temperature. If not serving immediately, cover the filled cups and keep them in the refrigerator.

To Serve Gently press the raspberries into the ganache filling, arranging them with their pointed ends facing upwards. Sift icing sugar evenly over the raspberries and serve at room temperature.

Chocolate and Pecan Yogurt Ice-Cream

Using yogurt as a base for ice-cream is a short cut well worth knowing. It saves a lot of preparation time, yet the result is just as good as ice-cream made with a custard or cream base. It's healthier too.

60 g (2 oz) good-quality dark chocolate
60 g (2 oz) pecan nuts
1 x 500 g carton natural bio yogurt
60 g (2 oz) caster sugar
1 large egg white
½ teaspoon vanilla extract

Serves 4–6

Preparation time: 20 minutes plus freezing

1 Finely grate the chocolate. Chop the pecans.

2 Mix all the ingredients together and churn in an ice-cream maker until firm. The freezing time will vary according to your machine – some take as little as 20 minutes. If you do not have an electric ice-cream maker, whisk the mixture well in a bowl, then pour into a freezer container. Place in the freezer until beginning to freeze (about 4 hours), then whisk or stir briskly with a fork and return to the freezer. Repeat this process twice more, then freeze until firm.

To Serve Scoop into glasses or bowls and serve immediately.

Chef's Tips

The pecans should not be chopped too coarsely or they will prevent the ice cream maker from working properly.

Organic bio yogurt and full-fat yogurt are best for ice-cream making. They have a lovely creamy texture.

If the ice-cream has been made or stored in the freezer you may need to soften it at room temperature for 10–15 minutes before serving.

Plum and cinnamon crumble

A traditional family favourite. A crumble is quicker and easier to make than a fruit pie or tart, yet equally as popular, especially for Sunday lunch. Plums and cinnamon are a winning combination.

750 g (1½ lb) ripe red plums
60 g (2 oz) caster or demerara sugar
1 teaspoon ground cinnamon

Topping
250 g (8 oz) plain flour
150 g (5 oz) butter, chilled
40 g (1½ oz) caster or demerara sugar

Serves 6–8

Preparation time: 20 minutes
Cooking time: about 10 minutes

1 Preheat the oven to 190°C (375°F) Gas 5. Halve and stone the plums and place them skin-side up in a large baking dish. Mix the caster or demerara sugar and cinnamon together and sprinkle over the plums.

2 Make the topping. Put the flour in a bowl, cut the butter into 1.25 cm (½ inch) cubes and add to the flour. Rub it in with your fingertips, using a light action, until the mixture resembles fine breadcrumbs and a few small lumps come together (this can also be done in a food processor). Toss in the sugar and mix through evenly.

3 Scatter the crumble mixture evenly over the filling and bake for 25–30 minutes until golden brown.

To Serve Spoon into bowls and serve with cream, custard or fromage frais.

Variations

For apple crumble, use Granny Smith apples cut into 5 mm (¼ inch) slices and the finely grated rind and juice of ½ lemon instead of cinnamon. Or use half apples and half cranberries or blackberries.

◆

For a crunchier topping, add 15 g (½ oz) roughly chopped nuts (eg walnuts, hazelnuts, pecans) with the sugar.

◆

Strawberries and blueberries also make excellent crumbles; so too does well-drained canned fruit or thawed frozen fruit. Good choices are pears, gooseberries, rhubarb (with a little chopped stem ginger), peaches and apricots.

Roasted fruit with mascarpone cream

Hot fruit and chilled cream make a sensational partnership, and an excellent choice for a winter or Christmas dinner party. Serve with a sweet dessert wine such as Muscat de Beaumes de Venise.

1 kg (2 lb) prepared fresh seasonal fruit
60 g (2 oz) butter
60 g (2 oz) walnut pieces
60 g (2 oz) soft brown sugar

Mascarpone Cream
finely grated rind of 1 large orange
juice of 2 large oranges
2–3 cardamom pods
250 g (8 oz) mascarpone cheese, well chilled

Serves 6

Preparation time: 20–30 minutes
Cooking time: 20 minutes

1 First make the mascarpone cream. Put the orange rind and juice in a small pan. Crush the cardamom pods and add the pods and seeds to the pan. Boil gently until syrupy and reduced to about 3–4 tablespoonfuls. Strain and leave to cool, then stir into the mascarpone. Transfer to a small serving bowl, cover with cling film and chill in the refrigerator until ready to serve.

2 Preheat the oven to 200°C (400°F) Gas 6. Spread the fruit out in an even layer in a large baking dish. Melt the butter in a small pan, mix in the nuts and sugar, then drizzle over the fruit. Bake for 10 minutes.

3 Remove the dish from the oven and carefully turn the fruit over. Return the dish to the oven and bake for another 10 minutes or until each piece of fruit is just tender and the syrup is bubbling hot.

To Serve Transfer the fruit to a large serving bowl or individual bowls and serve hot, with the chilled mascarpone cream handed separately.

Chef's Tip

Choose firm-textured but ripe fruit. You can use just one or two fruits or several. For a total prepared weight of 1 kg (2 lb), try the following combination: 2 pears and 1 large dessert apple, both quartered, cored and cut into thick slices; 6 dessert plums, halved and stored; 1 large mango, peeled, stoned and cut into cubes; 200 g (7 oz) prepared pineapple chunks and 6 fresh figs, halved. If using figs, add them when the other fruit are turned over halfway through cooking.

Crêpes suzette

Usually flambéed at the table in restaurants, Crêpes Suzette is quite difficult for the home cook to serve. Here is a really clever alternative that is both simple to prepare and serve, especially if you use ready made French crêpes.

140 g (4½ oz) butter, softened
90 g (3 oz) caster sugar
finely grated rind of 1 large orange
3 tablespoons Cointreau
8 ready made crêpes
200 ml (7 fl oz) orange juice (2 large oranges)

Serves 4–6

Preparation time: 15 minutes
Cooking time: 5–8 minutes

1 Preheat the oven to 220°C (425°F) Gas 7. Brush the inside of a large baking dish with 1 tablespoon of the butter. Put the remaining butter in a bowl and add 60 g (2 oz) of the sugar, the orange rind and 1 tablespoon of the Cointreau. Beat with a wooden spoon until smooth.

2 Take 1 crêpe and spread it thinly with some of the flavoured butter. Fold it in half and spread with another layer of butter. Fold it in half again to make a triangle, then place it in the dish. Repeat with the remaining crêpes and flavoured butter, placing them in the dish as they are done so that each one slightly overlaps the other.

3 Melt the remaining flavoured butter and pour it over the crêpes, then sprinkle with the remaining sugar. Bake for 5–8 minutes or until the crêpes are bubbling hot and the sugar on top is lightly caramelized.

4 Meanwhile, bring the orange juice and the remaining Cointreau to the boil in a small saucepan.

To Serve Remove the dish from the oven, pour the hot orange juice and Cointreau mixture over the crêpes and serve immediately.

Chef's Tip

Traditional sweet crêpes from Brittany are sold in many supermarkets. They are often quite large, about 30 cm (12 inches) in diameter, and are sold in packets of eight. If you make your own crêpes, they are likely to be smaller in size than the ready made French ones, so you will need 12 crêpes for 4–6 people. A recipe for crêpes is given *on page 372.*

Raspberry fool

An English classic, this fool can be made in minutes with fresh, simple ingredients from the supermarket. Rich and creamy, it is best served with light, crisp biscuits such as langues-de-chat or sponge fingers.

750 g (1½ lb) fresh or frozen raspberries
2–3 tablespoons caster sugar, or to taste
a few drops of lemon juice
300 ml (½ pint) prepared custard
300 g (10 oz) fromage frais
a few fresh raspberries, to serve

Serves 4

Preparation time: 15–20 minutes, plus chilling

1 Purée the raspberries in a food processor or blender, then sieve the purée to remove most of the seeds. Taste and add sugar and lemon juice to sweeten and accentuate the flavour of the fruit.

2 In a large bowl, mix together the custard and fromage frais. Stir in the raspberry purée until blended, or blend in half and streak the remainder through.

3 Spoon into 4 wine glasses or champagne flutes and chill in the refrigerator for at least 2 hours.

To Serve Top each serving with a few raspberries and serve chilled.

Chef's Tips

Strawberries can be used instead of raspberries, and canned fruit such as rhubarb or gooseberries also works well. To make the amount of fruit purée required for this recipe, drain the liquid from 2 x 539 g cans of fruit, then blend the fruit in a food processor or blender.

◆

You can make the fools up to 24 hours in advance and keep them, tightly covered with cling film, in the refrigerator. Top with fresh raspberries before serving.

Fragrant fruit salad

Delicate and refreshing, this is the perfect dessert to serve after a rich main course. It uses fruits that are good in winter, when soft fruits and berries are not at their best.

2 pink grapefruit
2 oranges
4 kiwi fruit
2 x 250 g (8 oz) tubs fresh mango slices
2 pears or dessert apples
juice of 1 lemon
2 tablespoons Cointreau
2 medium bananas
fresh mint sprigs, to serve

Spiced Sugar Syrup
150 g (5 oz) granulated sugar
1 cinnamon stick
1 cardamom pod, split
1 star anise or clove

Serves 6–8

Preparation time: 30 minutes, plus cooling syrup and final chilling

1 First make the spiced sugar syrup. Put all the ingredients in a saucepan and add 150 ml (¼ pint) water. Bring to the boil. When the sugar has dissolved, immediately remove from the heat, cover and set aside to cool.

2 Peel and segment the grapefruit and oranges, catching the juice over a large bowl. Cut the segments into bite-sized pieces. Peel and slice the kiwi fruit and cut each slice in half. Drain the mango and cut each slice crossways into three. Peel and core the pears or apples and slice them into bite-sized pieces.

3 Put all the prepared fruit in the bowl with the grapefruit and orange juice and add the lemon juice. Strain the cool sugar syrup over (you may not need all of it), add the Cointreau and stir gently to mix. Cover and chill for several hours.

To Serve Peel and thinly slice the bananas, then cut each slice in half and add to the fruit salad. Decorate with mint sprigs and serve immediately.

Chef's Tip

Ready prepared mango is an absolute boon for the busy cook because the whole fruit is very fiddly to prepare. Most supermarkets sell it in the chilled fruit section. Check that it is packed in natural juice rather than a sweetened syrup.

Ginger crème brûlée

Velvety and rich, with a spicy kick from the ginger, this is a dessert for a special occasion. It is best well chilled, so make it the day before serving, and keep it in the refrigerator until the last moment. The brûlée topping will stay crisp.

- 60 g (2 oz) drained stem ginger in syrup
- 200 ml (7 fl oz) double cream
- 200 ml (7 fl oz) milk
- 1–2 slices peeled fresh root ginger, about 15 g (½ oz)
- 125 g (4 oz) good-quality white chocolate
- 5 large egg yolks
- 125 g (4 oz) caster sugar
- 6 tablespoons demerara sugar

Serves 6

Preparation time: 20 minutes plus cooling and chilling
Cooking time: 30 minutes

1 Preheat the oven to 150°C (300°F) Gas 2. Finely chop the stem ginger and sprinkle it in the bottom of six 125–150 ml (4–5 fl oz) ramekins. Stand the ramekins in a roasting tin. Put the cream, milk and root ginger in a saucepan and bring just to boiling point. Remove from the heat. Break the chocolate into small pieces and add it to the pan a few pieces at a time, stirring, after each addition until melted.

2 In a bowl, whisk together the egg yolks and caster sugar until light in colour. Pour the hot liquid onto them and stir well. Strain into a jug, then pour into the ramekins. Pour enough hot water into the roasting tin to come halfway up the sides of the ramekins. Bake for 30 minutes, until barely set. Turn the oven off and leave the custards to cool in the oven, then cover and refrigerate for at least 4 hours.

3 Preheat the grill to high. Sprinkle the top of each dessert with 1 tablespoon demerara sugar and caramelize for 2–3 minutes. Leave to cool and set, then refrigerate until serving time.

To Serve Stand the ramekins on small plates or saucers and serve chilled. Each guest should crack open the crisp caramel with a teaspoon to reveal the rich yellow cream underneath.

Variations

For Cardamom Crème Brûlée, infuse the cream and milk with 3 crushed cardamom pods instead of the fresh root ginger, and use 90 g (3 oz) sugar instead of 125 g (4 oz). Leave the stem ginger in or omit it.

◆

For Vanilla Crème Brûlée, split a vanilla pod in half lengthways and scrape the seeds into the cream and milk before scalding. Leave the chocolate and stem ginger in or omit them.

Banana tart tatin

Upside-down hot fruit tarts are sweet and juicy, and very popular. This is an easy recipe in which everything is done in just one pan. Serve with a chilled cream like crème fraîche, or scoops of vanilla ice-cream.

200 g (7 oz) caster sugar
1 teaspoon lemon juice
4 tablespoons double cream
250–300 g (8–10 oz) ready made puff pastry
6 medium bananas

Serves 4–6

Preparation time: 30 minutes plus chilling
Cooking time: 30–35 minutes

1 Put the sugar, lemon juice and 4 tablespoons cold water in a heavy frying pan with an ovenproof handle. The pan should measure about 23 cm (9 inches) across the base. Place the pan over moderate heat and stir until the sugar has completely dissolved. Bring to the boil and boil rapidly until the syrup turns a golden caramel colour. Immediately remove from the heat and carefully stir in the cream. Continue stirring, off the heat, until a smooth caramel forms. Set aside to cool.

2 Roll out the pastry to a thickness of about 3 mm (⅛ inch). Cut out a large circle, about 30 cm (12 inches) in diameter, or the same diameter as the top of your frying pan. Prick the pastry all over with a fork.

3 Peel the bananas and trim off the ends. Cut the bananas into 2 cm (¾ inch) cylinders and stand them upright side by side in a single layer in the caramel sauce. Carefully place the puff pastry on top of the bananas, then put the pan in the refrigerator for 30 minutes. Meanwhile, preheat the oven to 200°C (400°F) Gas 6.

4 Bake the tart in the oven for about 30–35 minutes or until the pastry is well risen, golden and cooked through.

To Serve Place a large flat serving plate upside-down on top of the frying pan. Wearing oven gloves and holding both pan and plate tightly together, carefully invert both so that the tart is on the plate. Lift off the frying pan.

Chef's Tips

For speed, buy fresh puff pastry from the chilled section of the supermarket. Frozen puff pastry is just as good, but you have to wait several hours for it to thaw before you can roll it out.

◆

If your frying pan does not have an ovenproof handle, wrap the handle in several thicknesses of foil. This will protect it from the intense heat of the oven.

Lemon tart

Sharp and tangy, this classic French tart is amazingly quick to make, especially when you use a ready rolled sheet of shortcrust pastry to make the tart shell. It is good served perfectly plain, or with cream and berries as shown here.

1 sheet frozen shortcrust pastry, about 28cm (11 inches in diameter), thawed
6 large eggs
200 ml (7 fl oz) lemon juice
(4–6 large lemons)
200 g (7 oz) caster sugar
125 g (4 oz) butter

To Serve
icing sugar
cream
fresh berries

Serves 6–8

Preparation time: 15 minutes plus chilling
Cooking time: 15 minutes

1 Preheat the oven to 190°C (375°F) Gas 5. Put a baking sheet in the oven to heat. Line a 24.5 cm (9½ inch) loose-bottomed metal tart tin with the sheet of pastry and trim the edge. Line the pastry with foil and fill with baking beans. Place on the hot baking sheet and bake blind for 10 minutes. Remove the beans and foil and bake the empty tart shell for 5 minutes. Remove the tart shell from the oven and set it aside to cool in its tin on a wire rack.

2 Meanwhile, put the eggs, lemon juice and sugar in a saucepan and whisk well. Place over low to moderate heat and whisk constantly with a balloon whisk until thick enough for traces to be left by the whisk when lifted. Remove from the heat and strain into a clean bowl. Dice the butter and mix into the filling until melted.

3 Pour the filling into the pastry case and set aside to cool. Refrigerate for 1–2 hours or until the filling has set.

To Serve Remove the tart from the refrigerator, carefully remove the tart tin and set the tart on a serving plate. Leave to stand at room temperature for about 30 minutes, then sift icing sugar over the top. Serve with cream and fresh berries.

Chef's Tip

Boxes of round shortcrust pastry sheets are sold in the freezer cabinets of most supermarkets. They are rolled up individually, and need to be thawed before unrolling. The pastry is thin, crisp and light, perfect for making French-style tarts and quiches, but if you prefer to make your own, there is a recipe for sweet shortcrust pastry on page 373.

◆

For baking pastry blind, you can buy ceramic and metal baking beans at kitchenware shops, or use dried pulses or rice. Another way to bake blind is to put a cake tin on top of the foil inside the tart shell. Choose a tin that is slightly smaller in diameter than the tart tin.

DESSERTS

quick and easy ideas

Fresh fruit

• Sprinkle sliced mango or papaya with orange juice and a splash of Cointreau. Top with toasted shredded coconut if you like.

• Toss raspberries or loganberries with caster sugar and sprinkle with kirsch. Decorate with fresh mint sprigs.

• Sprinkle chunks or rings of pineapple with kirsch or rum.

• Halve or slice strawberries and sprinkle with a little balsamic vinegar. Turn the fruit gently in the vinegar.

• Grind black pepper lightly over halved or sliced strawberries. Sweeten to taste with caster sugar.

• Combine red fruit – cherries, raspberries, strawberries, blueberries – and toss in vanilla sugar. Or macerate in Cointreau and sugar. Serve well chilled.

• Heat sliced strawberries with butter, sugar, a splash of Cointreau and ½ teaspoon crushed green peppercorns.

• Macerate halved seedless grapes in whisky, honey and lemon juice in the refrigerator overnight. Serve chilled, with crème fraîche.

• Make frudités. Arrange a selection of fresh seasonal fruit on a platter and serve with a bowl of sweetened cream or fromage frais for dipping. Or mix the cream half and half with fromage frais, or with mascarpone cheese, Greek yogurt or soured cream.

quick and easy ideas

• Stir-fry mixed fresh fruit in a little sunflower oil, sprinkle with a little ground ginger, cardamom or five-spice powder. Serve hot, with chilled cream or Greek yogurt.

• Halve bananas lengthways and pan-fry in butter, brown sugar and orange or lime juice, or both. For a spicy flavour, add a pinch of ground cinnamon, cardamom or mixed spice. For a Caribbean kick, add a splash of rum. Serve hot, with vanilla ice-cream.

• Pan-fry apple slices in butter and sugar. Sprinkle with ground cinnamon before serving.

• Make Cherries Jubilee. Heat canned cherries in natural juice with brandy and pour over vanilla ice-cream.

• Make Peach Melba. Purée raspberries in a food processor, then sieve and sweeten to make a coulis. Slice peaches and fan out on individual plates. Top with vanilla ice-cream and pour raspberry coulis over the top.

• Put a few raspberries in the bottom of champagne flutes. Fill flutes with chilled champagne and serve immediately.

DESSERTS

quick and easy ideas

Creamy concoctions

• Fold together whipped cream and Greek yogurt. Layer in wine glasses with sliced or chopped fresh fruit, fruit purée or chopped nuts. Serve chilled.

• Whizz fromage frais or Quark in a food processor with fresh raspberries or strawberries, caster sugar and lemon juice to taste. Spoon into glasses, chill and serve topped with a single fresh fruit.

• Make syllabub. Whip double or whipping cream with a few tablespoons each of sweet white wine and caster sugar and 1–2 teaspoons finely grated orange or lemon rind. Spoon into tall glasses and serve well chilled. If you like, fold soft summer fruit like raspberries and chopped strawberries, peaches, nectarines or apricots into the syllabub. Or add chopped stem ginger.

• Cut a cross in the tops of fresh figs, open them out and fill with cream cheese or ricotta cheese sweetened with caster sugar.

• Fill bought meringue nests with sweetened whipped cream or a mixture of cream and fromage frais or Greek yogurt. Top with berries or sliced fruit, then cut passion fruit in half and scoop their flesh out onto the fruit and cream.

Chocolate

• Top warm brownies with scoops of vanilla ice-cream and drizzle with chocolate sauce. Sprinkle chopped pecans or walnuts over the sauce if you like.

• Scoop chocolate ice-cream into ready made meringue nests, drizzle with chocolate sauce and sprinkle with finely chopped pistachio nuts.

• Make a chocolate fondue by gently melting together equal weights of chocolate and double cream. You can use dark or white chocolate. Pour into a fondue pot and serve with chunks of fresh fruit, sponge fingers or cubes of sponge cake. Use fondue forks for spearing and dipping.

quick and easy ideas

• Make a chocolate sauce by heating together 250 g (8 oz) good-quality dark chocolate, broken into pieces, with 300 ml (½ pint) double cream. Stir in 1 teaspoon rum, Cointreau or peppermint essence if you like. Use as a warm sauce over ice-cream, bananas and crêpes.

Fillings for tarts

• Using a shortcrust pastry sheet, make a tart shell and bake it blind as in the recipe for Lemon Tart (page 339). Leave to cool, then fill with one of the following:

• Cream cheese, low-fat soft cheese or Quark sweetened with caster sugar. Stud the cheese filling with blueberries or raspberries, or a mixture of both fruit, arranging them attractively in concentric circles or wedges. If you like, coat with a red glaze made by boiling red jam with a little lemon juice. Sieve, then spoon over fruit.

• Ready made thick custard topped with peach halves placed cut-side down. Decorate between the peaches with shredded pistachios or toasted flaked almonds, then coat with an apricot glaze if you like. Boil apricot jam with a little lemon juice, then sieve and spoon over fruit.

And for the cheese course...

• Many people prefer fruit and cheese to dessert. The following combinations are good:
– Pears with Gorgonzola
– Figs with mascarpone
– Peaches with Dolcelatte
– Dainty fingers of rich fruit cake with Cheddar or Wensleydale
– Crisp apples with blue Stilton, Emmenthal or Gruyère
– Apricots with white Stilton
– Red or green grapes with Brie or Camembert

7

BASIC RECIPES

The recipes in this chapter range from stocks, the foundation of good home cooking, through to dressings and sauces, vegetables, pasta and pancakes. Some are used in the main recipe section of the book, others are not, but they are included here to provide you with a good basic grounding. You will also find a handy checklist of useful items to keep in your storecupboard, refrigerator or freezer, all of which feature in recipes in this book.

For freshness and flavour – and to be sure of what you are eating – there is no substitute for homemade. A homemade dressing or marinade will not only taste different from its bottled equivalent, it will also taste slightly different each time you make it, which is the beauty of home cooking. That said, for the keen cook with a hectic lifestyle, items like ready-made dressings, sauces, pastes and marinades are a huge help in cutting down on preparation time, as just about everything can be bought ready made these days. If you have a good stock of items like bottled sauces and dressings, spice mixes and flavoured butters, then all you have to do to put together quick and delicious meals is to buy a few fresh ingredients when you need them.

Many of the recipes provided here are for times when you prefer to make your own basics, or when you have run out of stock in your storecupboard. You can even fill your cupboard with with homemade basics for future use, because storage instructions and times are given with all the recipes where possible.

In the storecupboard

Stocking your storecupboard with the items listed here will cut down on your regular shopping time because you will only need to buy fresh fish, meat, vegetables, eggs, dairy produce and fruit when you need them. All are used in the recipes in this book, so you will be able to turn your freshly bought produce into a superb meal in next to no time. Check the labels for storage times and to see whether bottles or jars need refrigerating once opened.

Bottles and jars

Balsamic vinegar
Capers
Cider vinegar
Fish sauce (nam pla)
Honey
Malt vinegar (light)
Mayonnaise
Oil (sunflower, olive, nut and sesame)
Olive and tomato sauce
Olives (black and green)
Oyster sauce
Pesto (red and green)
Redcurrant jelly
Rice wine or sherry
Rice wine vinegar
Roasted peppers
Soy sauce
Sun-dried tomato paste (also in tubes)
Sun-dried tomatoes in olive oil
Tapenade (anchovy and olive paste)
Tomato ketchup
Wine vinegar (red, white and raspberry)
Worcestershire sauce

Cans

Anchovies
Chickpeas
Clams (also in jars)
Coconut milk
Consommé (chicken and beef)
Fish stock
Red kidney beans
Sweetcorn (plain, with sweet peppers and baby corn)
Tomatoes (whole and chopped)
Tomato purée (also in tubes)
Tuna

Dry goods

Chocolate (good-quality white and dark)
Cocoa powder
Cornflour
Couscous (quick-cooking)
Flour
Gelatine (powdered)
Lentils
Noodles (oriental)
Nuts
Pasta (long and short)
Polenta (instant)
Raisins or currants
Rice (long grain, short grain risotto, basmati and Thai)
Stock cubes
Sugar (caster, demerara, granulated, icing and soft brown)
Trifle sponges or sponge fingers

Hot flavourings

Chillies (crushed and whole dried red)
Green peppercorns in brine
Harissa (Tunisian hot chilli) paste)
Mustard (Dijon, English powdered and wholegrain)
Thai curry paste (red and green)
Wasabi (Japanese horseradish paste)

Dried herbs

Bay leaves
Herbes de Provence
Marjoram
Oregano
Rosemary
Thyme

Spices and seasonings

Cardamom pods
Cayenne pepper
Chilli powder
Cinnamon (ground and sticks)
Coriander (ground and seeds)
Cumin (ground)
Curry powder
Five-spice powder
Garam masala
Ginger (ground)
Juniper berries
Mixed spice (ground)
Nutmeg (whole)
Paprika
Peppercorns (black, white and mixed colours)
Saffron (threads or powder)
Sea salt
Sesame seeds
Star anise

Bouquet garni

This is a small herb 'packet' used to flavour foods cooked in liquid – especially soups, casseroles and stews. There are many good commercial brands available, both fresh and dried, but a bouquet garni is very easy to make yourself. The traditional combination is 1 bay leaf, 1 thyme sprig, a few parsley stalks and a celery leaf wrapped together in the green part of a leek and tied with kitchen string. If using dried herbs, wrap them in a small square of muslin rather than the leek.

Dry rubs

These ground spices and flavourings are mixed together and rubbed over fish, poultry or meat before grilling or roasting. The basic mixtures can be used on their own, or you can add one or more of the optional ingredients.

Basic spice rub

cayenne
garlic powder
paprika
salt

Optional extras

celery salt
coriander
cumin
dried basil
dried oregano
dried sage
ginger
ground black pepper
turmeric

Persian spice rub

anise
cardamom
cinnamon
coriander
cumin
ginger
mace

In the refrigerator

Aside from obvious ingredients you will regulary buy, like butter, cream, cheese and eggs, there are several invaluable homemade items you can store in the refrigerator – or freezer if you have one.

Roasted garlic

whole heads of garlic
coarse sea salt (optional)
good-quality olive oil

1 Preheat the oven to 180°C (350°F) Gas 4. Place whole heads of garlic on a baking sheet or bed of coarse sea salt and roast in the oven for 30 minutes. Allow to cool, then cut off the top third of each head of garlic and squeeze the flesh out of the skins. Use the flesh straight away, or put it in a sterilized airtight jar, cover with olive oil and seal the jar. The garlic can be kept in the refrigerator for several weeks.

Roasted bell peppers

whole peppers
good-quality olive oil

1 Preheat the oven to 190°C (375°F) Gas 5. Put the peppers in a roasting tin and roast for 40–50 minutes until the skins are charred and blistered on all sides. Turn the peppers several times during roasting.

2 Remove the roasted peppers from the oven and immediately place them in a plastic bag. Seal and leave to cool.

3 When the peppers are cold, peel off the skins and remove the cores and seeds. Pat the peppers dry and place in a sterilized airtight jar. Cover with olive oil and seal the jar. The peppers can be kept in the refrigerator for several weeks.

Basil pesto

For a different flavour, replace about half the basil with flat-leaf parsley and the pine nuts with walnuts.

3 garlic cloves
90 g (3 oz) Parmesan cheese
60 g (2 oz) fresh basil leaves
60 g (2 oz) toasted pine nuts
100 ml (3½ fl oz) good-quality olive oil
salt and freshly ground black pepper

1 Roughly chop the garlic and grate the Parmesan cheese. Place in a food processor with the remaining ingredients and work to a purée. Taste for seasoning.

2 Use the pesto fresh or transfer to a sterilized airtight jar, cover with a thin film of olive oil and seal the jar. Store in the refrigerator for up to 1 week, or in the freezer for up to 1 month.

Red pesto

60 g (2 oz) toasted pine nuts
60 g (2 oz) freshly grated Parmesan cheese
125 g (4 oz) well-drained sun-dried tomatoes in oil
100 ml (3½ fl oz) good-quality olive oil

1 Put the pine nuts, Parmesan and tomatoes in a food processor. Work to a purée, adding the oil through the feeder tube.

2 Use the pesto fresh or transfer to a sterilized airtight jar, cover with a thin film of olive oil and seal the jar. Store in the refrigerator for up to 1 week, or in the freezer for up to 1 month.

Basil coulis

This sauce is good tossed with pasta or served with cold meats or hot fish.

1 large bunch of fresh basil
salt and freshly ground black pepper
200 ml (7 fl oz) good-quality olive oil
a few drops of lemon juice (optional)

1 Wash the basil and remove the leaves from the stalks. Discard the stalks. Dry the leaves on kitchen paper, then place them in a food processor with salt and pepper to taste.

2 With the machine running, add the olive oil through the feeder tube in a thin steady stream until the basil liquefies and is smooth. Add a few drops of lemon juice if you like the flavour with basil. Store in a sterilized airtight jar in the refrigerator for up to 1 week.

Moroccan pickled lemons

unwaxed lemons
granulated sugar
coarse sea salt

1 Blanch whole lemons in boiling water for 2–3 minutes. Drain and plunge immediately into cold water. Cut the lemons into quarters and remove any pips. Toss in granulated sugar until well coated.

2 Sprinkle the bottom of a sterilized airtight jar with coarse sea salt. Layer the lemon quarters in the jar, sprinkling coarse salt between the layers and pressing them down well to extract some juice. Seal and leave in a cold place for at least 15 days. Rinse before using.

Mediterranean marinade

Use for chicken and lamb. If fresh oregano is not available, use 1 teaspoon dried oregano.

4 tablespoons lemon juice
125 ml (4 fl oz) olive oil
2 teaspoons chopped fresh oregano
2 tablespoons chopped fresh basil
salt and freshly ground black pepper

1 Whisk together all the ingredients, adding salt and pepper to taste.

Teriyaki marinade

Use for fish, chicken and meat. Minimum marinating time is 30 minutes; a few hours is ideal.

250 ml (8 fl oz) soy sauce
4 tablespoons rice wine vinegar
2–3 tablespoons caster sugar or runny honey
grated fresh root ginger, to taste
crushed garlic cloves, to taste

1 Whisk together all the ingredients. To use as a basting glaze, boil to reduce until syrupy.

Spiced yogurt marinade

Use for chicken and lamb.

300 ml (½ pint) natural yogurt
1 tablespoon mild curry paste
1 teaspoon cumin seeds
1 teaspoon black mustard seeds
1 tablespoon groundnut oil
salt and freshly ground black pepper

1 Whisk together all the ingredients, adding salt and pepper to taste.

Thai green curry paste

For a really hot curry paste, leave the seeds in the chilli. The Thais always do.

3 garlic cloves
60 g (2 oz) fresh root ginger
2 lemon grass stalks
1 small green chilli
1 large handful of fresh coriander
1 tablespoon groundnut oil
salt and freshly ground black pepper

1 Peel the garlic and ginger and cut into large pieces. Roughly chop the lemon grass. Halve the chilli. Put all the ingredients in a food processor fitted with the metal blade and work to a paste. Store in a sterilized airtight jar in the refrigerator for up to 1 week or in the freezer for up to 1 month.

Garlic butter

For fish, poultry, meat and vegetables.

125 g (4 oz) garlic cloves
salt and freshly ground black pepper
125 g (4 oz) butter, softened

1 Peel the garlic, cut each clove in half and remove the green germ from the centre. Blanch the garlic cloves in salted boiling water for 3–4 minutes until just soft. Drain and leave to cool.

2 Press the garlic flesh through a sieve and mix with the butter and salt and pepper to taste. Wrap or cover tightly and store in the refrigerator for up to 1 week or in the freezer for up to 1 month.

In the freezer

These items are useful to have in the freezer: Homemade pesto and curry paste; crêpes; filo pastry; puff pastry; shortcrust pastry; peas and petits pois; prawns; root ginger (grate from frozen); lemon grass and ice-cream.

Roasted red pepper butter

For pasta, fish and chicken. If you like garlic, process 4–5 roasted garlic cloves with the peppers and butter.

100 g (3½ oz) well-drained roasted peppers in oil
150 g (5 oz) butter, softened
salt and freshly ground black pepper

1 Process the peppers and butter until smooth. Press through a sieve to remove any pieces of skin. Season to taste. Wrap or cover tightly and store in the refrigerator for up to 1 week or in the freezer for up to 1 month.

Nut butter

For fish and vegetables.

100 g (3/oz) shelled almonds or pistachio nuts
125 g (4 oz) butter, softened
salt and freshly ground black pepper

1 Crush or process the nuts with a few drops of water to make a fine paste. Mix with the butter and season to taste. Wrap tightly and store in the refrigerator for up to 1 week or in the freezer for up to 1 month.

Maître d'hôtel butter

For pasta, meat and vegetables.

100 g (3½ oz) butter, softened
1 tablespoon finely chopped fresh parsley
salt and freshly ground black pepper

1 Beat the butter until pale and fluffy. Mix in the parsley and salt and pepper to taste. Wrap or cover tightly and store in the refrigerator for up to 1 week or in the freezer for up to 1 month.

Snail butter

For snails, pasta, meat and vegetables.

1 shallot
1 garlic clove
100 g (3½ oz) butter, softened
1 tablespoon finely chopped fresh parsley
salt and freshly ground black pepper

1 Chop the shallot and garlic very finely. Beat the butter until pale and fluffy. Mix in the chopped shallot, garlic, parsley and salt and pepper to taste. Wrap or cover tightly and store in the refrigerator for up to 1 week or in the freezer for up to 1 month.

Chicken stock

This is a basic chicken stock to which you can add flavourings of your choice, such as garlic and fresh herbs. Salt is not used in the making of the stock. It should be added at the time the stock is used.

about 1 kg (2 lb) chicken bones
500 g (1 lb) mixed onions, leeks, celery and carrots
1 bouquet garni
8 white peppercorns

1 Chop the chicken bones and place them in a stockpot or large, deep saucepan. Finely chop the mixed vegetables and add them to the pan with 2.4 litres (4 pints) cold water. Bring slowly to the boil, stirring occasionally. Add the bouquet garni. Cover and simmer for 2 hours, adding the peppercorns for the last 5 minutes. Strain through a chinois or other fine sieve. If not using immediately, cover and leave to cool, then chill in the refrigerator.

◆

Vegetable stock

Mild-flavoured vegetable stock is fat-free. If you like, you can use it whenever meat or chicken stock is called for, as a light alternative. The stock is not seasoned when it is made – seasoning should be added when the stock is used in a dish.

500 g (1 lb) mixed onions, leeks, celery and carrots
1 bouquet garni

1 Finely chop the mixed vegetables and place them in a stockpot or large, deep saucepan. Add 2.4 litres (4 pints) cold water and bring slowly to the boil. Add the bouquet garni, lower the heat and half cover the pan. Simmer gently for 1 hour.

2 Strain through a chinois or other fine sieve, pressing the solids to extract as much stock as possible. If not using immediately, cover and leave to cool, then chill in the refrigerator.

Brown stock

Ask your butcher to chop the meat bones for you. To degrease the stock before using, chill it in the refrigerator overnight. Any fat will solidify on the surface and you will be able to lift it off easily.

about 1 kg (2 lb) chopped beef or veal bones
500 g (1 lb) mixed onions, leeks, celery and carrots
200 ml (7 fl oz) dry white wine or water
300 g (10 oz) ripe tomatoes
30 g (1 oz) tomato purée
60 g (2 oz) mushroom trimmings
1 bouquet garni
8–10 black peppercorns

1 Preheat the oven to 220°C (425°F) Gas 7. Put the chopped bones in a roasting tin. Finely chop the mixed vegetables and add them to the tin. Roast until browned, about 40 minutes.

2 Transfer the bones and vegetables to a stockpot or very large, deep saucepan. Degrease and deglaze the roasting tin with the wine or water, then add to the pan with 2.4 litres (4 pints) cold water. Bring to the boil, skimming occasionally.

3 Roughly chop the tomatoes and add to the pan with the tomato purée, mushroom trimmings and bouquet garni. Cook very gently for 3–6 hours, skimming occasionally. Add the peppercorns towards the end.

4 Strain the stock through a chinois or other fine sieve. If not using immediately, cover and leave to cool, then chill in the refrigerator.

◆

Fish stock

Ask your fishmonger to chop the fish bones for you. When you get home, soak them in a bowl of cold water with a splash of lemon juice, then rinse them well under cold running water before use. This will get rid of any blood and impurities.

30 g (1 oz) butter or olive oil
250 g (8 oz) mixed onion, leek and celery, finely chopped
500 g (1 lb) chopped white fish bones
100 ml (3½ fl oz) dry white wine
1 bouquet garni
60 g (2 oz) mushroom trimmings
4 white peppercorns
juice of ¼ lemon

1 Heat the butter or oil in a large saucepan, add the mixed vegetables and sweat them until softened. Add the chopped fish bones and sweat these for 2–3 minutes.

2 Add the wine and cook until reduced by half, then add 1 litre (1¾ pints) cold water and bring to the boil. Add the bouquet garni and mushroom trimmings and simmer for 20 minutes, skimming occasionally. Add the peppercorns and lemon juice for the last 5 minutes.

3 Strain the stock through a chinois or other fine sieve. Cover and leave to cool, then keep in the refrigerator if not using immediately. Use within 24 hours.

◆

Chunky tomato sauce

This robust, low-fat sauce is good tossed with pasta, or it can be used in layered vegetable bakes or baked pasta dishes. It can also be served as an accompaniment to grilled or roast poultry and meat. To keep the fat content down, use the sun-dried tomatoes that are sold loose or in packets, not the ones bottled in oil.

500 g (1 lb) ripe plum tomatoes
30 g (1 oz) sun-dried tomatoes
1 x 400 g can chopped tomatoes
1/2 teaspoon sugar
2 teaspoons balsamic vinegar
salt and freshly ground black pepper

1 Halve the plum tomatoes lengthways and remove the cores and seeds. Roughly dice the flesh. Chop the sun-dried tomatoes.

2 Place the sun-dried tomatoes in a saucepan with the canned tomatoes and sugar. Bring to simmering point and simmer for 5 minutes.

3 Add the diced plum tomatoes and cook gently for 10 minutes, stirring occasionally. Remove the pan from the heat, stir in the balsamic vinegar and season to taste with salt and pepper.

◆

Tangy red relish

Cranberries and orange juice give this relish a sweet and sour flavour, while chillies and coriander give it a spicy kick. It is equally good served warm or cold, as an accompaniment to roast and grilled poultry and meat. It goes especially well with turkey, pork and venison.

- 1/2 teaspoon coriander seeds
- 2 shallots
- 1 red pepper
- 2 small red chillies
- 1 tablespoon olive oil
- 125 g (4 oz) fresh or frozen (thawed) cranberries
- 100 ml (3 1/2 fl oz) orange juice
- salt and freshly ground black pepper

1 Crush the coriander seeds with a pestle and mortar. Dice the shallots. Halve, core and deseed the red pepper and the chillies, then finely dice the flesh.

2 Gently heat the oil in a sauté pan, add the coriander seeds and fry for a few minutes to release their aroma, stirring all the time. When the seeds are nicely toasted, add the shallots, red pepper and chillies. Cook over low heat, stirring frequently, for 5 minutes or until softened.

3 Add the cranberries and orange juice, and add salt and pepper to taste. Stir well to mix, then simmer over moderate heat for about 10 minutes or until the orange juice has evaporated and the cranberries are soft. Serve hot, or cover and leave to cool, then refrigerate and serve chilled.

◆

Roasted tomato dressing

This is a basic purée to which you can add more oil or water depending on what you intend to use the dressing for. As it is, it can be spread over chicken or turkey, steaks or chops before grilling. Diluted, it can be used as a sauce.

500 g (1 lb) ripe plum tomatoes
3 tablespoons olive oil
2 tablespoons fresh thyme leaves
1 tablespoon fresh marjoram leaves
salt and freshly ground black pepper
½–1 teaspoon sugar, to taste (optional)

1 Preheat the oven to 170°C (325°F) Gas 3. Halve the tomatoes lengthways and remove the cores and seeds. Place the tomatoes cut side uppermost on baking trays and sprinkle with 2 tablespoons of the oil, half the thyme and marjoram leaves and a little salt and pepper. Make sure that each tomato half gets some herbs and seasoning.

2 Roast the tomatoes in the oven for 1 hour or until they are puckered and shrunken but still moist.

3 Place the roasted tomatoes in a food processor or blender and add 2 tablespoons cold water, the remaining oil and herbs. Add ½ teaspoon sugar if you think the tomatoes need it. Work until smooth, then taste for seasoning and add more sugar if you like. Turn into a bowl, cover and keep chilled in the refrigerator until required.

◆

VINAIGRETTE

The flavour of your vinaigrette will depend on the type of vinegar and oil used. Red wine vinegar is classic, sherry vinegar is slightly stronger, cider vinegar is mild. A neutral oil such as sunflower is good, but you may prefer the stronger flavour of olive oil, which can be fruity or peppery. Hazelnut and walnut oils are very strong in flavour, and best used in small quantities in combination with a light-flavoured oil such as sunflower.

BASIC VINAIGRETTE

Plain vinaigrette dressing can be kept in a screw-top jar in the refrigerator for several weeks; dressings which contain herbs, shallots or garlic will only keep for 1 week.

1 part vinegar
salt and freshly ground black pepper
2–4 parts oil

1 Whisk the vinegar with salt and pepper to taste, then whisk in oil until both the flavour and consistency are to your liking.

BALSAMIC VINAIGRETTE

1 garlic clove
1 tablespoon balsamic vinegar
salt and freshly ground black pepper
2 tablespoons olive oil
4 tablespoons sunflower oil

1 Finely chop the garlic. Whisk the vinegar with the garlic and salt and pepper to taste, then whisk in both kinds of oil until thick.

Mustard vinaigrette

2–3 teaspoons Dijon mustard
salt and freshly ground black pepper
2 tablespoons red wine vinegar
6 tablespoons olive oil

1 Put 2 teaspoons mustard in a bowl and add salt and pepper to taste. Mix well, then whisk in the vinegar. Gradually whisk in the oil until thick. Taste and add more mustard if you like.

Curry lime vinaigrette

finely grated rind of 3 limes
4 tablespoons lime juice
4 tablespoons mild curry powder or paste
125 ml (4 fl oz) groundnut oil
salt and freshly ground black pepper

1 Whisk all the ingredients together until evenly mixed, then taste for seasoning.

Yogurt and fresh herb dressing

Garlic and fresh herbs give this cool and creamy dressing lots of flavour. It is good with potato or cucumber salads, grilled or roast lamb or chicken, or any spicy food.

- 1 garlic clove
- 150 g (5 oz) low-fat natural yogurt
- 3 tablespoons skimmed or semi-skimmed milk
- 3 tablespoons chopped fresh herbs (eg chervil, flat-leaf parsley, dill)
- salt and freshly ground black pepper

1 Finely chop the garlic and place in a screw-top jar with the yogurt, milk and herbs. Shake until thoroughly mixed, then season generously with salt and pepper.

◆

Roasted red pepper dressing

This smoky flavoured dressing goes well with fish and salads, or it can be spread on crackers or crispbreads.

2 red peppers
2 tablespoons extra virgin olive oil
6 fresh basil leaves

1 Preheat the grill. Cut the peppers into quarters and remove the cores and seeds. Place the peppers skin side up on the grill pan and place under the grill for 5–8 minutes or until the skins are blistered and blackened. Place immediately in a plastic bag and allow to cool for at least 10 minutes or until completely cold.

2 Peel the skin off the peppers and place the flesh in a food processor or blender with the oil, basil, 2 tablespoons cold water and any liquid that has collected in the bag from the peppers. Work to a smooth paste.

◆

MAYONNAISE

The type of oil you use depends on whether you want a light mayonnaise or one with more colour and flavour. Sunflower oil makes a mild mayonnaise, whereas extra-virgin olive oil can be quite fruity, strong and peppery. A mixture of the two is a happy compromise. Because it contains raw egg, mayonnaise should be eaten within 2 days of making. Cover the surface of the mayonnaise with cling film and store in the refrigerator until ready to serve.

BY HAND

1 egg yolk
2 tablespoons Dijon mustard
salt and freshly ground black pepper
150–200 ml (5–7 fl oz) oil
juice of 1 lemon, or to taste

1 Whisk the egg yolk, mustard and salt and pepper in a bowl until well mixed and the salt has dissolved. Whisk in the oil a drop at a time until the mixture begins to emulsify, then whisk in a thin steady stream until the mayonnaise is thick. Add lemon juice to taste.

IN THE FOOD PROCESSOR

1 whole egg
2 tablespoons Dijon mustard
salt and freshly ground black pepper
150–200 ml (5–7 fl oz) oil
juice of 1 lemon, or to taste

1 Put the egg, mustard and salt and pepper in the bowl of a food processor and pulse to mix. With the machine running, add the oil through the feeder tube in a thin steady stream. Add lemon juice to taste.

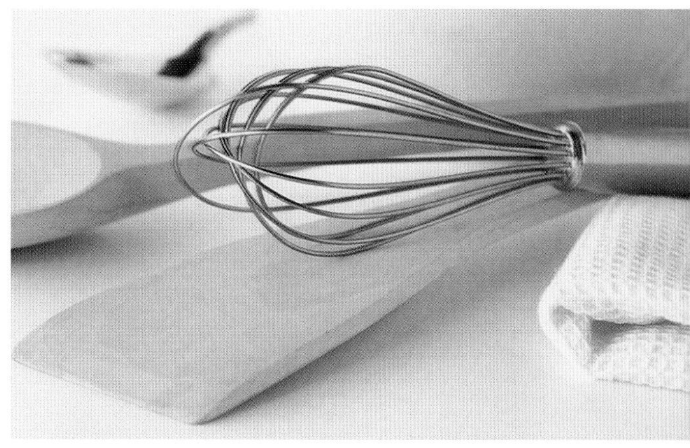

AÏOLI

This garlic mayonnaise from Provence is good with egg and fish dishes, and as a dip for crudités. Covered tightly with cling film, it will keep in the refrigerator for up to 2 days.

- 4 garlic cloves
- salt and freshly ground black pepper
- 1 egg yolk
- 300 ml (½ pint) olive oil
- a few drops of lemon juice, to taste

1 In a mortar, pound the garlic and ½ teaspoon salt to a paste with a pestle.

2 Add the egg yolk and whisk it in until evenly mixed, then add the oil a drop at a time, whisking vigorously until the mixture starts to emulsify.

3 Continue adding the oil gradually, whisking it in with a balloon whisk until all is incorporated and the aïoli is very thick. Add lemon juice and salt and freshly ground black pepper to taste.

Mayonnaise variations

Sun-dried tomato: Add 2 chopped sun-dried tomatoes in oil to the egg and seasoning mixture.

◆

Lemon: Add the finely grated rind of 1 lemon to the egg and seasoning mixture.

Pasta dough

Homemade pasta is lighter than bought fresh pasta. This a basic recipe for pasta with eggs (pasta all'uovo) that you can roll out thinly and use to make rectangles or squares for lasagne and cannelloni, or long strips to sandwich together with a filling to make ravioli. It can also be used for long strands such as tagliatelle and tagliarini. These can be made by hand but you will find it easier if you use a mechanical pasta machine. The quantity given here is sufficient for 4 servings.

250 g (8 oz) 00 pasta flour
1 teaspoon salt
large pinch of freshly grated nutmeg or ground mace
1 tablespoon olive oil
2 eggs
1 egg yolk
flour or semolina, for dusting

1 Mix the flour, salt and nutmeg or mace in a large bowl. Add the oil, whole eggs and egg yolk and mix to form a dough. Turn the dough on to a floured surface and knead for 5–10 minutes until smooth and elastic, adding a little more flour if necessary.

2 Shape the dough into a ball, wrap in cling film and leave to rest at room temperature for 20 minutes.

3 Roll the dough out thinly, either by hand or machine, and cut into the required shapes.

4 Dust the shapes with flour or semolina and leave to dry on floured tea towels for at least 15 minutes before cooking.

◆

Flavourings for Pasta

Tomato: *Add 1 tablespoon tomato purée with the egg yolks.*

Spinach: *Add 2 tablespoons well-drained cooked spinach with the egg yolks.*

Herb: *Add 2 tablespoons chopped fresh herbs with the egg yolks.*

Saffron: *Add a generous pinch of saffron powder to the dry ingredients.*

Mash

King Edward, Desirée and Maris Piper potatoes have a floury texture which is ideal for fluffy, smooth mash. This recipe is for basic mash. If you like, you can flavour the potatoes with seasonings like freshly grated nutmeg, a few cardamom seeds or a spoonful of coarsegrain mustard. Crisp, browned onions, spring onions or leeks also make good flavourings. If you are serving the mash with fish, add a little grated lemon rind and juice to the potatoes. This quantity of mash is enough for 4 servings.

1.4 kg (3 lb) floury potatoes
salt and freshly ground black pepper
60 g (2 oz) butter
200 ml (7 fl oz) hot semi-skimmed milk
finely chopped fresh parsley, to serve (optional)

1 Peel the potatoes and cut them into even-size pieces. Put them in a saucepan, cover with cold water and add 1 teaspoon salt. Bring to the boil and simmer until very tender, 20–30 minutes.

2 Drain the potatoes and return them to the pan. Dry them by shaking the pan over low heat.

3 Mash the potatoes, then add the butter and hot milk and beat well to mix. Season with salt and pepper. Serve hot, sprinkled with chopped parsley if you like.

◆

Celeriac purée

Celeriac is a winter vegetable that makes a very tasty purée to serve with meat. It goes especially well with venison and other game. You can serve it in neat mounds or shaped into ovals. This quantity is enough for 3–4 servings.

375–400 g (12–14 oz) celeriac
30 g (1 oz) butter
salt and freshly ground black pepper
about 4 tablespoons low-fat crème fraîche

1 Thickly peel the celeriac. Dice the flesh finely and evenly. Melt the butter in a wide shallow pan, add the celeriac and season with salt and pepper. Cover with a piece of greaseproof paper and a tightly fitting lid and cook over low heat, testing after 10 minutes to see if it is tender enough to mash with a fork. If necessary, cook uncovered to evaporate excess moisture.

2 Turn the celeriac into in a food processor and purée until smooth, then tip into a saucepan. Warm gently and beat with a wooden spoon as you add enough crème fraîche for the mixture to just hold its shape. Season well with salt and pepper.

◆

CUCUMBER AND MINT RAITA

Cool and refreshing, raita is the ideal accompaniment for spicy foods, especially Indian curries, and it is also good with hot Indian bread and pitta bread. It can be made several hours ahead of serving.

½ large cucumber
1 teaspoon salt
90 ml (3 fl oz) natural yogurt
½ tablespoon white wine vinegar
freshly ground black pepper
6 fresh mint leaves
4 tablespoons shredded nori seaweed, to garnish (optional)

Serves 3–4

Preparation time: 10 minutes plus draining and chilling

1 Peel the cucumber, cut it lengthways in half, then crossways into thin slices. Toss with the salt and place in a colander to drain for 30 minutes.

2 Mix the yogurt and vinegar together and add peppper to taste. Finely shred the mint and stir it into the yogurt mixture.

3 Turn the cucumber into a clean tea towel and press gently to remove excess water. Add to the yogurt and mix well. Chill in the refrigerator for at least 20 minutes before serving.

To Serve Sprinkle with shredded seaweed if you like. Serve chilled.

Variations

Fresh coriander can be used in place of mint, or you can use a combination of both.

Chopped garlic can be added to the yogurt with the mint.

Instead of the seaweed garnish, sprinkle chopped fresh mint over the raita just before serving.

Thin egg pancakes

These are oriental-style pancakes that can be used to add protein to stir-fries. Here they are sliced into ribbons, but they can also be left whole and used to wrap around fillings.

2 eggs
salt and freshly ground black pepper
about 1 tablespoon vegetable oil

1 Beat the eggs with 50 ml (2 fl oz) cold water and a little salt and pepper. Heat a little oil in a non-stick frying pan and add one-quarter of the mixture, tilting the pan to cover the base with egg. Cook until lightly golden on the underside, about 2–3 minutes. Do not turn the pancake over. Remove the pancake from the pan and repeat to make 3 more pancakes, adding more oil as necessary.

2 Roll each pancake into a cigarette shape, then cut crossways with a sharp knife into 5 mm (1/4 inch) ribbons.

◆

Herb and yogurt pancakes

Yogurt, herbs and Parmesan cheese make these pancakes very tasty and filling. Use them to wrap light vegetable fillings.

150 g (5 oz) self-raising flour
350 g (11½ oz) low-fat natural yogurt
1 egg
salt and freshly ground black pepper
2 tablespoons chopped fresh herbs (eg basil, chervil, parsley, marjoram, oregano)
1 tablespoon grated Parmesan cheese
about 6 tablespoons milk
vegetable oil for frying

1 Sift the flour into a bowl. Beat the yogurt and egg together and season well. Add to the flour, stirring until fairly smooth. Add the herbs and Parmesan, and enough milk to thin the mixture down to the consistency of a thick batter.

2 Brush a non-stick 18 cm (7 inch) frying pan with a little oil and heat until hot. Drop about 2 tablespoonfuls of the batter into the pan and spread it out with a palette knife, then cook until bubbles rise to the surface and the underside is golden. Turn the pancake over and cook until the other side is golden, then remove the pancake from the pan. Repeat with the remaining mixture to make about 8 pancakes altogether, adding more oil as necessary and stacking the pancakes on top of each other as they are done (this will keep them warm).

◆

Crêpes

This recipe makes twelve 15–18 cm (6–7 inch) crêpes. The batter can be made in a food processor but it will need to be sieved before using, to remove any lumps.

- 100 g (3½ oz) plain flour
- 15 g (½ oz) caster sugar
- pinch of salt
- 2 large eggs
- 300 ml (½ pint) milk
- 1 teaspoon vanilla extract
- sunflower oil

1 Mix the flour, sugar and salt together in a bowl. Make a well in the centre and add the eggs. Mix the eggs with a balloon whisk, gradually drawing in the flour. Continue whisking and gradually add the milk until all is incorporated. Whisk in the vanilla extract and 2 teaspoons oil.

2 Heat a non-stick omelette or frying pan until very hot. Dip a wad of kitchen paper in oil, then wipe over the pan and heat until very hot. Whisk the batter well, then ladle a few tablespoonfuls into the pan and swirl around to coat the base. Cook for 1 minute or until golden underneath, then flip the crêpe over and cook for 30–60 seconds on the other side. Slide onto a plate.

3 Repeat with the remaining batter to make 12 crêpes, stacking them on top of one another and coating the pan with oil as necessary.

Sweet shortcrust pastry

This rich dough, called pâte sucrée in French, is ideal for all sweet tarts. The quantity here is enough to line two 24.5 cm (9½ inch) tart tins. If not using it all, the remainder can be stored in the freezer for up to 1 month. To bake blind, see the method on page 339.

300 g (10 oz) plain flour
150 g (5 oz) chilled butter
60 g (2 oz) icing or caster sugar
1 medium egg
1 medium egg yolk
¾ teaspoon vanilla extract

1 Put the flour in a food processor. Cut the butter into 1.25 cm (½ inch) cubes and add to the flour. Process until the mixture looks like breadcrumbs. Add the sugar and pulse once to mix.

2 Mix the egg, egg yolk and vanilla extract. With the machine running, add the egg mixture and process until a rough dough forms.

3 Turn the dough out onto a work surface and form into 2 balls. Flatten both slightly and wrap in cling film. Chill 1 ball in the refrigerator for at least 30 minutes. Freeze the other.

4 To line a tart tin, roughly roll the chilled dough out on a floured surface with a floured rolling pin, then press it into the tin with your fingertips.

8

WEEKEND ENTERTAINING

Most of us have a little more time to spend preparing food at the weekend than during the week. You may have invited friends for a Saturday dinner party, family for a special Sunday lunch, or a few people round for an informal soirée or al fresco lunch in the garden. Maybe you plan an intimate dinner for two or you may have a houseful of guests for the whole weekend. These are very different occasions, but for all of them you will need to plan, shop, prepare and cook more than usual.

The recipes in this book are easy, but the results are sensational. All main courses are arranged according to their main ingredient – fish and shellfish, chicken and duck, beef, lamb and pork. On the following pages is a selection of menu ideas to help you put these main course dishes together with recipes from elsewhere in the book.

Read your chosen recipes through carefully and prepare and assemble the ingredients before starting to cook. Plan your occasion well in advance and make a timetable of what you have to do and when, working backwards from serving time. Don't forget to build in extra time for drinks and nibbles before the meal – and the possibility of someone arriving late. This way you can make every special occasion relaxed, for both you and your guests.

Weekend entertaining menu ideas

Celebration dinner party

Smoked Duck with Broccoli and Almonds
•
Seafood Fricassée
Boiled New Potatoes
Mangetouts with Herbs
•
Lemon Tart
≈

Sunday roast lunch

Courgette and Roasted Garlic Soup
•
Roast Lamb with Garlic and Thyme
Normandy Carrots
Green Beans with Leeks and Tomatoes
Mashed Potatoes
•
Plum and Cinnamon Crumble
≈

Thai lunch or dinner

Prawn and Ginger Soup
•
Thai Chicken with Peppers
Jasmine Rice
•
Fragrant Fruit Salad
≈

Summer lunch party

Layered Vegetable Terrine
•
Scallops with Tomato and Saffron
Boiled Rice
Leafy Mixed Salad
•
Raspberry Fool
≈

Winter dinner party

Warm Scallop Salad
•
Duck Breasts with Honey Coriander Sauce
Spinach with Coriander and Cream
Gratin Dauphinois
•
Chocolate Vacherin
≈

Seafood dinner party

Grilled Mussels with Lime and Pesto

•

Sole with Smoked Salmon

New Potatoes with Butter and Herbs

•

Ginger Crème Brûlée

≈

Chinese meal

Asparagus with Soy and Wasabi Dressing

•

Chicken and Cashews

Egg Noodles

•

Fragrant Fruit Salad

≈

Al fresco summer lunch

Cucumber and Dill Soup

•

Fish Kebabs with Lime and Rosemary

Boiled Rice

•

Eton Mess

≈

Saturday dinner party

Warm Potato Salad

•

Salmon with Rosemary Cream

Roasted Mediterranean Vegetables

•

White Chocolate and Cream Cheese Tart

≈

Indian curry lunch

Chicken Jalfrezi

Rice Pilaf

Cucumber and Mint Raita

•

Cardamom Crème Brûlée

≈

French bistro supper

Seared Scallops with Roasted Pepper Coulis

•

Coq au Vin

Gratin Dauphinois

Green Salad

•

Crêpes Suzette

≈

Italian summer party

Fresh Tomato and Pepper Soup with Basil

•

Risotto with Peas and Prosciutto

•

Saltimbocca

Roasted Fruit with Mascarpone Cream

≈

Dinner à deux

Avocado with Grapefruit and Vinaigrette

•

Steak with Green Peppercorn Sauce

•

Chocolate and Pecan Yogurt Ice-Cream

≈

CONVERSION TABLES

Please note that all conversions given here are approximate. You should follow either the metric or imperial systems throughout a recipe, not a mixture of the two.

WEIGHTS

Ounces	Grams
½	15
¾	20
1	30
1½	40
2	60
2½	75
3	90
3½	100
4	125
5	150
6	175
7	200
8	250
10	300
12	375
16/1 lb	500
1¼ lb	625
1½ lb	700
2 lb	1000/1 kg
3 lb	1500/1.5 kg

SPOON SIZES

Spoon	Fluid ounces	Millilitres
1 teaspoon	⅛	5
1 dessertspoon	⅓	10
1 tablespoon	½	15

TEMPERATURES

°C	°F	Gas Mark
140	275	1
150	300	2
165	325	3
180	350	4
190	375	5
200	400	6
220	425	7
230	450	8
240	475	9
250	480	–

VOLUME

Please note that there are 20 fluid ounces to a pint in the UK, but 16 fluid ounces in the US.

Fluid ounces (UK)	Millilitres	Cups (US)
1	30	⅛
2	50	¼
3½	100	–
4	125	½
¼ pint	150	–
7	200	–
8	250	1
½ pint	300	–
14	400	1½
¾ pint	450	–
16	500	2
1 pint	600	2½
1½ pints	900	3½
1¾ pints	1000/1 litre	4
2 pints	1.2 litres	–
2½ pints	1.5 litres	–
3 pints	1.8 litres	–

INDEX

Page numbers in **bold** indicate illustrations.
Page numbers in *italics* indicate the Quick & Easy Ideas sections.